The Kleist Variations

Three Plays

Based on plays by Heinrich von Kleist

THIRD EDITION

Eric Bentley

Northwestern University Press
Evanston, Illinois

Northwestern University Press
Evanston, Illinois 60208-4170

Third edition

Printed in the United States of America

10 9 8 7 6 5 4 3 2 1

ISBN 0-8101-2115-8

Front cover: Bronze sculpture of St. Michael and the Devil, by Jacob Epstein, found on the south side of Coventry Cathedral. Photograph used by kind permission of the Chapter of Coventry Cathedral.

Frontispiece: Heinrich von Kleist, courtesy of Maurice Sendak. This portrait shows Kleist modernized for the twentieth and twenty-first centuries, much like the Kleist of Eric Bentley's variations.

page 211: Portrait of Eric Bentley courtesy of Lamont O'Neal

Library of Congress Cataloging-in-Publication Data are available from the Library of Congress.

∞ The paper used in this publication meets the minimum requirements of the American National Standard for Information Sciences—Permanence of Paper for Printed Library Materials, ANSI Z39.48-1992.

The Kleist Variations

Heinrich von Kleist, by Maurice Sendak

Not everyone can or will do that: give his specific fears and desires a chance to be of universal significance.

–Robert Coles

Contents

Worship: Its Wonder and Guises

In an age in which uncertainty has become one of the sure things we can depend upon, and in which cult belief has grown as a counter for our tattered souls, what is it that you can say you believe in?

A reply by Eric Bentley

> *It is not the problem of "an age" but a problem for all time, because, as Samuel Butler put it, "life is the art of drawing sufficient conclusions from insufficient premises." A corollary of this is that one should not draw excessive conclusions, as do not only the "cults" your questionnaire cites but most of the religious outlooks and all of the quasi-religious political outlooks: religion and quasi-religious politics will settle for nothing less than paradise, whether in heaven or on earth. However, retreats from millennialism to pure skepticism or conservatism will not avail us either. As Maimonides said, to repudiate the Messianic idea altogether is to repudiate the whole Torah. . . . What is it I can say "I believe in"? Not, certainly, that the Kingdom of God is at hand. But still it must be for God one waits, not for Godot. Is this theological language something I can say "I believe in"? No; not in a literal sense. But I can find no other language to express, however figuratively, what I truly believe. No other language—except the even more figurative language of my plays.*
>
> —From *Confrontation* magazine, Summer, 1979

Concord
A Comedy

Based on *The Broken Jug*

Preface: In the Matter of Heinrich von Kleist

(The interviewer Jerome Clegg investigates Eric Bentley's tamperings with the masterpieces of Heinrich von Kleist.)

CLEGG: Three of them was it — *The Broken Jug, Penthesilea,* and *Das Kätchen von Heilbronn?* Why just those three?

BENTLEY: I liked them. I still like them.

CLEGG: *Das Kätchen von Heilbronn:* what commended it to you?

BENTLEY: That there's nothing like it in English.

CLEGG: Except, now, your play *Wannsee?*

BENTLEY: Which is not like it. Which is merely a by-product of my own infatuation with it, an excuse for keeping the German text close company. Intimacy I enjoy!

CLEGG: If you didn't hope to create the special quality of *Das Kätchen* in English, what did you hope to do?

BENTLEY: Draw on some of the magic of that play for a few conjuring tricks of my own.

CLEGG: Plagiarism? "Based on" equals "stolen from"?

BENTLEY: But in an anarchistic utopia where there is no distinction between *stolen* and *borrowed!* I take it where I find it, says Molière. Shakespeare does not even bother to tell anyone that *Measure for Measure* is "based on" another play.

CLEGG: You are Shakespeare?

BENTLEY: Who said works of art owe more to other works of art than to life?

CLEGG: Brecht?

BENTLEY: E.H. Gombrich. But Brecht was listening. "Anyone can be creative," he once told me, "what takes talent is re-writing someone else."

CLEGG: And whether it takes talent or not, you propose to do it? Rather than merely translate — reproduce — someone else?

BENTLEY: Merely? That is sometimes the hardest thing of all. I think I know German, but I don't think I can "merely" translate, reproduce, *Das Kätchen von Heilbronn:* if "reproduce" means, as surely it should, "reproduce all its effects"—all the effects it has upon a reader of the German.

CLEGG: Then why didn't you just walk away?

BENTLEY: I did. But it walked with me. The characters, the story, lingered in my mind. And story is all—did someone say that?

CLEGG: You just did.

BENTLEY: But stories must be re-told—with subtractions and additions.

CLEGG: *Wannsee,* may I conclude, was not intended to be *Das Kätchen* minus something, or *not only* minus something, but definitely plus something? Isn't that rather arrogant?

BENTLEY: Arrogant or not, am I entitled to answer your question or to write my play? Should one rob Kleist of much of his poetry, and not make him a present of anything in return—just to show *you* one is not arrogant?

CLEGG: You made him a present of much Anglo-Saxon humor. I laughed.

BENTLEY: Too much? Too little? Or shouldn't you have laughed at all?

CLEGG: Ar you imitating Tom Stoppard?

BENTLEY: No.

CLEGG: Are you sure?

BENTLEY: Yes.

CLEGG: OK. Is your adaptation problem—

BENTLEY: My what?

CLEGG: Solved merely by replacing poetry with comedy?

BENTLEY: No.

CLEGG: Then?

BENTLEY: In *Wannsee,* I wanted to create a single world in which both romantic poetry and extravagant, even coarse, comedy had a part.

CLEGG: You also wanted to put Heinrich von Kleist on stage.

BENTLEY: His ghost, anyway.

CLEGG: *Das Kätchen* is imbued with Christian optimism; yet its author committed suicide.

BENTLEY: I wanted to dramatize just that contradiction.

CLEGG: Why?

BENTLEY: Why not?

CLEGG: To show Kleist's inconsistency?

BENTLEY: Is that interesting?

CLEGG: You tell me.

BENTLEY: What is . . . contrary to the appearances . . . is potentially interesting.

CLEGG: To all appearances, Kleist was a pessimist. And pessimists try to talk themselves into optimism.

BENTLEY: Poor Kleist talked himself into suicide till it was too late to talk himself out of it!

CLEGG: But—

BENTLEY: The optimism of *Das Kätchen von Heilbronn* was authentic and heartfelt. I didn't try to counteract it. On the contrary, I hoped, in my own way, to endorse it.

CLEGG: So you fell in love with Kätchen. And then with Penthesilea?

BENTLEY: The woman or the play?

CLEGG: Does it matter?

BENTLEY: Yes. The woman I could love. Do love. The Kleist play, though . . . that's an antagonist to fight off rather than embrace.

CLEGG: Yet not to put behind you. You commissioned a translation of it years ago for one of your anthologies. Incidentally, why didn't you translate it yourself?

BENTLEY: Too difficult. I couldn't . . .

CLEGG: You took on the creative job—a play "based on"—as the easy way out?

BENTLEY: It wasn't easy.

CLEGG: My notes tell me you did buckle down and write this play years later—late Seventies? why?

BENTLEY: One of my students said I wrote plays for men only and asked when women (she was one) would find their way into my work? (I had written an *Antigone* but students don't know everything. Besides, I had not written the plays on Emma Goldman and Rosa Luxemburg that I'd dreamed of writing.)

CLEGG: I've read *The Fall of the Amazons.* Is this a play "about women"?

BENTLEY: Women and men. The war of the sexes.

CLEGG: Thurber!

BENTLEY: Yes.

CLEGG: Strindberg!

BENTLEY: Almost. Or let's say: in content but not in form. Strindberg's form was domestic tragedy. He was a camera. He gave us Sweden, 1900.

CLEGG: Whereas you?

BENTLEY: Shouldn't *you* answer that one?

CLEGG: No.

BENTLEY: I was a plagiarist. At least to begin with. Because the play I dreamed of writing had already been written. It was *Penthesilea* by Heinrich von Kleist.

CLEGG: So now we have *The Fall of the Amazons, really* by Heinrich von Kleist.

BENTLEY: I'm afraid Kleist wouldn't agree to *that* proposition. Too much, in the later play, that is un-Kleistian.

CLEGG: So you tried to—improve on him? Like those various 18th-century mediocrities who "improved on" Shakespeare?

BENTLEY: I risked that—that ignominy.

CLEGG: Why?

BENTLEY: I suppose because some things in Kleist's text were unacceptable to me.

CLEGG: Like what?

BENTLEY: I know I can't answer that—adequately. There were matters of style. Maybe he is "right," and I am "wrong," but one can't write that way now.

CLEGG: You replaced poetry with prose. Was that an essential factor?

BENTLEY: I don't know. I only know it was one, perhaps inevitable result of my encounter with him. If you want, you can put it down to my limitations.

CLEGG: Let's get beyond modesty.

BENTLEY: By all means.

CLEGG: You changed the style of the dialogue—of all the discourse between people in the play. Is that the most significant change?

BENTLEY: It's for others to say what my play signifies, let alone whether it is significant. I can only say what writing it signified.

CLEGG: Which was?

BENTLEY: One doesn't write a play in order to achieve a particular style of dialogue, let alone to change someone else's style. It's a matter of the substance—a theme, perhaps, or a character—

CLEGG: You find something—in Kleist or wherever—you like it and wish to preserve it, even enhance it?

BENTLEY: No. That's how one makes use of an inferior writer: borrowing, improving. A great writer is a challenge, even a threat. One cannot surpass him, perhaps one cannot even match him, but one can respond to him, make a counter move, perhaps even, in some matters, correct him.

CLEGG: To be specific?

BENTLEY: I was repelled by the last act of *Penthesilea,* by Kleist's account of Penthesilea's death, by the image of woman implicit in it. *This must all be seen another way,* I felt, and reached for my typewriter.

CLEGG: What "other way"?

BENTLEY: *The Fall of the Amazons* is the answer to that question.

CLEGG: Then one last query on *Penthesilea.* If you were going to reject Kleist's handling of the story, why use his play at all? Why not work directly from the legends he worked from?

BENTLEY: Ancient legend relates that Achilles slew Penthesilea, the Amazon queen, but that, as she lay dying in his arms, their eyes met, and he fell in love with her. Kleist changed this. His idea is that Penthesilea did not die when Achilles struck her down but lived on to kill him: in remorse for which deed she kills herself.

CLEGG: Just drops dead, doesn't she? Has a rather convenient heart attack?

BENTLEY: And that part I find highly acceptable! Inspired! I wouldn't want to change the outline, the scenario, and it is not ancient, so far as I've been able to discover, it is Kleist's contribution to myth . . . What did you make of *Concord?*

CLEGG: It reminded me of Stefan Zweig's version of *Volpone* in which all the positive values of Jonson's original are thrown overboard. Kleist may have been suicidal—

BENTLEY: *May* have been!

CLEGG: But Kleist retained a vestigial belief in 18th-century patrons, benevolent despots, wise father figures—

BENTLEY: So much the worse for him! And his being *really suicidal* shows he wasn't convinced by his own suppositions! Kleist was aware of the death of God—

CLEGG: That's a phrase from the late 19th century—Nietzsche—

BENTLEY: No, one thing in my own play that is simply lifted from Kleist is Adam's statement that recent thinkers had killed God but had left the Devil alive.

CLEGG: You're changing the subject. We were talking about 18th-century patrons—

BENTLEY: Chief of whom was God. The one slightly dubious item in Kleist's masterpiece *The Prince of Homburg* is the Elector. He's too nearly a god. On the other hand, Kleist did seem aware of the problem and gave the Elector an imperfection or two. Moral perfection is admirable but uninteresting; and that's the trouble with Kleist's superior Judge in *The Broken Jug.*

CLEGG: So you made him an ineffectual Liberal!

BENTLEY: Worse, I suppose: he's the angel (messenger) from the God who isn't there, the ambassador from the Good Society and the Just Government that also are not there. To worship him would be the lowest form of idolatry since he's an idol *and* has feet of clay.

CLEGG: Now you're agreeing with me that you have undermined Kleist's noble, edifying 18th-century comedy with your damned modern nihilism!

BENTLEY: It's a *19th*-century comedy—

CLEGG: Barely: you're really quibbling now—

BENTLEY: What I should be saying is that, by looking to the Higher Judge for my positive values, my criteria, you are barking up the wrong tree.

CLEGG: Because there is no *right* tree.

BENTLEY: Is my play so profound it's obscure?

CLEGG: You threw in a bit of feminism—maybe just for good measure, maybe as modish updating of the material, maybe to express a personal prejudice?

BENTLEY: A bit of feminism?

CLEGG: The *un*taming of a shrew, or how the little feminine milque-toast can *become* a shrew, shrews being what we nowadays approve of. Kleist must bow to Ibsen and Shaw: the doll must walk out on her guy.

BENTLEY: Just to show her power?

CLEGG: Ha?

BENTLEY: Why does she walk out?

CLEGG: To give you your modern ending.

BENTLEY: I have no objection to a modern ending—*Concord* does have to be a modern play after all—but I still hope she isn't just walking out in order to walk out, in order to resemble Nora or Eliza, or even to register a protest against marriage.

CLEGG: What was on your mind, then?

BENTLEY: That we mistrust each other. We are all cynics today. "When I consider life, it's all a cheat:" it isn't just the mafiosi who believe this—except in the sense that today we are all mafiosi or their victims—and their victims don't dispute their premises, they only fail to get picked for membership in the mafia . . . Watergate was above all consoling. What it proved was: if even the Top Man does it, little you needn't feel bad.

CLEGG: But I already *said* your play was cynical: you took the one character in the Kleist who was above all the skulduggery and brought him down into it.

BENTLEY: How about Kleist's heroine?

CLEGG: She was above it only in a conventional and by now quite unbelievable way: she swallows her pride and meekly marries the guy who's insulted her up and down, called her a Whore, and so on . . .

BENTLEY: Kleist gives her some words about trust which I find touching. Her fiancé should have *trusted* her . . .

CLEGG: Kleist's treatment of the romance is not only conventional but boring: all this pother about whether she'd be a virgin on her wedding day . . .

BENTLEY: Well, that's a pother that entertained Western Civilization for centuries.

CLEGG: And now doesn't any more.

BENTLEY: True. Re-writing the story, I either had to have her defend being a non-virgin, or have her put quite a different interpretation on her "fidelity"—not preservation of her hymen, which does not interest you, me, or my audience, but her respect for her own promises, whatever they might be, her trustworthiness. When, as playwright, I come to her boyfriend, I must ask what is his capacity for trust. I did ask that, didn't I? And I depicted her as trustworthy. Which sounds like a rather ordinary virtue to attribute to someone, only I placed it in the context of a war of all against all, where mistrust is the rule, and trust so far the exception one might think it is one of those values that are becoming obsolete.

CLEGG: Good God, then Eve is your mouthpiece! You've given her your editorials to read aloud!

BENTLEY: That I must leave others to judge. All *I* need be aware of is that I am strongly identified with the stand Eve takes: "Hier stehe *ich,* ich kann nicht anders."

CLEGG: She's the Martin Luther of Feminism! But that is not the note on which your play ends, or it would be very affirmative, very optimistic, and I feel it is not. It ends with the replacement of one judge by another. The first judge was a rascal but the new one seems likely to be an avenging angel which, in your terms, will be an avenging scoundrel. . . . My title for your play would be: Out of the Frying Pan. Is that fair?

BENTLEY: As far as I can judge, it is a fair response to what I wrote, and is not in contradiction to what was on my mind throughout—

CLEGG: Which was?

BENTLEY: Original sin. That we are all sinners, therefore that there's no such thing in this life as replacing a sinner by a non-sinner. "Seven times a day sinneth the just man."

CLEGG: You are turning to religion?

BENTLEY: Did I ever turn away from it?

CLEGG: Yes.

BENTLEY: And no. Human thinking, human fantasy even, always has human substance . . .

CLEGG: But the substance in this case! Doesn't *Concord* say, with *Waiting for Godot,* "Nothing to be done"?

BENTLEY: I hope not. I think I am more "religious" than Beckett . . . a little closer to the optimism of the New Testament—or even the Old. *Now* do you see why my heroine is so important to *Concord,* as to *Wannsee?* But I must stop before I start holding forth on what these plays *should* mean. What they do mean, they themselves say.

A play that has a protagonist is a concerto for solo and orchestra. The playwright has a solo instrument in mind: often writes the role for the physique, especially for the voice – timbre and intonation – of a particular performer. The question throughout is: can I see him doing this, hear him saying that? I asked the question while writing the role of Judge Adam, though the actor was no longer alive. I dedicate the play to the memory of Z.M.

In Adam's fall
We sinned all.

– New England Primer

The devil is a traitor to justice and a lover of power.

– St. Augustine

Cast (in order of appearance)

Adam, the Concord Judge
Mr. Light, Clerk of the Court
Manservant to Judge Walter
Maggie, Adam's housemaid
Walter, a Judge from Boston
Mrs. Martha Bull, a shopkeeper's widow
Eve, her daughter
Mr. Thomas Tumpel, a farmer
Robert, his son
Old Bridget, a crone, Mr. Tumpel's aunt

The Time: in the early days of the Republic. A Tuesday morning in January.

The Place: Concord, Massachusetts. The scene is laid in the Courthouse, which is also where Judge Adam lives. *Outside:* snow.

Prologue

(The cast sings the following hymn, to the tune of 'O Sacred Head, Now Wounded,' and, if they can, in the four-part harmony by Bach.)

All men were sold to Satan
By the first Adam's fall
Till Christ, a second Adam,
Was slain to save us all.
And now in clouds descending
Christ fights the final fight
And hurls the serpent's legions
Down to infernal night;

Down into foul Gehenna
Land of eternal pains
Where sinners dwell with devils
In darkness, fire, and chains.
But there's another country
The chosen can expect:
The Lord's eternal heaven
The home of the elect.

Arise, young men and maidens
Chaste, undefiled, and pure
Though Satan sorely tempt you
By God's grace ye endure.
Curb thy unruly body!
All lustful thoughts put down!
Foregoing carnal pleasures
Ye win a heavenly crown.

The church shall be completed
The chosen gathered in
The King in glory seated
Subdued and banished, sin:
The sheep from goats be parted

In paradise to dwell
The goats condemned to fire
And brimstone down in hell.

The world is full of evil
The times are waxing late
Be ready, all, keep vigil
The Judge is at the gate –
The Judge who comes in vengeance
The Judge who comes in might
Who comes to conquer evil
Who comes to crown the right.

(Courtroom. A large baldheaded man sitting on the floor, half-dressed, fingering cuts and bruises on his body.)

A SMALLER MAN *(entering):* Heaven and hell, what has become of you, Judge Adam? You've stumbled over something?

ADAM: Must there always be a something one stumbles over, Mr. Light?

LIGHT: Ha?

ADAM: Is not *homo sapiens* a stumbler? Who has his stumbling block within? That's philosophy, Mr. Light.

LIGHT: Theology, Judge Adam: we all go back to the first Adam, who fell in Act One, Scene One, of the comedy.

ADAM: Tragedy.

LIGHT: Tell me about *your* fall then, Judge.

ADAM: The fall from . . . bed! I fell out of bed this morning. No, that's not it. Begin again. I got out of bed, a song in my heart—Concord's my garden of Eden—tripping, free from care, to meet the day, then, presto! I fell on my face and wrenched my foot. How's that?

LIGHT: Which foot?

ADAM: Which foot?

LIGHT: Was it . . . your club foot?

ADAM: You know everything. All right, more philosophy! *(He clears his throat.)* What foot of humankind is no club foot?

LIGHT: A normal foot can skate on thinner ice.

ADAM: What good is that? Where one foot skates, the other foot must follow.

LIGHT: My God, your face!

ADAM: My face *is* normal.

LIGHT: There's a bit of cheek missing!

ADAM: Give me that mirror.

LIGHT: *(Handing Adam a mirror so he can inspect the damage to his face).* Somewhere in Concord, a piece of human skin hanging from a thornbush! Or did some female try to scratch your eyes out?

ADAM: My cheek, my nose—

LIGHT: Your eye—

ADAM: Which one? Or have I lost both?

LIGHT: You've blackened both.

ADAM: *(looking in the mirror).* No. My right eye is red. Look at this great red weal!

LIGHT: Remember when you were a farmhand!

ADAM: Me, a mere peasant? Never!

LIGHT: It looks like your farmer hit you one!

ADAM: I think the bone's damaged.

LIGHT: That's not bone.

ADAM: And I felt nothing.

LIGHT: Soldiers in battle feel nothing. Who was the enemy?

ADAM: A goat.

LIGHT: There are no goats in Concord.

ADAM: In my room –

LIGHT: You don't mean that . . . goat's head . . . ?

ADAM: Above the stove. Solid iron.

LIGHT: Start over.

ADAM: I'm climbing out of bed. Punch drunk with sleep, unsteady on my pins, I reach for my pants. Got them soaked last night in the snow, they're hanging on the stove to dry. Once I have my pants on, suspenders and all, I'll be steady as Plymouth Rock. But something's wrong. Could it be the Devil's handiwork?

LIGHT: It could be.

ADAM: It must be. The suspenders snap! The trousers drop! I fall over them and hurtle across my room – crash, bang! –

LIGHT: You've hit –

ADAM: The goat. The iron head. Above the stove.

LIGHT: *(giggling).* It *is* a comedy.

ADAM: A tragedy, you bastard: Adam's second fall.

LIGHT: The fall of man – from bed – that's comedy.

ADAM: Tragedy! Just look. *(He points to his wounds.)*

LIGHT: Comedy – look here. *(He points to his own grinning face.)*

ADAM: What brings you here anyway?

LIGHT: You weren't expecting me?

ADAM: Is it Tuesday!

LIGHT: *(nodding).* So we're in session.

ADAM: Later.

LIGHT: I came early with an urgent message. Get up off the floor! Get your pants on! There's no time to lose!

ADAM: What is it?

LIGHT: An unexpected visitor from Boston!

ADAM: Not an Inspector?

LIGHT: *(nodding).* A very high-up Judge—empowered by the Supreme Court of Massachusetts—to inspect the courts of all the Commonwealth!

ADAM: *(not moving).* Next year, I presume? Next autumn? Next week?

LIGHT: Today.

ADAM: You're crazy.

LIGHT: He did Lexington yesterday. Today: Concord.

ADAM: Concord, New Hampshire?

LIGHT: Massachusetts.

ADAM: New Englanders gossip too much. It's another idle rumor.

LIGHT: I had it from Jeremy.

ADAM: The farmhand?

LIGHT: The same.

ADAM: He wouldn't know my face from the back of my head.

LIGHT: Because you're bald.

ADAM: *(glares at him).* A very high-up Judge?

LIGHT: Name of Walter.

ADAM: A high-up Judge wouldn't do this to me, he'd give advance notice so I could—

LIGHT: That was Judge Falter.

ADAM: This is Judge Palter?

LIGHT: This is Judge Walter.

ADAM: A man, I hear, that respects local customs and traditions . . . Maybe one can do business with him.

LIGHT: They hadn't expected him in Lexington either. He marches straight to the record room and examines the accounts—

ADAM: What?!

LIGHT: Half an hour later Judge Peter was suspended.

ADAM: What's the world coming to?

LIGHT: That's not all. Placed under house arrest, Judge Peter tried to hang himself. He was dangling from the rafters in his barn when they came in this morning and cut him down.

ADAM: My God, will he live?

LIGHT: Maybe. They're rubbing him. Sprinkling him with things.

ADAM: But professionally speaking?

LIGHT: Dead already—courtroom doors locked, an inventory in progress and, oh yes, he's been replaced.

ADAM: Already? He wasn't even corrupt as this world goes. You know how this world goes, don't you, Mr. Light?

LIGHT: It's a world of lies and deceit.

ADAM: Corrupt to the core. By comparison with the world, Judge Peter was almost honest.

LIGHT: They say he was a lecher, though.

ADAM: And they say true. I could a tale unfold . . . *(He rolls his eyes.)* Who got his job?

LIGHT: Mr. Paul.

ADAM: His clerk? Clerk of the Lexington court?

LIGHT: Yes, He's no lecher.

ADAM: Just power-mad. There's nothing like a power-mad Puritan, is there, Mr. Light?

LIGHT: Of course the Inspector's been delayed by the suicide attempt.

ADAM: Till tomorrow?

LIGHT: Till about eleven.

ADAM: It *is* about eleven.

LIGHT: Ten forty three, I believe.

ADAM: Then you and I must come to an understanding.

LIGHT: Understanding?

ADAM: Opposite of *mis*understanding. Life is mainly misunderstandings, Mr. Light!

LIGHT: Ha?

ADAM: One hand washes the other. *(Pause.)*

LIGHT: If you scratch my back, I scratch yours?

ADAM: I know what you're after.

LIGHT: After?

ADAM: You're Clerk of the *Concord* court, Mr. Paul. Mr. Light. You're after my job.

LIGHT: Your job?

ADAM: Stop echoing me! You deserve my job, Mr. Light. You are welcome to my job. Not today, that's all. Suffer this cup to pass from thee, do you mind?

LIGHT: Me? The Concord Judge? Me?

ADAM: Why not? You're educated. You've heard of Cicero! On occasion you can rise to a bit of Ciceronian eloquence, isn't that so?

LIGHT: Oh, I don't know, Judge—

ADAM: I do! And all I have to add on *this* occasion is: not today, Mr. Light. For the unbridled ambition of power-mad Puritans, even if Judge Walter's partial to them, there will be other days.

LIGHT: Power-mad Puritan? Want your job? But we're cronies—birds of a feather—almost friends! *(Adam gives him a steady, level look.)*

ADAM: Who was Demosthenes?

LIGHT: Oh, um, I'd say—

ADAM: The greatest orator of them all. Why do I invoke his memory?

LIGHT: There you have me.

ADAM: The greatest orator of them all well knew when to keep his trap shut.

LIGHT: He did?

ADAM: And his arch-enemy Philip of Macedon knew how to show gratitude on a more than colossal scale.

LIGHT: Did he?

ADAM: I may not be built on quite that scale but I too know how to show gratitude. You look rather dazed.

LIGHT: I am.

ADAM: Hm. Are there stories about me?

LIGHT: Oh yes!

ADAM: About my handling of public monies, not to mention the Flood Fund?

LIGHT: I did hear one little rumor—

ADAM: Keep it little, Mr. Light. Reduce it to zero. I can't

imagine what such a rumor would be. *(Light starts to tell him, but Adam stops him.)* The whole episode was just a prank, to be laughed off as such! *(He bursts out laughing and continues to laugh until Light is induced to join in.)* Little rumors are born in the night: let them not live till day!

LIGHT: Ha?

ADAM: Do you agree?

LIGHT: Oh, I agree.

ADAM: Then we shall go to the record room and conduct a little, swift research. Should we wish to tidy up a bit, there's a fire in the fireplace. *(Enter a Manservant.)*

MANSERVANT: Judge Adam? God bless! My master Judge Walter is in Concord.

ADAM: Already? *(Calling for the Maid:)* Maggie!

MANSERVANT: He'll leave for Amherst before evening.

ADAM: The man's a lightning flash! A thunderbolt!

LIGHT: Send him a message of welcome! Tell him—! *(Enter Maggie, the Maid.)*

MAGGIE: Here, sir!

LIGHT: But first put your pants on *(Maggie giggles.)*

ADAM: *(putting on his pants).* Who said, "Here Sir!" The Judge?

MAGGIE: *(mimicking a male voice).* Here, sir!

ADAM: That little sexpot Maggie. Help cover my nakedness, Maggie!

LIGHT: Here's your coat.

MAGGIE: The vest first, silly! *(Light and Maggie help Adam finish dressing.)*

LIGHT: *(repeating his prepared speech for both Adam and the Manservant).* "Welcome to Concord! We await your arrival at the courthouse with eager anticipation!"

ADAM: *(to the Manservant).* Adding that, um, Judge Adam humbly begs to be excused.

LIGHT: What?!

ADAM: Where is he anyway?

MANSERVANT: At the tavern. We had an accident. Our coach fell apart. He's called in the smith.

ADAM: That's good news: the Concord smith is a real slowpoke. "Judge Adam humbly begs to be excused, he broke his neck."

MANSERVANT: You broke your neck, sir?

ADAM: Broke his leg. Look at that wound. And I'm about to have diarrhea, my good man.

LIGHT: Calm down, Judge, it's not the end of the world.

ADAM: How do you know? *(He holds his behind and runs across the room.)* It's like I'd taken an irresistible laxative!

LIGHT: *(to the Manservant).* He'll be all right in a minute. *(Light and the Manservant are on one side; Adam and Maggie on the other.)*

ADAM: Maggie!

MAGGIE: Yes, Sir?

ADAM: You're too skinny, Maggie, eat more!

MAGGIE: Now, sir?

ADAM: On the contrary: remove the food and drink from the record room before the Inspector arrives!

MAGGIE: All that butter and cheese—

ADAM: The ham, the sausage, everything! All bottles, empty and full! *(Pinching her behind.)* Hm. When are you going to say Yes at long last? Say Yes!

MAGGIE: Oh no, sir! I'm a good Puritan girl, sir!

ADAM: *(mimicking a female voice).* "Call me Priscilla!" Very well. And bring my wig from the bookcase.

MAGGIE: Yes, sir. *(She leaves.)*

LIGHT: You seem to have had a rather troubled journey?

MANSERVANT: By Sleepy Hollow Cemetery the carriage turned right over.

ADAM: *(still on the other side of the room).* There's an open wound in my foot, I can't get my shoe on!

LIGHT: *(still talking to the servant).* Turned right over, eh? But no harm done, I trust?

MANSERVANT: The Judge sprained his wrist. Oh, and the shaft of the coach was shattered.

LIGHT: His poor wrist! Did the smith arrive?

MANSERVANT: To repair the shaft? Yes.

ADAM: *(overhearing some of this).* You mean the doctor, Mr. Light.

MANSERVANT: For the shaft?

ADAM: For the wrist, stupid! Be off!

MANSERVANT: *(leaving).* Courthouse or madhouse? Which?

ADAM: You meant the doctor.

LIGHT: I meant the smith!

ADAM: Now don't be touchy, Mr. Light. We all get confused sometimes!

LIGHT: Touchy? Me? *(Maggie comes back in with an armful of food roughly wrapped in parchment).*

ADAM: What have you got there?

MAGGIE: Boston sausage!

ADAM: Wrapped in court records!

LIGHT: Confused, am I?

ADAM: Back to the record room with all that!

MAGGIE: The sausage?

ADAM: The court records! *(Maggie starts to go.)*

LIGHT: Touchy, am I? Hm. We shall see.

MAGGIE: *(turning in the doorway).* Couldn't find your wig, sir.

ADAM: I have two wigs!

MAGGIE: The second one's at the barber's being cleaned.

ADAM: Then give me the first one!

MAGGIE: Don't you remember? You came home last night in the wee hours without your wig.

ADAM: Not possible. Where there's a Judge there's a wig!

MAGGIE: You said you'd taken a fall. I washed the blood off your head.

ADAM: Sh! Now don't tell fibs, Maggie!

LIGHT: You've had the wound since yesterday, Judge?

ADAM: No, no. Wig—yesterday. Wound—today. I removed it—

LIGHT: The wound?

ADAM: The wig. Along with my hat. As I came in the door.

LIGHT: And, also yesterday, she washed—your what?

ADAM: "Washed my what?" What a question!

MAGGIE: It was like this –

ADAM: Maggie! Our friend the Sexton can lend me *his* wig. *(He signals to her to leave, and she does so.)*

LIGHT: How'll you put it to him?

ADAM: *(reciting).* My cat's a dirty pig
And she's littered in my wig!

LIGHT: You'll tell him your cat –

ADAM: Littered in my wig under the bed, which is where it is now, befouled with –

LIGHT: The cat?

ADAM: The wig. Five kittens. Black and yellow. No: one is white. Gonna drown the black and yellow ones in Walden Pond. Want the white one?

LIGHT: A dirty pig
Littered in your wig?

ADAM: A dirty cat –

LIGHT: Littered in your hat?

ADAM: I'd left it on a chair.

LIGHT: The cat?

ADAM: The wig. On my way to bed, I touch the chair, the wig tumbles to the floor –

LIGHT: The cat takes it in her mouth, drags it under your bed, and . . .

ADAM: In her mouth – the cat?

LIGHT: Or you, the Judge?

ADAM: Right: I kicked it under the bed this morning!

LIGHT: I see.

ADAM: How much lower can the lower animals get – forever fucking, conceiving and delivering all over the floor?

MAGGIE: *(returning, the food this time in a basket).* That word, fucking, Judge Adam!

ADAM: Maggie? I'd put you in the stocks but you're so skinny you'd wriggle out! You must eat more!

MAGGIE: Now?

ADAM: No! Talk to the Sexton's wife. Tell her I'll return the wig unharmed before the day is out. You needn't mention it to the Sexton.

MAGGIE: Very good, sir. *(She leaves.)*

ADAM: Mr. Light, I have a feeling this won't be my day.

LIGHT: Will it be mine?

ADAM: I doubt it.

LIGHT: Why?

ADAM: Does not the Bible say: "Everything tends toward nothing"?

LIGHT: No.

ADAM: It doesn't?

LIGHT: No.

ADAM: "All is vanity"?

LIGHT: Yes.

ADAM: "Chaos and old night"?

LIGHT: No.

ADAM: And court in session! Just to heap Pelion upon Ossa!

LIGHT: They aren't in the Bible, either. Judgment Day: *that* is.

ADAM: So it *is* the end of the world.

LIGHT: And plaintiffs at the door!

ADAM: That's what I dreamt of last night: plaintiffs—dragging me before the bench. But I was also on it. Judge *and* Defendant. Passing judgment on myself. Sending myself to jail—an iron collar round my neck. The Dream of a Judge Disgraced!

LIGHT: Will it come true?

ADAM: How dare you? *(He raises his fist.)*

LIGHT: I meant: to some other Judge? Then again, you *will* be disgraced if you don't do all the right things today! Judge Peter—

ADAM: I *shall* do all the right things today! *(Enter Judge Walter.)*

WALTER: Judge Adam, I believe?

ADAM: *(miserably).* The very same, alas!

WALTER: Alas? I'm Walter from Boston.

ADAM: *(joyfully).* Why didn't you say so? Welcome to Concord! We have awaited your arrival with eager anticipation!

WALTER: May you not live to change your mind! The Supreme Court of Massachusetts wants to, well, raise the plane of legal practice in the Commonwealth. I'm no Avenging Angel. Concord can't be all concord, ha? But I hear rumors it's been lagging behind the times.

ADAM: It has, it has! Even Boston's not Heaven, and Concord's not Boston. It's pre-George Washington. Slightly George the Second. What are you going to do about it?

WALTER: Isn't there much red tape?

ADAM: Mountains of it!

WALTER: We have too many meaningless regulations?

ADAM: Do we!

WALTER: So let's . . . sift them, shall we?

ADAM: Sift'em, sift'em, throw out the chaff!

WALTER: And this is the Clerk of the Court?

ADAM: Mr. Light, yes.

LIGHT: At your service, your worship.

WALTER: Very important job. How long have you had it?

LIGHT: Nine years, come Pentecost.

WALTER: And ready for better things, I'll wager!

ADAM: *(nervously).* You were in Lexington, Judge?

WALTER: *(nodding).* You heard what happened?

ADAM: Judge Peter under house arrest? He tried to hang himself?

WALTER: What he hoped I'd find to be mere incompetence proved to be no less than embezzlement.

ADAM: And the clerk of the court's a saint, is he?

WALTER: Mr. Paul?

ADAM: He'll keep his hand out of the cookie jar?

WALTER: I was favorably impressed by him.

ADAM: *(to Light).* He's about to be impressed by *me,* isn't he, Mr. Light?

LIGHT: You?

WALTER: You've collected money from the people of Concord for several Funds?

ADAM: Five.

WALTER: I thought four?

ADAM: Until the floods. The Concord River was in flood. So we had a Flood Fund.

WALTER: Last spring when the snow melted. The money's still there? *(Pause.)* Who are the people in the lobby—litigants?

LIGHT: Every Tuesday, the court's in session.

WALTER: And the crowd outside?

LIGHT: Waiting to come in and watch.

WALTER: Good. Let's see how you handle these things in Concord. *(Enter Maggie.)*

MAGGIE: *(to Adam).* Greetings from the Sexton's wife but there's a funeral service in church this morning and the Sexton's wearing one wig. The other one's worn out. She'll send you the one he's wearing, later.

ADAM: *(waving Maggie out of the room).* Thank you, Maggie. *(She leaves.)*

WALTER: What's this?

ADAM: An accident. I've been trying to borrow a wig. But I was born bareheaded, and bareheaded I'll be today.

WALTER: Bareheaded in court? Tsk, tsk, tsk.

ADAM: Does my dignity as a judge depend upon mere externals?

LIGHT: Yes.

ADAM: All right: I'll borrow one from the farmer I used to work for. I've come up in the world, your worship. I'm a success story.

WALTER: A farmer? Out in the country? Is there no one in Concord? The minister, the teacher?

ADAM: Both *corrupt,* your worship! I had to deprive them of . . . certain perquisites, so they don't love me. It's this farmer—

WALTER: *(shaking his head).* We're late already. I'm going on to Amherst.

ADAM: What do I do? Put some powder on my head? Let me at least offer you a hearty breakfast—Boston sausage, Nut-brown ale from New York—

WALTER: I've had breakfast, thanks . . . Those bruises, Judge! You mentioned an accident?

ADAM: I fell out of my bed as if into my grave! But, it was only the bedroom floor, so um—

WALTER: The damage isn't too serious?

ADAM: Let me tell you something, Judge: no damage, however serious, comes between Adam and the performance of his duty!

WALTER: That's splendid. Show me.

ADAM: Show you what? The sights of Concord: the river, the bridge, the wineglass elms?

WALTER: Bring in your first Plaintiff and Defendant. And let me watch quietly from the side.

ADAM: You heart's set on that? Ah well, at least we won't put you, so to speak, below the salt: you must have the seat of honor, my very own Judge's bench: up here.

WALTER: And where will you do your judging?

ADAM: At this humble table, Judge, like our ancestors before us.

WALTER: Well, thank you. *(He takes the Judge's seat, which is elevated and central, facing a long table at stage level, at which Adam will conduct his interrogations, seated at one end—the party being interrogated at the other end.)*

ADAM: I still can't talk you out of it? No? Then, while the presiding Judge retires to don his robe, if not his wig, let the contestants enter.

LIGHT: Spectators, this way *(indicating the front of house)*; litigants, this way *(indicating chairs placed behind the table and facing front)*.

(Four litigants enter, and we imagine a crowd of spectators to be entering at the same time. The litigants are Martha Bull, plaintiff and her daughter Eve; Robert, defendant, and his father, Thomas Tumpel).

MRS. BULL: I claim damages! Where's Judge Adam?

MR. TUMPEL: No need to scream! If you're right and can prove it, you'll win.

MRS. BULL: Win? Some things can't be mended. Try getting an egg back into its shell.

MR. TUMPEL: A jug's been broken. That's all!

MRS. BULL: But *what* a jug! Why,—

MR. TUMPEL: If it can't be mended, it can be replaced.

MRS. BULL: A human being can't be replaced. My jug was *human!*

MR. TUMPEL: So what are you asking the Judge to do?

ROBERT: Let her rant and rave, Father. It's not the jug that's geting her goat, it's her daughter Eve—

MR. TUMPEL: Your fiancée—

ROBERT: *(looking straight at Eve).* My ex-fiancée. I leave for Boston in the morning. Six months training in the Militia. When I return, that girl and I will be strangers.

EVE: Robert!

ROBERT: That's my name.

EVE: You've refused to see me in private. I must speak now in public.

ROBERT: Why?

EVE: You could still see me in private.

ROBERT: Oh, no!

EVE: Then it must be here and now.

ROBERT: Public or private, all I have to say is that you are a— *(He stops.)* Do I have to say the word?

EVE: *I* have to say one thing—

ROBERT: Me too. You are a WHORE.

(A silence.)

EVE: You asked me the big question: "will you have me?" Would I have you in my bed one day and no man else? I said: Yes. You believed me, trusted me, chose me because I was *to be trusted,* would be *loyal.*

ROBERT: A century ago.

EVE: Three months. In which time you heard things.

ROBERT: And *saw* things, too. Things that spoke volumes.

EVE: People, Robert can be deceived and often are. Suppose there was deception in *this* case? You've been misled, and so you were in error. But meanwhile you'd rejected me. With violence. How would I feel?

ROBERT: Cut the cackle, girl: you are a—

EVE: I would feel: he did *not* trust me. He would give me the benefit of no doubt—

ROBERT: What doubt was there?—

EVE: Yet now he finds that he's been wrong, comes to me all apology, "Forgive me, I was wrong." *Could* I forgive you?

ROBERT: I'm not sure I follow.

EVE: I could forgive you, but would that help?

ROBERT: Ha?

EVE: When you had so mistrusted me, could *I* trust *you?* Forget *as well as* forgive . . . still love you?

ROBERT: Your questions!

EVE: My questions! I . . . beg you to consider them!

(She goes down on her knees. A silence.)

ROBERT: Oh, my God!

MRS. BULL: Get up off your knees, girl! I've lined up a real man for you, a go-getter: Corporal Pegleg. Yeah, he *gives* the beatings in the Militia! This . . . peacock will just receive'em. Forget him.

EVE: *(getting up).* Drop your suit, Mother. The Concord potter will repair the jug.

MRS. BULL: It's too far gone!

EVE: Buy another jug. I'll give you my savings.

MRS. BULL: And we all know why: your honor is at stake! But this jug's enemies are yours. They must be defeated here in court: the Concord Judge is the Concord potter who'll repair our jug. Ah! *(Judge Adam has just re-entered—in his robe but without his wig.)* Judge Adam!

ADAM: Mrs. Bull! One word, first, with your daughter. *(Taking Eve to one side)* What goes on? Robert and his father here? Not going to accuse *me* of anything, I hope? Make me pass judgement on—*(He points to himself)?* Even in my wildest dreams —ugh! *(He shudders to recall last night's dream.)*

EVE: *(pulling away from him).* Let's drop the suit, mother!

ADAM: Yes, let's!

MRS. BULL: Not on your life!

ADAM: *(taking Light on one side).* What is the case about?

LIGHT: Something and nothing. Someone broke a jug.

ADAM: A jug! What next? *Who* broke it?

LIGHT: The jug?

ADAM: Yes.

LIGHT: Who broke it?

ADAM: Yes.

LIGHT: You should be at the table, Judge. That's where you'll find who broke the jug.

ADAM: *(going back to Eve).* Eve!

EVE: No.

ADAM: One question.

EVE: No.

ADAM: What brings *you* here?

EVE: Go away.

ADAM: Eve! Tell me what this is about!

EVE: If you don't leave me alone, I shall have to—

ADAM: Sh!!*(He returns to Light.)* I'm sick, Mr. Light. Must be this gaping wound on my shin. Got to go back to bed. *You* hear this case!

LIGHT: Are you taking leave of your senses?

ADAM: *(returning to Eve).* Eve, by the wounded head of Christ, what brought you here?

EVE: You'll find out—from the judge's bench.

ADAM: A suit about a jug?

EVE: Yes.

ADAM: A jug—and nothing else?

EVE: Leave me alone.

ADAM: You're a brainy girl. Are you going to *use* your brains?

EVE: You are without shame.

ADAM: *(taking her further from the others and speaking in a whisper).* Aren't you forgetting what can happen to a Boston militia man if we don't take counter-measures? I hope you haven't lost those papers: they prove—

WALTER: Judge Adam! It is improper for the presiding judge to confer privately with the parties!

ADAM: What's that, your worship? What was your gracious command?

WALTER: Your place is at the table: I'm here to see a *public* trial!

ADAM: *(to himself).* Wish I could remember—I do recall a crash as I was leaving—

LIGHT: Judge!

ADAM: *(not hearing).* And I thought I'd put the thing securely on the shelf!

LIGHT: *(partially overhearing).* Put what on what shelf, Judge?

ADAM: *(to himself).* Well, well, what does not bend must break!

LIGHT: Are you deaf? Judge Walter is speaking to you.

ADAM: What can I do for you, your worship? Start the trial?

WALTER: You're so pre-occupied, Judge. Now why is that?

ADAM: It's the guinea hen I bought—off a ship that came in to Boston from the Indies. It has the pip. And what do you do for a hen with the pip? You cram it. If you can. I can't. She can. That girl there. I was just consulting her on the subject. I think of my chickens, Judge, as my children—I'm a bachelor, don't you know.

WALTER: Sit down, Judge. *(Adam sits at the table.)* Now call the Plaintiff. Question him or her, and have your Clerk take down the minutes.

ADAM: *(very humble).* Your worship!

WALTER: Yes.

ADAM: Would you want all the formalities observed? Or shall I do what's customary in Concord?

WALTER: Is it customary to observe the laws of Massachusetts?

ADAM: *(puzzled).* Ha? Well, I'm sure I know what you want. All set, Mr. Light?

LIGHT: We are all waiting, Judge.

ADAM: *(taking a deep breath).* Let Justice—implacable though blind—now take its course! Who's the Plaintiff?

MRS. BULL: Me, your honor.

ADAM: Step forward! *(She does so.)* Who are you?

MRS. BULL: Who am I?!

ADAM: Yes: name, address, social standing . . .

MRS. BULL: You must be kidding.

ADAM: Jesting is the word in court. Right, Judge?

MRS. BULL: You must be jesting, your honor.

ADAM: Well, I'm not. The law, the law we all hold sacred, requires me to know, ma'am, who you are.

MRS. BULL: You peep in at my window every Sunday on your way to your cottage near Walden Pond.

WALTER: You know this woman, Judge?

ADAM: Martha Bull? Naturally. She lives just round the corner—where the path cuts through the hedge. Shopkeeper's widow, a midwife nowadays, regular churchgoer, excellent reputation . . .

WALTER: Walter, Superior Judge from Boston, Mrs. Bull. Judge Adam, have the Clerk write: "Well-known to the Court."

ADAM: *(to Light).* His Honor doesn't stand on ceremony! D'you have that, Mr. Light?

(Light nods, and writes.)

WALTER: Now what's the subject of the complaint?

ADAM: A jug.

WALTER: You know about the case already?

ADAM: Put down "jug," Mr. Light, and add: "Well-known to the Court."

LIGHT: It's *only* about a jug? It is not possible that—?

ADAM: Just a jug, right, Mrs. Bull?

MRS. BULL: *(embarking on what might be a tirade).* This jug here, smashed to smithereens as you all can see—

ADAM: So: no pedantic scruples, Mr. Light! *(To Walter:)* I hit the trail and follow it, Judge, looking neither to the right nor to the left!

LIGHT: May I, however, ask—

ADAM: No, you may not! *(To Walter:)* And I maintain strict discipline in court! *(To Mrs. Bull:)* Who broke the jug? *(Pointing at Robert.)* That good-for-nothing!

MRS. BULL: Yes, your honor.

ADAM: *(to himself).* So far, so good.

ROBERT: Your honor, that's not true!

ADAM: *(not hearing).* The Old Adam rides again—rides, if all goes this well, to victory!

LIGHT: There's been an objection, Judge.

ROBERT: She lies in her throat!

ADAM: We'll have an iron collar round *your* throat before you can say George Washington! D'you have that, Mr. Light, the one word: jug? And the name of this good-for-nothing who broke it?

WALTER: Judge, judge, this is violence, not law.

ADAM: Ha?

WALTER: Don't you propose to look into the case before—

ADAM: What?

LIGHT: Wouldn't you care, Judge, formally to—

ADAM: No, no, his Honor doesn't stand on ceremony!

WALTER: Do you know how to conduct a trial, Judge? If not, I'm afraid we may have to replace you.

ADAM: Ha? With who?

WALTER: I'm favorably impressed with the Clerk of the Court.

ADAM: That seems to be a habit of yours. Hm. I offered him the job just this morning. He wouldn't take it! He had a severe attack of Christian humility!

LIGHT: Well, um—I'm not worthy, I—!

ADAM: *(to Walter).* You said: do what's customary in Concord.

WALTER: I was hoping it was customary to do what's lawful.

ADAM: Well, Judge, there are certain time-honored customs, certain hallowed traditions, from which I, as Concord's favorite son, would not presume to deviate by a hair.

WALTER: Now, Judge—

ADAM: I'm a somewhat educated man. Cracker barrel philosopher, if you like. I know the world. I've been to Boston—several times. I've read the Constitution of the United States—all three volumes. *(Judge Walter raises his eyebrows.)* Ha? All right: give me one last chance and, if I must, I'll try this case according to the law.

WALTER: One last chance, then. Start the trial again.

ADAM: *(starting over).* Your complaint, Mrs. Bull?

MRS. BULL: Can I tell about the jug?

ADAM: Now is your opportunity! That right, Judge?

MRS. BULL: Well, d'you *see* the jug?

ADAM: I should: you've been waving it around for the past half hour!

MRS. BULL: You see what's left of the jug. The best part's gone forever. Know what that part was like?

ADAM: *(looking at Walter).* Who asks the questions in a Court of Law? Judge or Plaintiff?

MRS. BULL: "The Life of Sir Walter Raleigh, Discoverer of America."

ADAM: Ignorant peasant! *I* know who discovered America, it was—

MRS. BULL: Sir Walter Raleigh! And named Virginia for the Virgin Queen! She was here—

ADAM: In Concord?

MRS. BULL: Here—on the jug—

ADAM: You're pointing to a hole.

MRS. BULL: That's right. And there Sir Walter threw his cloak down in the mud, so the Queen's pretty feet would not get wet!

ADAM: All this was painted on your jug?

MRS. BULL: *(nodding).* His whole life story. Voyage to Guiana. Imprisonment in the Tower of London. Second Voyage to the Americas . . . And, here, see this?

ADAM: More hole.

MRS. BULL: Sir Walter's head is missing.

ADAM: He was beheaded! I know my history, Judge!

MRS. BULL: His head fell in the basket.

ADAM: I don't see any basket.

MRS. BULL: It's missing.

LIGHT: How then, Judge, does the Court know that his head was *ever* in the basket?

ADAM: Everyone knows it was in the basket, idiot!

LIGHT: But if someone had moved the basket—say, 18 inches to the left—the head would just have rolled away . . .

(His eyes seem to follow such a rolling head.)

MRS. BULL: Rubbish! It was the jug that rolled away. Part of the jug, the artistic part, the historic part!

ADAM: Prove it! This court demands proof beyond a reasonable doubt!

WALTER: Mrs. Bull, may we ask that you stick to the point? Mr. Light—

LIGHT: My records now have a complete description of the jug.

WALTER: So can we go on from there?

MRS. BULL: To the history of the jug itself?

WALTER: Well, I rather think Judge Adam will rule that out.

MRS. BULL: *(as Adam starts to speak).* He wouldn't dare! This jug is a historic landmark!

ADAM: Really? Now that's of interest to all Concordians, Judge. I'll have to let her tell *this* story!

WALTER: One minute?

ADAM: It's hard to pack all this history into one minute! Two minutes, Mrs. Bull.

MRS. BULL: It began with Burgoyne at Saratoga. The jug belonged, or so they say, to the General himself. They also say he'd brought it from old England, a gift from his lady mother. She in turn—

WALTER: Are we going to have the life story of General Burgoyne's mother? How old *is* the jug?

MRS. BULL: Some say it's from the time of Raleigh himself, others say even earlier—

WALTER: How then could the jug portray Sir Walter?

ADAM: Well now, isn't that what is called folklore, Judge?

WALTER: *(tartly).* Suppose you hold the Plaintiff to the facts of history?

MRS. BULL: It's history, patriotic history, for it was a common soldier, a plain democratic American, who grabbed the jug from General Burgoyne's sweetly perfumed hands! *(To Light:)* His name was Freddy Feargod.

LIGHT: *(writing it into the record)* Fear-god, a good Puritan name!

MRS. BULL: Only drank from the jug three times in all his life, Freddy. The Puritans were never friendly to firewater: Freddy mixed pump water with it. Well, at sixty three, he married and thereafter had sixteen children—

ADAM: *(hooting with pleasure).* Whoo!

WALTER: Is this pertinent, Judge?

MRS. BULL: Yes, because the third and last time Freddy drank from the jug was at her funeral.

ADAM: *(grinning).* What a story!

WALTER: I asked if it was pertinent?

ADAM: *(calling himself to order, harshly to Mrs. Bull).* It's not pertinent, you fool!

MRS. BULL: Yes it is. Remember the great fire in New York?

WALTER: There have been many great fires in New York.

MRS. BULL: This was in '89.

ADAM: The jug was in *that* fire?

MRS. BULL: It was.

ADAM: Heaven and hell! What happened to it?

MRS. BULL: Nothing.

ADAM: Nothing at all?

MRS. BULL: Nothing at all.

WALTER: Then, Madam, may I ask why you are telling us?

MRS. BULL: History records that the jug at that time – the time when nothing happened to it in the great fire – actually, it was all the better for a burnishing and a glazing! – belonged to, can you guess?

ADAM: Thomas Jefferson?

MRS. BULL: Mr. Bull. My husband. Ran the general store here.

WALTER: What of that?

MRS. BULL: And so it came to me, the jug! And so it comes to this court today – though in smithereens! To sum up –

WALTER: You're allowing a summation, Judge?

ADAM: *(to Mrs. Bull).* Thirty seconds more history to go!

MRS. BULL: Then first, the jug was beautiful and English and had a picture of the great Queen on it! And second, the jug's historic and American, coming down to us in a fine native tradition from Washington's army to yours truly in Concord, Massachusetts! A jug, in short –

WALTER: Short!

MRS. BULL: – to grace the lips of the Mayor of Boston or the First Lady of these United States! So how dare he –

ADAM: The Mayor of Boston?

MRS. BULL: That good-for nothing! *(She points at Robert.)*

ADAM: Ah yes! How dare he what? Just for the record!

MRS. BULL: How dare he break such a jug?

ADAM: Got all that, Mr. Light?

ROBERT: Get this too, Mr. Light: she's a liar.

ADAM: Speak when you're spoken to! Proceed, Mrs. Bull.

MRS. BULL: Well, yesterday at eleven –

ADAM: In the morning, yes?

MRS. BULL: No, in the evening. I'm in bed, just about to put out the light, when I hear a noise, voices, men's voices, from my daughter's room at the back of the house. Phew! You'd think the Devil himself had broke in! I rush over. The door's been forced! More noise! More voices! I strike a light, and what do I see?

ADAM: The Devil himself?

MRS. BULL: This jug. In pieces. All over the floor.

ADAM: And nobody around?

MRS. BULL: Her *(pointing to her daughter)* wringing her hands! And that peacock *(pointing to Robert)* shouting his head off!

ADAM: I'll be damned.

MRS. BULL: What?

ADAM: That . . . peacock?

MRS. BULL: How dare he come here in the dead of night, I ask, breaking my jugs as he goes?

ADAM: His answer?

MRS. BULL: "It wasn't me! It wasn't me!"

ADAM: Wasn't him that—?

MRS. BULL: Knocked the jug off the shelf. It was someone who'd jumped out of the window.

WALTER: Who was that!

MRS. BULL: Who knows?

ADAM: *No one* knows!

MRS. BULL: Meanwhile he *(pointing at Robert)* sounds off against me and my daughter.

ADAM: A gambit, Judge Walter, a red herring.

MRS. BULL: I look at Eve. She's petrified. "Eve!" I shout. He's still gabbing, that's why I'm shouting. "Eve," I shout, "Was someone else here?" "Someone else?" Says she. "Someone else," I answer, "was another man here?" "Another man? Oh, oh," cries she: and swears that there was not.

EVE: Swears? No.

MRS. BULL: You swore it was Robert.

EVE: I did not.

ROBERT: Hear that, Judge?

ADAM: Silence! Wait your turn!

MRS. BULL: "God above," you said—

EVE: I didn't *swear* by Him—

ADAM: Swear or not swear, what did she say? I'd like to get God off the hook!

WALTER: *(shocked.)* Judge Adam!

MRS. BULL: Wait a minute, is she saying now it was not Robert? There was *another* man in her room!!

EVE: That's not what I said.

ADAM: That's not what she said.

MRS. BULL: She said yesterday it was Robert.

ROBERT: She lied.

ADAM: Silence! You're in contempt of court, young man. Mr. Light, did you get all this down?

WALTER: All what? That, yesterday, the girl confessed something, and even then not on oath?

ADAM: Now Judge Walter—

WALTER: Don't push the evidence, Judge!

ADAM: I won't. That was very wrong of me!

WALTER: So anxious to pin suspicion on this young man! Anyone might think you broke the jug yourself! *(A silence.)*

ADAM: Keep on talking, Judge! I could listen to you till the cows come home!

WALTER: Pull yourself together and question him.

ADAM: Him?

WALTER: He's the Defendant, is he not?

ADAM: Or the indefensible, which?

WALTER: Your jokes, Judge, are out of place. I'm really afraid your legal career is drawing to a close.

ADAM: Hey, it's that bad? I'm going to be fired?

WALTER: Proceed with the trial.

ADAM: Absentminded, that's my trouble. Never think of anything but that guinea hen, the one with the pip. It should have dropped dead in the Indies! The noodle dumpling, don't you know . . .

WALTER: We are discussing dumplings now?

ADAM: Well, I was going to give the hen a noodle dumpling.

WALTER: Set that aside now, and do your duty.

ADAM: My duty! *That's* what I should be doing! Defendant! That's you, you fool. Who are you, etcetera?

ROBERT: Robert, son of Thomas Tumpel, farmer, Concord, Mass.

ADAM: You heard what Mrs. Bull had to say about you?

ROBERT: Yes, your honor.

ADAM: D'you have the gall to deny it, the effrontery to disavow one jot or tittle of it? I'm suggesting that you open these proceedings with a full and contrite confession.

ROBERT: Not a word she spoke was true.

ADAM: *(cupping hand to ear).* What's that? I can't hear you. And anyway, can you prove it?

ROBERT: Yes!

ADAM: No! Mrs. Bull says—

WALTER: Excuse me, Judge: you must not quote one witness to another—

ADAM: What? Can I stand idly by and—I'm a Deacon of the Concord Baptist Church—

WALTER: We need Robert's testimony. Mr. Light—

LIGHT: Yes, your worship?

WALTER: Do *you* know how to conduct a trial?

LIGHT: Me? Conduct this trial? Well, since you insist—*He heads for Judge Adam's chair, but Adam gets there first.)*

ADAM: Robert! Don't just stand there, you're not a cow in your father's pasture! Testify this minute! *(To Walter:)* That the idea, Judge?

ROBERT: Testify—to what?

WALTER: *(gently).* Just tell us your story, Robert.

ROBERT: It must've been before ten last night. It's January, and snow on the ground, but it was mild and felt like Spring. I said to Father: "Mind if I go over to the Bulls' place? I'd like to see Eve." We were engaged. I thought her quite a girl, no wallflower. She can work! You should see her handle a rake at harvest time! Hay flies from her rake like mice from a cat! It hadn't taken me long to ask her: would she have me? She gave me a saucy answer: "how you do cackle!" But later she said: "Yes."

ADAM: *(taking notes).* "How you do cackle but later she said yes." *(To Walter:)* Oh, these peasants!

WALTER: Let him talk.

ROBERT: Father acted like he didn't hear me. I said, "Outside. Under her window. We'll just talk for a while." Father spoke for the first time. "Outside! You'll *stay* outside?" "I give you my word," I said. Another pause but shorter. Then: "Very well, be back by eleven."

ADAM: Father said, I said, Father spoke, I said . . . Are we boring you, Judge?

WALTER: That isn't the question, is it?

ADAM: *(to Robert).* Keep going!

ROBERT: "It's a bargain," I replied. I was thinking to get there in fifteen minutes but the snow held me up. "Oh dear, oh dear," I thought, "the Bulls' garden gate will be locked!" They lock it every night when the clock strikes ten.

ADAM: Is this evidence admissible, Judge? It's verging on the indecent.

WALTER: Quiet. *(To Robert:)* Yes, and then?

ROBERT: You know about the Concord elms? Wineglass elms the finest ones are called. *(His hands indicate the shape.)* Others bend outwards at the top. Some of these, just near the Bulls' place, form a vaulted archway. Avenue of the Elms, Judge Walter, that's what we locals call it, and dark as a cathedral. Down this avenue I walk towards the Bulls' place. I hear the sound of a latch on a garden gate, *their* garden gate. It must be Eve. I look in that direction, and . . . and . . . *(He stops.)*

WALTER: Yes?

ROBERT: What's the matter with my eyes?

ADAM: Maybe you're blind, ha, ha, ha! Excuse me, Judge.

ROBERT: That was my first thought. Yet I saw too much. Was seeing believing? No, my eyes were liars! Worse. They were scandal-mongers! Yet worse. They were—!

ADAM: *(to Judge Walter).* Isn't he a character? Such gift of gab! *(To Robert:)* You should run for Congress sometime!

WALTER: Ask him what he saw, Judge.

ADAM: You, um, *saw* something? You imagined it, didn't you?

ROBERT: I knew Eve—by her clothes.

ADAM: You saw *Eve!* Well, that's all right. Get it down, Mr. Light. He saw Eve.

LIGHT: Eve . . .

ROBERT: And a man.

ADAM: Order in the court! The Court disallows impropriety!

WALTER: *(dryly).* A court can't investigate impropriety without mentioning it, Judge Adam. *(To Robert:)* Name the man.

ADAM: *(on the point of heading for an exit.)* Name—!

ROBERT: I only wish I knew! In the dark all cats are black.

ADAM: You *can't* name him! Have that, Mr. Light?

WALTER: You have no idea?

ROBERT: There's an apprentice to our Concord cobbler runs

after Eve. Last Fall I told her, "That bastard's hanging around, I don't like it, throw him out!" But, says she, "You bother me!" What she tells the fellow could be taken two ways. *I* threw him out!

ADAM: *(cheering him on now).* Yeh! That's how we handle lechers in Concord, Judge! And you wanted his name, didn't you? The Defendant will now give us his name.

ROBERT: His name is Rupert.

ADAM: Once you have a name—didn't need a law school to teach me this—the rest is a snap! You took down that name, Mr. Light?

LIGHT: *(nodding).* Rupert.

ADAM: Proceed, Robert, my son!

ROBERT: I'd always left at ten. It was long after. I go through the garden gate. Hide behind the hedge. Lots of whispering, lots of hanky-panky, pulling, pushing, O my God—there are horns sprouting on my brow!

EVE: Eavesdropper, spy!

MRS. BULL: Wait till I sink my claws in you!

ADAM: *(benignly).* Quiet, ladies, order in the court! *(To Robert:)* Proceed, my son.

ROBERT: Who's marrying who around here, I ask myself! I'd been there who knows how long when the two of them, not stopping to see the minister on their way, slipped inside the house.

EVE: Mother, I'm going to speak now, come what may!

ADAM: *(as Mrs. Bull starts to speak).* Ladies, silence, I say! We have law and order in Concord despite those rumors you've been listening to, Judge Walter! Law and order, ladies, and no uncalled-for gossip! Proceed, young gentleman!

ROBERT: I'm gonna burst a vein. Two buttons snap right off my coat. "Air! Give me Air!" I check the door. Locked *and* bolted. But what's a cottage door? I bang on it with my fists and scream. No response. I break in. Kick the door down.

ADAM: Samson in Gaza!

ROBERT: The door crashes to the floor, and what do I see? A jug falls from a shelf, and whisk! in that same instant a man jumps out the window!

WALTER: Who? Who?

ROBERT: All I saw, really, was his coat tails.

ADAM: Ah! You saw Rupert's coat tails?

ROBERT: Yes.

ADAM: You have that, Mr. Light?

LIGHT: Yes, Judge.

WALTER: But, Judge—

ADAM: Continue, Robert, lad!

ROBERT: The girl just stands there, helpless. I dash to the window. He hasn't made a getaway! He's got stuck in the trellis—where the vine's entwined on the wall! He's hanging there and can't pull free! Well, when I'd broken in, the doorknob came off in my hand. I was still holding it, and his head was within reach. I whacked him with it.

ADAM: *(surreptitiously feeling the dents in his head).* It was a doorknob!

ROBERT: *(thrown).* What?

ADAM: It was a—?

ROBERT: Oh, a doorknob, yes. So now he falls—down off the trellis—to the ground. He's not dead, but that can be corrected! I climb on to the window sill, prepare to jump down right on top of him . . . All goes blank! The world's not there any more!

ADAM: The world—not there! Where's it gone?

ROBERT: He's thrown sand in my eyes, a handful of coarse, sharp-edged sand!

ADAM: Hm. Sand, eh? Thrown by this . . . Rupert?

ROBERT: Yes, sir.

ADAM: Mr. Light?

LIGHT: Rupert.

ADAM: Oh, what a scoundrel, eh, Judge?

ROBERT: If it *was* Rupert.

ADAM: You just agreed with me—But go on, sonny.

ROBERT: I sit up, wipe the sand from my sore eyes. She comes over. "Dear God, Robert," she cries, "you're hurt?" I tried to kick her. Kicked thin air!

ADAM: Still blinded, eh?

ROBERT: Yes, sir.

ADAM: He must've been a pretty good shot?

ROBERT: That's what *I* was thinking.

ADAM: You have that, Mr. Light? Rupert—an excellent shot with a handful of sand! *(Light nods.)* Proceed, Robert.

ROBERT: I pick myself up. Why dirty my hands with her, I was thinking now, why not throw that word at her?

ADAM: What word?

ROBERT: WHORE. But when Mrs. Bull came in with a lamp, and I saw that the girl was in tears, I wished I *was* blind, wished I'd given my eyes to kids to play marbles with. *I* burst out crying . . . the rest you know.

WALTER: I don't. What happened to the man who threw the sand?

ROBERT: Who knows? That was at the back of the house. We were all at the front.

WALTER: We all?

ROBERT: Before midnight, all Concord was on the scene. It began with their nextdoor neighbors, Herb and Sam, then *their* nextdoor neighbors, then theirs, then all the Bulls' relatives, Cousin Susie, Cousin Lisa, and none of them could leave their kids at home, so all the kids of Concord came, and the kids couldn't leave their pets at home, so all the pets of Concord came, it was like when the Circus comes around in July! Mrs. Bull then asks for quiet and, when you could hear a pin drop, asks our young lady in front of all those people: who smashed the jug? Me, she said, making no mention of the Cobbler's apprentice and the hole in his head.

ADAM: Hm. Interesting point. You have it, Mr. Light—Rupert "had a hole in his head"? *(Light nods.)* Satisfied now, Judge?

WALTER: By no means. Mrs. Bull hasn't finished.

ADAM: *(to her.)* Mrs. Bull?

MRS. BULL: My side has a witness.

ADAM: But young Robert has just told us the whole story.

MRS. BULL: Young Robert has crept into my chicken coop and strangled a chicken.

ADAM: A chicken?

MRS. BULL: The truth!

ADAM: You're gonna have to prove it!

MRS. BULL: *(pointing to Eve.)* With the aid of this witness.

ADAM: Your own daughter? That's illegal!

WALTER: What?

ADAM: Yes, Judge, the law book says—*titulo quarto* or at worst *quinto*—"when jugs and such like, who knows?—are spoiled, smashed, pulverized, annihilated, etcetera—by young punks and such like, sons, daughters or whatever cannot be witnesses for their own mothers who bore them and the like . . . "

WALTER: Surely the girl could make a Statement?

ADAM: The law book says that? Sorry, your worship: of course the law book says that! *Titulo sexto!* "Sons, daughters and such like can make Statements." Too bad what she says can't be believed.

WALTER: Let's not judge a Statement we've not heard! *(To Eve:)* Step forward, child.

ADAM: *(before Eve can move).* May we confer, your worship—you and I?

WALTER: You're the presiding judge! *(The two judges confer privately.)*

ADAM: I believe in compromise!

WALTER: Between what and what? We don't yet have the facts.

ADAM: Not from the legal but from the philosophic viewpoint? I often take that viewpoint, don't I, Light?

LIGHT: *(cryptically). Very* often.

ADAM: Two possibilities! It could be Robert or it could be Rupert. Which?

WALTER: Having stuck your hand in a bag of peas, you are just groping around.

ADAM: Which? That's a philosophical question!

WALTER: Can you answer it?

ADAM: No.

WALTER: So then where are we?

ADAM: Where we come up with another question: couldn't it be both?

WALTER: Both what?

ADAM: It could be Robert, it could be Rupert—

WALTER: Or it could be both! I take that back.

ADAM: Don't. That was the answer! The first answer. Will you advance with me to the second?

WALTER: *(sweating).* Perish the thought! No, no. Let's have the Statement.

ADAM: What Statement?

WALTER: The young lady's.

ADAM: Oh her! That's you, Miss Eve. Speak, do! But remember it's Judgment Day: your life, your eternal soul, depend on what you now shall say! *(He coughs.)* You could say it was Rupert. Why not? Maybe it *was* Rupert! Same with Robert. Why not say it's *him,* ha? Very good solutions, both of those! On the other hand, Miss Eve, to bring up a third name . . . a fourth, a fifth and so on up to a five-hundredth – that might create discord in Concord! Time consuming, for one thing. For another, not a soul would believe you, you'd find no witnesses: and white walls tell no tales, ha? There are hazards. You might pick a third man who knows a thing or two. Or one who has a hold over your Robert –

WALTER: What *are* you talking about, Judge?

ADAM: I know, your worship, I'm a country bumpkin, born and bred. In Boston I can't make myself understood. In Concord, though, even an ignorant girl understands me, eh, Miss Eve?

MRS. BULL: *(to Eve).* What is he talking about?

EVE: Be patient with me, mother.

ROBERT: When you have a bad conscience, it's hard to speak out!

MRS. BULL: That's enough out of you. *(To Eve:)* Then who was it?

EVE: *(overcome).* Lord Jesus, Lord Jesus!

MRS. BULL: It was the Lord Jesus?!

ADAM: No blasphemy in this court. How's that, Judge?

MRS. BULL: He called her a WHORE, didn't he?

ADAM: Which you confirmed by saying she'd been doing it with Jesus!

WALTER: *(sternly).* Judge Adam!

MRS. BULL: Her father used to say, "Listen, Martha, if my girl should prove a WHORE and I turn over in my grave, give the gravedigger a penny to turn me on my back again."

ADAM: You see, Judge, Concord is *still* a good Puritan town. Honor thy father and thy mother!

MRS. BULL: Was it the cobbler's apprentice?

ROBERT: I'm beginning to feel sorry for her again. Now I wish I *had* broken the jug!

EVE: Well, don't! Don't wish that!

ROBERT: Ha?

EVE: Tell me something, Robert, Why weren't you willing to *pretend* you'd broken it?

ROBERT: Pretend? Lie? It's a world of lies and deceit, this world! I should join you there?

EVE: There are white lies. Good lies. What's a bad lie, for that matter? A breach of trust, isn't it? Whereas, it you'd lied for me then, what would it have shown?

ROBERT: That I'm a liar in a liars' world.

EVE: It would have shown you trusted me. *(As he starts to expostulate:)* Suppose, then, that you'd looked right through the keyhole, seen me drinking with a man—yes, from this jug. You could have told yourself: it will be explained sometime—before Judgment Day.

ROBERT: I can't wait that long.

EVE: You could if you trusted me. If you felt I was bound to be loyal.

ROBERT: What?

EVE: Circumstances, oh yes, can be uncertain and unclear. Should our loyalties be uncertain and unclear? In this "world of lies and deceit," isn't loyalty something—the one thing, maybe—we have to have?

ROBERT: Disbelieve my own eyes and ears? Wait till Judgment Day for the reason why?

EVE: Suppose it *was* Rupert. I'd have told you, wouldn't I? Told you alone. Might there not be good reason *not* to tell others, not to have all Concord buzzing with the story? If you trusted me—and your trust was real trust, total, indestructible—I could have *pretended* the man was you and not Rupert—could've pretended this quite safely, without fear of any misunderstanding—

ROBERT: *(to Judge Walter).* There's still the stocks in Concord for her kind. *(To Eve:)* But if you can get off by naming me, you're welcome.

EVE: You have understood nothing!

ROBERT: Maybe one *should* fear misunderstanding.

WALTER: Don't let them bicker, Judge.

ADAM: Children, stop bickering!

WALTER: And now pursue the obvious line of questioning.

ADAM: You wouldn't want me peering through the keyhole, would you, the *bedroom* keyhole?

WALTER: *(shaking his head ruefully).* Young lady, are you telling us the man in your room was not Robert?

EVE: Robert has already told you that.

MRS. BULL: It was not Robert?

EVE: It was not.

MRS. BULL: Then you lied to your own mother . . . words fail me . . . I'm gonna beat you black and blue!

WALTER: Now, Mrs. Bull . . .!

ADAM: You know nothing about it. You weren't there. The young lady *was* there. She knows the man was either Robert or Rupert. If not Robert, then—

MRS. BULL: Rupert? It was Rupert?

ADAM: *(winking at Eve).* Hear that, my girl? Even your mother concedes it *must* be Rupert!

EVE: How dare *you* say that?

WALTER: How dare you ask, young woman? Disrespect for a presiding judge is inadmissible!

EVE: Respect for this judge is impossible! *He* knows who the man was in my room! *He* knows it wasn't Rupert! May I ask him one question? *(Adam starts to remonstrate. Walter raises his hand.)*

WALTER: Let me hear it.

EVE: *(to Adam).* Did you, yesterday, dispatch Rupert to Boston with a certified letter to the Militia?

ADAM: Ha? What if I did?

EVE: If you did, then he wasn't in Concord last night.

ADAM: Tsk, tsk, tsk. We've all agreed, have we not, that it must be either Robert or Rupert? You're not helping the court to discover which!

ROBERT: This time she's *not* a liar: I saw Rupert on the Boston Road at eight o'clock last night.

ADAM: And if you did?

ROBERT: If I did, there's a third man in the case.

WALTER: Question her. *(Adam is at a loss.)* Then I must. *(To Eve:)* Tell the court, at long last, what occurred.

ADAM: *(Suddenly finding his tongue).* Excuse me, your honor, this young thing can't do that! She was only confirmed last week!

WALTER: Can't tell the truth?

ADAM: No! She'll only enlarge the area of, um, misunderstanding. *(To Walter, whispering:)* New England girls are all the same. They do it in the dark, then, in court next morning, deny everything.

WALTER: You want me to excuse her?

ADAM: *(nodding).* Her father was a very dear friend of mine! Should she suffer all her life long for a single slip?

WALTER: *(to Eve).* You fear that you'll be mercilessly punished? This is not Salem, 1692. Tell us who broke the jug.

EVE: I've told the court who didn't.

WALTER: Very well then, who did! Tell the court that.

MRS. BULL: Tell your mother that.

EVE: I will tell you, Mother. But not here, not now.

WALTER: And why not?

EVE: Sometimes, when you tell one thing, another thing's revealed.

WALTER: What?

EVE: Secrets leak out that aren't your own.

WALTER: That's all you're prepared to say!

EVE: Yes.

WALTER: Your witness isn't much use to you, Mrs. Bull.

MRS. BULL: Worse than that, she's perjured herself.

WALTER: Tell the court about that.

MRS. BULL: Perjury, as I've known it, can be understood: you're in the place of shame, the stocks, you perjure yourself to get back home, the place of honor. The perjury we hear of now can*not* be understood: this girl has an honorable home yet with a lie will get herself into the stocks.

WALTER: Suppose it was no lie?

MRS. BULL: Oh, your honor, if the man wasn't Robert, I should show Eve and door and say: "From your mother, you've inherited long hair: use it as a rope to hang yourself!"

EVE: Mother!

WALTER: Mrs. Bull!

MRS. BULL: He broke my jug, yet they both deny it! There must be a sinister secret! Some hidden scandal!

WALTER: Yes? Then what?

MRS. BULL: Robert's in the Militia, due to leave for Boston. When one of these modern boys has a girlfriend, oh sir, there's no treason he won't dream up.

WALTER: Such as what?

MRS. BULL: He could run off to California. Take her with him.

WALTER: They could afford that?

MRS. BULL: She knows where my money is. She has the key. Talking of trust, how I have trusted that . . . ! *(She can't say "Whore.")*

WALTER: Your daughter would agree to—?

MRS. BULL: She'd resist his suggestions. I overheard her doing something of the sort. But later she'd—

EVE: Mother, you're making all this up!

ROBERT: Adding insult to injury!

MR. TUMPEL: We'll sue *her* now, my son!

WALTER: Everyone come to order! *(They all sit.)* The subject is a jug. Mrs. Bull, can you prove Robert broke it?

MRS. BULL: Yes.

WALTER: How?

MRS. BULL: By producing a surprise witness.

WALTER: You have a surprise witness?

ADAM: Who?

MRS. BULL: Old Bridget.

ADAM: Old Bridget!

MR. TUMPEL: My Aunt Bridget?

MRS. BULL: *(nodding).* The jug was broken at eleven. Old Bridget was in the garden at half past ten. Found him at that time—Robert, yes—talking to my daughter.

ROBERT: My Great Aunt Bridget found me with Eve?

ADAM: *(to himself).* The Devil's on my side! All I need now is two minutes alone with the girl.

WALTER: *(to Adam).* Bridget must testify.

ROBERT: Why? This is all false!

ADAM: Must testify, by all means! Mr. Light, go and fetch her. *(Light leaves.)*

MR. TUMPEL: *(to Robert).* I'm going to beat the hell out of you!

ROBERT: You believe her!

MR. TUMPEL: Playing around in the garden at half past ten? Then went indoors – against my orders – you admitted as much –

ROBERT: Yes, and I told you how and why! I told the court too! Why go off half cocked?

MR. TUMPEL: If you kept this secret from your own father, who knows what else you've been keeping dark?

ROBERT: Why d'you believe them and not me?

MR. TUMPEL: You're hiding some scandalous secret. I can tell!

ROBERT: Hang Mrs. Bull! And if she really says all this, hang Great Aunt Bridget head downwards from the nearest tree!

MR. TUMPEL: Yesterday you were packing. Why?

ROBERT: I'm going to Boston. For my training.

MR. TUMPEL: A week ago you had no idea when the training would start.

WALTER: Mr. Tumpel, if you know something, tell the court what it is.

MR. TUMPEL: Oh dear, Judge. This about flight and scandal and treason is such a shock! D'you know why I came to court today?

WALTER: Why?

MR. TUMPEL: To get back a silver chain my Robert gave Eve when they got engaged . . .

ADAM: What time is it?

WALTER: The half hour just struck. Why?

ADAM: Past ten?

WALTER: Past eleven. Why?

ADAM: That clock's out of its mind. You must be worn out, Judge!

WALTER: I, um, think we should –

ADAM: Adjourn for a couple of minutes?

WALTER: Continue!

ADAM: *(cupping hand to ear).* Ha? I can't hear you.

WALTER: *(louder).* I want to see you get some business done, Judge Adam!

ADAM: I can't till Old Bridget comes. So how about stretching our legs, everyone, and getting a breath of air? *(Everyone except Walter starts to move.)*

WALTER: The parties to the case must stay in the courthouse.

ADAM: Why? Oh, that's the law, of course, the dear old law! For that matter, the refreshments can be served right here!

WALTER: Refreshments? In the courtroom?

ADAM: An old Concord custom. You wouldn't have me break that tradition?

WALTER: One glass of wine, then.

ADAM: From the celebrated Concord grape. Maggie! *(Maggie appears in the doorway.)* Wine for his honor, oh, and Maggie, butter—

MAGGIE: Freshly churned this morning—

ADAM: —And the Vermont cheese—

MAGGIE: And that smoked goose from Maine? *(Adam nods and Maggie exits.)*

WALTER: Oh, I couldn't, Judge, Besides, there isn't time—

ADAM: It's Firewood Day. The women are out collecting kindling. Old Bridget will take hours to get here.

ROBERT: Nonsense. She hasn't collected wood for years. She's much too old.

ADAM: How do you know?

ROBERT: She's *my* Great Aunt.

ADAM: Prove it! Beyond a reasonable doubt! This is a courtroom, sir!

WALTER: In recess, however. He doesn't have to prove it. Let's taste your wine.

ADAM: *(to himself).* Damnation! *(To Walter:)* And our food!

WALTER: One slice of bread at most with a little salt, no butter.

ADAM: *(to himself).* How'm I to get those two minutes alone with the silly filly? *(Shouting:)* Maggie, dry bread, salt! *(To Walter:)* A piece of Vermont cheese would bring out the bouquet of the Concord grape!

WALTER: A very small piece then.

ADAM: Not being blessed with children, we bachelors are blessed with food and drink!

WALTER: That wound, Judge! How did you get it?

ADAM: What wound?

WALTER: There's a hole in your head!

ADAM: Oh, that. I fell.

WALTER: Last night?

ADAM: This morning. Getting out of bed!

WALTER: Fell *over* something?

ADAM: Yes.

WALTER: What?

ADAM: Myself! And, falling, hit an iron stove!

WALTER: I see two wounds now, one front, one back. *(Maggie has brought food and drink and placed them on the table.)*

ADAM: Thank you, Maggie! Yes, I fell forwards on the stove, recoiled, and then fell backwards on the floor! Your wine, Judge. *(He pours a first glass.)*

WALTER: If you were a married man, one would assume a female had tried to scratch your eyes out.

ADAM: *(Coughing.)* Out of the question!

WALTER: Out of the question, eh? A bachelor's life *is* enviable.

ADAM: Some prickly branches for my silkworms were drying out on the stove . . . Your health! *(They drink.)*

WALTER: To lose your wig so strangely the same day! It would at least have concealed your wounds!

ADAM: They say every evil has a twin! *(Cutting a piece of Vermont Cheese:)* The cheese is rich. May I?

WALTER: *(taking the cheese).* Thanks. Vermont cheese, ha?

ADAM: Straight from Brattleboro.

WALTER: But how the Devil—pardon my profanity—did it come about?

ADAM: The cheese?

WALTER: Your losing of your wig.

ADAM: Well, sitting down last night to . . . study some deep law books, bending low like this to follow every precious word—I'd mislaid my glasses—I pushed my head right into the candle flame. Fire from heaven upon the worst of sinners! The wig flares up like

Sodom and Gomorrah, burning Cities of the Plain! I was lucky not to have my real hair all burnt off—the three or four hairs I have left!

WALTER: And your other wig is where?

ADAM: At the barber's being cleaned. But, um, as you said, your worship, shouldn't we be getting business done?

WALTER: Your turn to push ahead now? Why would that be?

ADAM: I'm a push-ahead kind of person.

WALTER: *Does* Rupert have a hole in his head?

ADAM: Ha? We had testimony to that effect. Your health! *(He drinks.)*

WALTER: And even if it's not Rupert, a man with a head wound will be noticed on the street. Your health! *(He drinks.)* Your Concord grape is good.

ADAM: I was weaned on it!

WALTER: Really? *(Walking over to Mrs. Bull.)* Mrs. Bull, how high did you say your daughter's window was?

MRS. BULL: Nine feet at most. The vine is on a trellis just underneath. Jumping down, you get caught in the vine: it would take a wild boar and his tusks to cut through!

ADAM: *(to himself).* Oh, to be a wild boar with tusks!

WALTER: *(as Adam re-fills his own glass).* What was that?

ADAM: Your health, dear sir!

WALTER: *(calling over to Robert).* Robert! Where was it you hit the culprit—on the head?

ADAM: *(quickly).* A re-fill, sir?

WALTER: No, no, I'm fine.

ADAM: *(insisting on the re-fill).* For what saith Pythagoras?

WALTER: I'm sure I don't know!

ADAM: *(reciting).* "Down three glasses! In your third glass, each drop will be a shining sun."

WALTER: Pythagoras, eh?

ADAM: *(nodding, and continuing).* "After one glass you're still Master. After two comes Chaos! After three, Cosmos!" Your health!

WALTER: *(calling as before).* Robert! How often did you hit the sinner?

ADAM: And was he the sinner or the goat?

WALTER: What?

ADAM: He might have been more sinned against than sinning! Shakespeare, your worship! *(To Robert:)* Hey! The Judge asked you something. Feel free to say you don't remember!

ROBERT: Hitting him with the doorknob?

ADAM: *(shuddering).* Doorknob.

WALTER: You said you leaned out the window and whacked him.

ROBERT: Oh yes, twice.

ADAM: *(to himself).* He does remember. And I'm not getting those two minutes alone with Eve.

WALTER: You could easily have killed him!

ROBERT: Pity I didn't. Then we'd have the body, and you'd know my whole story was true.

ADAM: *(to himself).* As it is, Old Bridget heard him talking with Eve. Hm.

WALTER: Could you see him at all? Did you ever get to see him?

ROBERT: It was dark. And he threw sand in my eyes.

ADAM: Third and last glass! *(He is filling the glasses a third time.)* And let every man drink to what he loves best!

WALTER: To Justice, then, Brother Adam!

ADAM: Make it: Justice and Concord! *(They drink the toast. As they do so, Mr. Light returns bringing an old woman with him. She stays in the doorway while Light reports.)*

WALTER: That's Madam Bridget?

LIGHT: Yes, your honor, a redoubtable old lady.

WALTER: What's that in her hand?

LIGHT: A wig, your honor.

WALTER: How did she come by it?

LIGHT: It was caught in the trellis on Mrs. Bull's wall.

MRS. BULL: In my trellis?

LIGHT: Among the vine leaves—looking like a bird's nest, she says.

WALTER: *(going to Adam, lowering his voice).* Is there anything you'd care to tell me in confidence, Judge?

ADAM: I've no idea what you mean, your worship. *(And he goes over to Old Bridget and snatches the wig.)* Thanks!

WALTER: So it *is* yours!

ADAM: Found at last! And all that peacock's fault! *(He points at Robert.)* The indefensible Defendant!

LIGHT: Robert?

ROBERT: Me?

ADAM: Let this unseemly eating and drinking cease! Maggie! *(She starts to gather in the glasses and tidy up.)* The Court will come to order. *(It does so.)* Defendant, do you remember the wig I gave you to take to the barber's for cleaning?

ROBERT: Yes, sir.

ADAM: What did you do with it, ha?

ROBERT: I *took* it for cleaning. And left it at the barber's.

ADAM: No, you didn't.

ROBERT: Yes, I did.

ADAM: Mutiny on the Bounty!

ROBERT: I did. I did.

ADAM: Benedict Arnold, thou art mighty yet!

ROBERT: You're insane.

ADAM: You dropped the wig among Mrs. Bull's vine leaves! How? When? Why? Judge Walter, I propose to examine this lady forthwith.

WALTER: That's what you're supposed to be doing.

ADAM: Madam Bridget!

OLD BRIDGET: Yes, Sir Judge?

ADAM: What happened last night?

OLD BRIDGET: I was on my way to my granddaughter's. She was in childbirth and having a hard time of it. Passing Mrs. Bull's garden gate, I heard a girl's voice bawling someone out, but so hoarse, so panicky, it took me a minute to realize it was my Eve. "Pfui! Have you no shame, you low-down scoundrel? How dare you, I'll call Mother!" Fast and furious! I thought the Redcoats were back! "Eve," I shout, over the hedge, "What *is* the matter?" Silence! "Eve! Answer me!" Then Eve – in a quiet voice – almost her usual sweet self – "Yes, Aunt Bridget?" – she calls me Aunt – "What *are* you up to?", I sing out. "Three guesses!" she now cries pertly and kind of laughing. "Oho," I ask, "is it Robert? This was a lovers' quarrel?" "That's it, that's just it," she calls out quickly, "now run along!" Run! At my age!

MRS. BULL: A question, Judge –

ROBERT: Several questions, Judge –

WALTER: First let her finish.

OLD BRIDGET: There are two Judges?!

ADAM: I'll say! Me, Adam, and *(pointing)* Judge Walter, my infinitely superior! Was it a boy?

OLD BRIDGET: Two boys.

ADAM: Twins?

OLD BRIDGET: Eight pounds apiece. All three thriving.

ADAM: Hey? Concord isn't through yet, eh, Judge? "Be fruitful and multiply!" The Bible also says—

WALTER: Finish, Madam Bridget.

OLD BRIDGET: It was well after midnight when I left my granddaughter's place but as I passed behind Mrs. Bull's cottage, someone picked himself up off the ground.

WALTER: What?

OLD BRIDGET: He must have been in a dead faint. Staggered to his feet. If they were feet. Had a bald head, too.

WALTER: If they were feet, you say?

OLD BRIDGET: One foot wasn't a foot. It was a hoof.

WALTER: A what?

OLD BRIDGET: It was a horse's hoof.

WALTER: Is that possible!

OLD BRIDGET: No. Not if he was human, Judge Two. This . . . creature gave off an odor . . . like the horrid vapor that rises from pitch or sulphur . . . "God save us," I cried, and, no, it wasn't blasphemy, Judge Two, because it would take God to save us from this. I turned round. He was disappearing in the distance. You know how rotting wood gives off a faint light sometimes, phosphorescent, is that the word? Well, his bald head lit up like that!

MRS. BULL: What has all this got to do with my jug?

ROBERT: Auntie, are you asking us to believe it was Satan himself?

MRS. BULL: There was a rumor you're plumb crazy.

OLD BRIDGET: My nose knows what it smells.

WALTER: *(smoothly).* We could decide this was the Devil, Ma'am, but where would it get us? We can't arraign the Devil. Name someone else.

OLD BRIDGET: *(shaking her head).* The Clerk of your own court will bear me out.

WALTER: Mr. Light, you, too, assert this creature was the Devil?

LIGHT: The Devil? No. The bald head, the horse's hoof, the stench? Yes.

WALTER: Thank you. Proceed, Ma'am.

OLD BRIDGET: Well, today, Judge Two, all Concord was a-buzz with the mystery of the jug. Clue to the mystery: someone had jumped down from on high. Now who does things like that? Who's the greatest Jumper Down of 'em all, jumping down as He did at the beginning of time from Heaven itself? I returned to the scene of the crime and what did I find? *(She stops.)*

WALTER: Go on, go on, what *did* you find?

OLD BRIDGET: It'd been snowing again and, look! on the fresh snow, fresh tracks!

WALTER: As there must have been last night all over Massachusetts.

OLD BRIDGET: New England is peopled by Christians, Judge Two. Christians have human feet. This creature's left leg leaves the track of a hoof!

WALTER: Such talk borders on the dangerous, Madam.

OLD BRIDGET: The tracks aren't clear by the trellis. That's where he must have fallen in a faint. Just lay there, who knows how long! But, once he took to his heels, two prints: foot and hoof, foot and hoof, across the garden like the serpent in Eden and out into the world!

ADAM: *(pointing at Robert). I* know, Judge: that peacock disguised himself as the Devil!

ROBERT: *I* did that? I—?

OLD BRIDGET: Ever hunted badgers, Judge Two? *(He nods.)* How d'you feel when you find badger tracks! *(Before he can answer:)* That's how *I* felt when I found Devil tracks! I agree with you: no use arraigning *this* customer! He's already doing life in Hell, life and eternity with no parole!

WALTER: Your advice, Mr. Light?

LIGHT: I saw the tracks ten minutes ago. They're still there.

WALTER: A horse's hoof?

LIGHT: A man's foot, your honor, but taking, shall we say? the *form* of a hoof.

WALTER: So well put!

ADAM: This interests me—theologically. Why, it's like having old Jonathan Edwards back with us in New England! But then came the Atheists and proved God doesn't exist.

WALTER: What interests you?

ADAM: That they never proved the Devil didn't exist.

WALTER: Ah! And so?

ADAM: I propose we take this case to the Supreme Court of the United States.

WALTER: What?

ADAM: Raise the jurisdictional issue: is the Concord Court entitled to reach such a conclusion?

WALTER: As what?

ADAM: That the Defendant's name, if we had a Defendant, would be Mr. Be-elzebub.

WALTER: What's *your* judicial wisdom, Mr. Light?

LIGHT: Why don't we hear the rest of Old Bridget's story, *then* put it all together?

WALTER: Very sagacious. Good, conclude, Madam Bridget.

OLD BRIDGET: Well, I said to Mr. Light just now, "Why don't we *follow* these tracks for a spell?"

WALTER: And Mr. Light replied?

OLD BRIDGET: "They may lead straight to the courthouse."

WALTER: So you didn't follow the tracks?

OLD BRIDGET: We did.

WALTER: And did they lead to the courthouse?

OLD BRIDGET: They did.

ADAM: Here? Where *I* live?

OLD BRIDGET: That's it.

ADAM: Phew! He must have passed right through!

OLD BRIDGET: No.

ADAM: Right through!

OLD BRIDGET: Tell him, Mr. Light.

LIGHT: The tracks end at the back door. If he passed through, they'd begin again at the front door.

ADAM: *(pursuing the same thought as above).* So, Judge Walter, if there's something wrong with my records, if my accounts aren't in perfect order, we'll know why! Devil or not, he did pass through!

LIGHT: He did not pass through.

ADAM: Did NOT pass through? Heaven and hell, then he must be in the record room right now!

WALTER: *(to Light, in a whisper).* Brother Adam always keeps one foot concealed. I must get to see it. *(Aloud:)* Judge!

ADAM: Your worship?

WALTER: Could you let me have a pinch of snuff?

ADAM: Delighted! Maggie, pass my snuffbox to his worship!

WALTER: Bring it yourself, would you? I want to whisper something in your ear. *(But Maggie has brought the snuffbox already.)*

MAGGIE: Here, your worship.

ADAM: I'll have to wait for your whisper, your worship!

WALTER: *(to Mr. Light).* Check, but not checkmate. *(Loudly:)* Who in Concord has misshapen feet? I address you all!

LIGHT: I suggest you address Judge Adam.

WALTER: Judge Adam?

ADAM: Yes, I'm an expert! In this job I've watched the feet of Concord coming and going, coming and going, for ten years now. What feet! All of them perfect!

WALTER: *(to Light).* Whom did you have in mind?

MRS. BULL: *(as Light hesitates).* Ask me that question, would you, Judge?

WALTER: Whom, then, have *you* in mind?

MRS. BULL: Judge Adam.

ADAM: Me? This Judge Adam?

MRS. BULL: Yes, How about *your* feet? You're always hiding at least one of them.

ADAM: Oh. Oh! *(A double take.)* Mrs. Bull has guessed my secret! I am a person of the highest cosmic status: Satan, King of Hell! *(He roars with laughter, then shows his right foot.)* If the Devil had a foot like that, he'd be the Beau of the Boston Ball! *(In a whisper:)* What did you want to whisper in my ear?

WALTER: *(whispering).* Retire from the case. Adjourn the session.

ADAM: *(whispering back).* I've got to hear Old Bridget out. Madam Bridget?

OLD BRIDGET: I have my doubts about the wig.

ADAM: How's that?

OLD BRIDGET: Would the Devil agree to wear it? Isn't it too greasy?

ADAM: Not necessarily. What do *we* know of current fashions in Hell? How much grease *do* demons have in their wigs? Then, too, the Devil might wear a wig as a disguise – to get him in among people of quality, eh, Judge?

WALTER: A moment ago you said this Devil was a *man* in disguise!

ADAM: Again the philosophical approach: two possibilities –

WALTER: No! Now, in the hearing of all, I must ask the presiding Judge to retire from this case and adjourn the session!

ADAM: No, no, I have a question – and it's a matter of credibility, including yours, Judge – would any American, let alone a Judge, leave his wig hanging in some peasant's trellis?

WALTER: Not if it's already gone up in flames like Sodom and Gomorrah!

LIGHT: Or if it's still under the bed where the cat's had kittens in it. *(Walter and Light smile at each other.)*

ADAM: *(looking from Light to Walter and back).* Hm. Appearances *may* be against me . . . but you're a gentleman, your worship: you realize that I'm confronted, now, with the possible loss of my honor . . . where would I be without my honor? Hm? As for the legalities, the evidence is circumstantial, and goes for nothing where law rules. All this talk, talk, talk, while the one witness you need for direct evidence – dear Miss Eve here – is silent. For legal purposes, for practical purposes, you have nothing on me. Nothing. Ha?

LIGHT: Your worship, this wig –

ADAM: Call that wig mine, Mr. Light, and I'll sue you in the State Supreme Court.

LIGHT: I dare you to put it on!

ADAM: Help me on with it, Maggie. *(He winks at her, and she helps him put it on crooked.)* See? It's not my size!

LIGHT: *(straightening it on Adam's head).* It is just your size. *(Convinced that Adam is the Devil, Old Bridget screams.)*

WALTER: *(as Adam tears off the wig and raises his fist to Light).* Bring these proceedings to a close, sir!

ADAM: Ready! Ready, your worship, with verdict and sentence!

WALTER: Ah! This we have to hear.

ADAM: Defendant Robert: guilty as charged.

MR. TUMPEL: I object—

ADAM: I also find him in contempt of court, and sentence him to sit in the Concord jail with an iron collar round his neck.

ROBERT: Jail? In irons?

MR. TUMPEL: We appeal to you, Judge Walter.

WALTER: Let Judge Adam finish. What about the jug?

ADAM: Two possibilities? The Defendant may choose to replace the jug. Then again he may not. How's that for impartiality?

MRS. BULL: I protest—

WALTER: *(raising his hand for order).* Enough. I now declare the session ended.

EVE: With Robert in jail? Sentenced by *him?*

WALTER: You have heard.

EVE: Then the one witness you need you can have: Robert has nothing more to lose. It was Judge Adam in my room. It was Judge Adam who broke the jug. *(Silence. Adam begins to edge towards the window.)*

WALTER: Thank you.

ROBERT: Now I make mincemeat of him.

WALTER: *(Quickly).* Oh, no, you do not. The dignity of the law is also at stake here.

ROBERT: Who's going to stop me?

WALTER: I am. By calling the Bailiff.

EVE: A Bailiff in Judge Adam's court? He'll be off drinking at the tavern. Go ahead, Robert. Pull down this monstrous idol, right here in his sanctuary.

WALTER: No! The sanctuary *is* sacred! Bailiff! *(Adam has now reached the window. Maggie is standing beside it. He gives her his judicial robe.)*

ADAM: It's true, the Bailiff was given a short leave of absence. Bye! *(He pinches Maggie's behind and jumps through the window.)*

EVE: He's jumped out of the window! Again! Grab him!

WALTER: *(As Robert starts to move).* No one is to leave the courtroom! *(Robert stops in his tracks. To Eve:)* And thanks again for the confession.

EVE: I didn't finish. Robert won't be released from the Militia in six months. By secret orders from Washington, he'll be shipped West to fight the Indians.

WALTER: I don't follow. What could Adam do about that?

EVE: He has influence in Washington. Can get the secret orders rescinded. Robert could be released after his training if only, in the meanwhile, I became . . . Judge Adam's WHORE.

WALTER: God in Heaven!

EVE: I was trapped. If I said No, Robert was lost. If I said yes . . . What could I do but play for time, hold back, even lie a little . . .

WALTER: *(having looked the papers over).* These, my child, are forgeries. Washington would not do such a thing. Nor will Robert be imprisoned. *(To Robert:)* I hereby release you from the verdict and the sentence. No, don't thank *me* but your faithful . . . *(He points to Eve.)*

ROBERT: Saint! And hero! To suffer all this, and my abuse as well! Can you ever forgive me?

EVE: Forgive? Yes, in time.

ROBERT: Angel! Goddess! Let me kiss you. When shall we be married?

EVE: Forgiven is not forgotten, Robert. I shall remember you: as the man who did not trust me. *I* cannot trust *you*—now.

ROBERT: We'll soon take care of that! I'm gonna show you what I'm made of.

EVE: You did: alas!

ROBERT: No, no! *(He tries to take her in his arms.)*

EVE: No kisses! No wedding bells! Eve's leaving the Garden of Eden—alone. *(She walks out of the courtroom. At first Robert is inclined to follow. Then he stops, and returns to his father's side.)*

LIGHT: *(at the window).* Just watch him run—Judge Adam—at his age—his wig bobbing up and down at his back! Like a man running from the gallows!

MR. TUMPEL: Send Robert after him, your honor, bring him back! Let him taste the jail and irons he had in store for others!

WALTER: Ha? Oh, yes, he has forfeited his judgeship. Off to Boston with you, Robert, and be a good Militia man!

ROBERT: Thank you. And now—

MR. TUMPEL: Sentence Judge Adam!

WALTER: An eye for an eye? A tooth for a tooth?

MR. TUMPEL: That's in the Bible!

ROBERT: *(nodding).* That is Justice!

WALTER: But this is Concord. And it's not in the Bible that Adam is Satan. Or is it, Madam Bridget? There's an Old Adam in each of us. By that token, this Adam is no worse than his neighbors: and by *that* token, the Commonwealth must make room for him. Shorn of authority, he'll be harmless.

LIGHT: Shorn of authority?

WALTER: Yes, and you get his job. *(Light bows low.)* A happy ending! Concord in Concord! I can leave for Amherst. God be with you, friends. *(He leaves. All bow.)*

OLD BRIDGET: Such a nice man!

MR. TUMPEL: A real peace maker.

MRS. BULL: And congratulations, Judge Light *(She kisses his hand.)*

OLD BRIDGET: Judge Three!

ROBERT: Long may you reign!

LIGHT: *(tense, his eyes unfocused).* I feel funny. *(He is dizzy.)* "Shorn of authority, he'll be harmless." What about me, *acquiring* the authority? An Old Adam in each of us, eh? *(Vertigo overcomes him, he sinks down on a chair, eyes closed.)*

OLD BRIDGET: Poor thing, he doesn't seem quite right in the head.

MRS. BULL: It takes one to know one.

ROBERT: *(cutting in as Bridget starts to protest).* Judge Walter doesn't know where God lives. Mr. Light was trying to tell us. *Judge* Light. It ain't a happy ending—yet! Eh, Judge Light?

MR. TUMPEL: I shall hate that Adam to the end of my days.

OLD BRIDGET: I still say he's the Devil.

ROBERT: He did rob me of my bride when all's done. I'm supposed to overlook that? After he conspired against me, blackmailed her—

MR. TUMPEL: The Bible does say an eye for an eye!

OLD BRIDGET: The Devil's the Devil!

MRS. BULL: What was this trial all about? My jug! And nothing has been done about my jug!

ROBERT: *(sarcastically).* But then our new Judge has been enjoined to—

MR. TUMPEL: Temper justice with mercy! And let this devil go!!

OLD BRIDGET: Never! Fight Satan where you find him! We found him *(pointing at the table)* there!

MRS. BULL: *(looking at Light).* His honor is so quiet. Wake up, your honor! Remember my jug?

MR. TUMPEL: Remember the conspiracy, the blackmail, the threat to New England womanhood?

OLD BRIDGET: With the Devil in the woodpile!

ROBERT: But the Defendant isn't here. If you'll try the case, Judge Light, I'll go out and get him. *(Light opens his eyes.)* Well, Judge, well?

LIGHT: *(and it is a different Mr. Light, speaking in a voice we have not heard before.)* Go out and get him. *(He stands up.)* I came, I saw, I have Concord. Maggie!

MAGGIE: Yes, sir?

LIGHT: My robe. *(He puts on Judge Adam's robe. Meanwhile Robert has left.)*

OLD BRIDGET: See that? *(We see nothing).* See that, everyone? *(Nothing.)* He's there—in the clouds—Satan himself—see what he's up to! Yes, yes, he's calling the witches together—see their broomsticks?—the witches of Salem!

LIGHT: *(who has taken up the Judge's position on the bench, grandly).* Let there be Light!

MAGGIE: *(at the window).* Poor Judge Adam! When he gets back—when he gets out of jail—I'm gonna tell him Yes.

The Fall of the Amazons
A Tragedy

Based on *Penthesilea*

Preface: On Hating the Other Sex

I

It gets harder to believe all the time, but there was a day when I was twenty-four years old and a graduate student at Yale. Which would have been quite bearable had I not met a freshman whom I considered charming.

What is charm? One can take a negative view, and many have: to charm is to bewitch, and behind witchery, we well know, is the Devil. But a positive view need not be heretical: it's love that makes the world go round. Aristotle thought so. And love uses charm, personal charm, to call attention to itself. But then I am speaking of a time when all this was no excuse, a time when charm was not permitted. Or rather when the freshman was permitted to be charming but when I was not permitted to be charmed. He could throw me the ball but I must not catch it.

Since I *had* caught it, however, I must now take care no one sees me ball in hand. Had even Fred – that was his name – actually seen me catch the ball, or could he perhaps tell himself it was some other ball, thrown by another, or a ball I just happened to bring with me that afternoon?

No simple matter! It could not be disposed of by the admission, however large the capital letters, "My interest is SEXUAL." Because, if *that* is what sexual means, let me quickly put in that I would not have been appeased by any of those brief encounters in dark alleys which "our culture" did concede even then, if strictly on the condition that no further demands be made. Even then I sensed, however dimly, that the associations I craved would not be over in a hurry, nor should they be shrouded in darkness, literal or figurative.

One well-known gambit of Eros is to steer conversation towards sex even while pretending the subject has no present bearing on ourselves, but my relationship with Fred remained so tenuous that sex never got mentioned at all. All that got mentioned for a while was things like the weather. At some point I elicited the big news that Fred was a freshman; at another point the even bigger news that he hailed from Topeka, Kansas. And perhaps both of us felt that the Danger Area had been entered when I asked where he was living and volunteered that for my part I was to be found nightly in the Hall of Graduate Studies. The ultimate question posed by Western civilization, My place or yours? might then have seemed to hover, and a conspiracy to commit the gravest of all crimes—with ivy if not vine leaves in our hair—might have seemed just round the corner.

Alas, it was not. I would seek Fred out in public places, and say "Hi," and he would dart his charm back at me, but one day he must have "got the idea," because after that he would smile less, or not at all, and slip away before those Hi's could be uttered. "I am really going to have to talk to this boy," I was saying to myself, without knowing what it was I could say, when a letter came in the campus mail from the Dean of Freshmen. It was that a freshman, naming Fred, had complained to the dean that he was receiving unwelcome attention from me. Might the Dean suggest, then, that his ward Fred be spared such attention in future? That was all. No accusation. No mention of the hovering crime against nature. It is probably the mildest communication I have ever received on a non-mild subject, a masterpiece of gentlemanly tact, worldly wisdom, and WASP reticence. And it had the intended effect: it scared me out of my wits.

Why? How could it? asks 1982. To which I can only answer—my training, after all, was in history—"You have to understand the period. And me as a man of my period." Unenlightened 1982 will find it just as hard to realize that the Dean of Frosh was actually raising *my* consciousness while dutifully enabling Fred to stay virginal, or at least straight. Hadn't I known what I was up to? Had I not heard the music to which the little things that had happened were but an overture? Yes and No, the "No" being that I felt it was safer in this world not be any more self-aware than one had to be. The Dean had forced me to see as a social fact—visible to the neighbors—what I had blithely assumed would be invisible to all except me and, when the time came, Fred. "You should have gone straight to that Dean," this is 1982 speaking, "and said you liked Fred and it was none of his damn business." But it was 1940, so I went to the bathroom, felt I was going to vomit, and actually did have diarrhea. Rising like vapor from the toilet came the decision never to see Fred again—as if I ever *had* seen him! If we bumped into each other on the sidewalk, I would turn away. And so it was. And for a considerable period, I limited my sex life to solitary masturbation. A spiritual victory: I had more time for study and would walk away with the prize for the best doctoral dissertation of the year.

ONE SIMPLY MUST NOT LOVE PERSONS OF THE SAME SEX: if it had taught me nothing else, Yale did seem to have taught me this. One's enemies—one should love *them*. Jesus said so. One's fellow males, no. Not love. Not (a fortiori) lust. And not tender affection. There: I have it now. What I had felt for Fred was tender affection. Tinged with sensuality? I should hope so! But I am expressing this hope in 1982: in 1940 I did not hope to feel such hope. I had been raised, not to be sure in New Haven, but in that same Protestant and Puritanic tradition which feared and loathed all lust, even the "natural" kind. What I was learning now was that even affection is taboo if it is for the wrong person. The good life was a life of love only if that love found the correct object. If it found the incorrect object, you were a worse person than one who did not love at all, even than one whose life was all hate. To love persons of the same sex was to lead the worst of lives. To give that love physical expression was to commit the worst of crimes. . . . This much Yale had taught its star graduate student of the year.

Ah yes, had Fred been a girl, I could have invited him, without blush or shame, and with few preliminaries, to the Yale Prom or, if that was too long a wait, a football game, after which there could have been SEX. Officially, yes, the parents, in those far away days, disapproved of pre-marital sex, and the colleges themselves raised various barriers against it, but . . . first things first, and the first thing, erotically speaking, was to pick the right sex, which was the other one. How far had I come? As far, I think, as to receive a keen impression that, if Society let me, I could love members of my own sex. Society, I gathered, would not let me. But I was not at the end of my rope because I had also received a keen impression that I would love members of the "opposite" sex, and it seemed as if Society had given its stamp of approval to that in advance, had promised, indeed, to confer every kind of congratulation and reward upon proven and consummated heterosexuality. (Those were the days when, in Mussolini's Italy, the government gave you an additional subsidy for every child you begot. The American government still does something of the kind by way of I.R.S. exemptions.)

Do books have an effect upon real life? Bookish persons like myself flatter ourselves that they do, and when Yale drove me from the New Haven streets and quadrangles into its own library stacks—for me another form of romance—I was led by luck or fate to the works of Nietzsche and Strindberg. Oh yes, I had already seen real life's war of the sexes. My own parents fought it unremittingly, as did various uncles and aunts. Still, it was a shock to find that exactly the same thing had been going on decades earlier in Germany and Sweden. Even more awful to contemplate was the *argument* of the two great misogynists. At the very least one realized that the Great Sexual War was by no means limited to Germany and Sweden or to recent times.

How far had I *now* come? To realize that the same Society which has banned my love for the same sex, has placed on my love for the other sex a heavy and enduring curse. What kind of a Society was this which forbade a love one felt, and then placed a curse upon the kind of love it was commending and subsidizing?

Not all my own experience confirms Nietzsche and Strindberg. On the contrary. I came in time to reject their teaching, and any effort I make today to lift the stigma off homosexuality is unaccompanied by the wish to switch the stigma to heterosexuals. I have lived to hear men shout the slogan "Gay is twice as good as straight!" but I wonder how any such ratio, even if true, could be established? I have read a gay psychologist who eagerly implies that the sensations of gay sexual intercourse are stronger than those of straight. For him, this is true, I will readily assume. But how are the sensations of millions to be correlated with those of millions of others?

And who cares? If I myself seem to have implied, a moment ago, that homosexuality might be a refuge from the sexual wars, I should proceed at once to declare that, in fact, the love-hate of men and women gets duplicated by a love-hate of men and men, women and women. And if heterosexuals are wrong to make outcasts of homosexuals, banishing them from the nuclear family and its licensed, respectable homes and territories, homosexuals are wrong to create ghettoes which they regard as a sort of Utopia for the enlightened, particularly if each sex retires into itself and there is little contact of gay men with Lesbians, let alone of gay and straight. Years ago James Baldwin wrote an eloquent, and to me cogent, warning to gay men against locking themselves up in any such "male prison."

II

William Blake says we are put on earth "that we may learn to bear the beams of love" but the conditions of our life have made this quite difficult since, in all the history we know, men have been the masters and women the slaves.

Whenever there are masters and slaves, the former will propose and *im*pose an ideology, and it will be the one over-riding ideology of their culture. It will begin by declaring that slaves are an inferior species, and it will go on to generously venture that no one—no master—will hold this inferiority against the slaves if they will in turn be generous on one point and refrain from questioning the ideology, which means that they must accept their inferiority either as fact or as unquestioned assumption: they thereby accept "I know my place" as their motto whether they actually feel they know their place or merely fear for their life should they say they don't. Oppressors don't mind about the metaphysics, provided everything goes according to plan. Blacks whom South Africans call Cheeky, whom Southern American Whites have called Uppity, are to be discouraged and eliminated so that Uncle Tom may be the name of every Black alive. . . .

Sometimes, indeed often, it may seem to the philosophic observer of the human scene that all things work together for oppression. Certainly all conservative philosophers claim that human nature is theirs: it favors them, and only they really understand and accept it. Luckily for the rest of mankind, they have made a misjudgement that undermines their whole case: they have failed to realize that homo sapiens is by nature uppity. Man is the cheeky animal. Not exclusively so, of course. He is also passive, submissive. Cowardice or expediency lead him to play Possum (a.k.a. Tom). But he resents having to do it to such an extent that when he is not in revolt he is sullenly resentful, as the more realistic anti-liberals from Nietzsche to Kipling have perceived. The Uncle Tom pose is hard to sustain, and homo sapiens does not sustain it indefinitely. Nor does woman, the slave of the sexual wars. Centuries of male force, male indoctrination, and male conditioning have impelled woman toward the one clear goal: that she should be a Patient Griselda. How hot a brainwashing that would be is suggested by the cold fact that many women were still Shrewish. Shakespeare's *Taming of the Shrew*, often dismissed as lightheartedly unreal, is a historical document of horrifying candor. Incidentally it would kid us into thinking a Shrew can be turned into Griselda in short order. The reverse is closer to the truth. Give all these fake Griseldas half a chance, and they will happily revert to type, and unmask themselves as unreconstructed Shrews.

The revolt of women over the course of the past hundred years is the most prolonged and insistent of all the slave revolts, but to say this is only to underscore that, to modern men, every woman has been a potential Nat Turner in a slave revolt that seems never to be over.

Many men, it will be said, have bowed to feminism as to the inevitable, but one would have to be naive to assume that such men are usually good losers. On the contrary, they take their resentment with them, and will never forgive the women for what has been a series of setbacks and humiliations and may prove a definitive defeat. The hope may linger, though, that, while all those battles have been lost, the war might someday be won.

Do men hate women more than women hate men? Probably. For though women, being the vanquished for so long, had the more reason to feel hatred, hatred is not a matter of reason, and something had happened to blow the glowing embers of male resentment into a blazing conflagration of sheer hate: the men had been fooled by the women's Uncle Tom act. They thought Griselda was a face, not just a mask. They considered themselves accepted, recognized, as the Master Sex without cavil or mental reservation. But now they know the women were only biding their time: for they have emerged as Shrews, if not Amazons, and even Mr. Andy Warhol can rouse them to man-killing fury.

Women have become the equivalent of the Red Threat on the international scene: safety is sought in a preponderance of weapons, and if it is not always easy to have more guns than the Russians, the men will, I think, find it possible to harbor more hate than the women.

But one should not minimize women's hatred of men, it goes back to the beginning of time. Men can cry: "Don't blame us for what our ancestors did to you!" This is what Whites say to Blacks, but the crime against the Africans only goes a couple of centuries back, while the crime against women has been traced to the point in time when Eve was refused a mother and given instead two fathers, her husband and Old Yahweh, the original Supermale. Two thousand years ago the new religion of Christianity was put together by a housebroken Yahweh, a second Adam, twelve disciples, all male, plus a thirteenth disciple more influential than the other twelve combined, Paul of Tarsus. It seems to have been Paul who first made Christian Anti-feminism explicit.

As all slaves have prayed for the annihilation of the masters, so women have prayed for a world without men, a paradise supervised by the Great Goddess and occupied by an Eve with no husband and not a rib to spare. If the Great Goddess has not answered their prayers, it is because She knew no way—or wanted to know no way—of enabling women to beget just women or of enabling women to give birth at all without the help of men. Impasse.

Or not? Someone—some female—must have thought not when she proposed that (a) the man's help could be limited to those few minutes when he gets an erection, has an ejaculation and impregnates the female and that (b) the male fruit of such encounters could be destroyed. Implicit in the proposal, obviously, is a manpower pool elsewhere for future copulations. These men are The Enemy, and may only be fucked after we, the women, have defeated them and put them in shackles. Such is the Amazon Solution. No one knows who the female was who first proposed it, but it could hardly be the Great Goddess. The proposal is against her principles.

The principle at the basis of Amazonism is all male. It must surely have been funnelled through to the women by a female thoroughly brainwashed by men, some super-"realist," who thinks of violence as "the only language they understand." Our Western "statesmen" talking about the Russians, or vice versa. The paranoid style is appropriate: the style is the man. Or the woman.

What resentment can ever match the resentment of men by women? Only the resentment of women by men. Both parties have so much to resent. And the resentment is so deeply rooted in history and pre-history, has been handed down almost reverently for so long from one generation to another. Yet nothing good can come of it. Are we put on earth merely to dominate or be dominated? If so, the end is clear and by this time in sight: destruction of the earth and ourselves along with it. But no: ". . . we are put on earth a little space/That we may learn to bear the beams of love." Human beings have sometimes managed to believe this. I think they always need to.

Blake's words do not imply that it is easy. To give up the wish to dominate would be to give up all defensiveness, to stand revealed as defenseless, totally vulnerable. This, it might well be concluded, is to ask to *be* dominated. I would prefer to say: it is to *risk* being dominated, but to achieve a degree of trust which guarantees that the risk will be taken.

Is not this the deeper meaning of the much-discussed "sacrifice of Isaac" in the Bible? Abraham can only prove he loves God by letting himself be dominated by God. (Christianity would later put it: "In Thy service is perfect freedom.") It seems to have escaped the commentators that the boy Isaac is following suit – he is letting himself be dominated by Abraham. Is God cruel throughout this episode? Yes, but to be kind. In seeming to be about to hurt both father and son, he has enabled them to find, in total vulnerability, total love. This is the note struck by Heinrich von Kleist in at least two of his plays, and for years now I have felt it reverberate within me: my Kleistian plays, *Wannsee* and *The Fall of the Amazons* are the result. My risk-takers are Cathy of Heilbronn and Achilles. As to the latter, I follow Homer in ignoring the legend of his 99% invulnerability. An invulnerable man risks nothing. My Achilles risks everything, is vulnerable all over, and especially in his soul. As I re-wrote this pagan story, it is possible that a Christian voice was whispering in my ear: "My strength is made perfect in weakness" (II Corinthians, xii, 9).

The Fall of the Amazons, which follows here, has a grisly story to tell, but its author would be the last to deny that, so long as we still have our hour, our "little space" on earth, love will still be dreamed of.

And hoped for.

Wannsee is the story of a woman's love but there are few parts for women in the play. A young poet, who is also a student of mine, Linda Lavorgna, suggested I write a play with more parts for women in it, a play which would be, in a degree, a play *about* women. This is how the following play came to be written, and it is gratefully dedicated to Linda. I'd like to think too, that the writings of a number of women I admire—Barbara Deming, Brigid Brophy, May Sarton—steered me away from certain errors and towards certain truths.

> . . . the gates of paradise are closed to those who have committed an act of sodomy, particularly those who have been the object of the action: If all *active* sodomists were doomed to go to hell, the kings would be the first to be sent there. Haven't they, after all, been the buyers, breeders and promoters of the best and most beautiful young slaves of the world. . . . The slave does to his wife what the kings did to him. He pretends to be the master at home while he is the slave in the bigger home, society at large. Just as he was a piece of meat for the kings and masters of society, his wife and other people with whom he sleeps become pieces of meat for him. This is very important in understanding the sources of Iranian history and the cannibalism of its monarchy.
>
> —Reza Baraheni in *The Crowned Cannibals*

Cast

The people of this play (with one exception) fall into two groups: the males are Greeks fighting the Trojan War, the females are Amazons, hovering in a troop on the plains near Troy. The Amazons in turn form two sub-groups: soldiers and civilians. The latter are either priestesses or little girls. What the size of these groups should be in the theatre is entirely a matter of that theatre's resources – or of the director's interpretation of the play. But clearly the rival armies could be represented by small squads – say, of ten soldiers apiece.

A list of principals will be slightly misleading as a non-principal delivering a messenger speech may have more lines than a principal. With that proviso, these are the principals:

Amazons:
Queen Penthesilea
Prothoe
Meroe
Asteria
High Priestess

Greeks:
Agamemnon
Ulysses
Achilles
Diomede

The one character who is not a Greek and not now an Amazon is a Sibyl.

Setting: The setting, a single one, represents a battlefield on the plains not far from Troy. There is a slope, the highest point of which serves as a hilltop from which off-stage action is seen. There is a bridge for armies to march across and for Penthesilea to try to throw herself into the water from.

While it is not desirable to fill up the stage with naturalistic detail—rather, the action lends itself to platforms and ramps—emblems of the rival armies would be in place, as would stage use of symbols from the text itself. The emblem of the Amazons was a golden crescent. The symbol of Amazon power was the golden bow carried by the Queen. It is Kleist's idea that the bowstring responds like a musical instrument in moments of crisis: when the Amazon order is collapsing, the bow performs a brief dirge as it tumbles to the ground.

Music: Incidental music for this play would have to cover several territories: there must be Amazon martial music that is meaningfully different from the martial music of the Greeks. The lyric side of Amazon life needs to be heard in the scene with the little girls. When Penthesilea feels the approach of the Blessed Ones, a serene spirituality is required. There should be music, in the appropriate spots, to suggest the sacred memory (or dream, if you will) of The Mothers at the dawn of human history.

Research Materials: Though they may have historical connections, myths are not history: it would be wrongheaded to go out in search of "the facts." But the myths themselves have a history, and it could be of interest to check out how the ancients saw Amazons. A 5th-century painting shows Penthesilea being killed by Achilles: it is reproduced in various books, for instance, *The Horizon Book of Ancient Greece,* p. 106. An Etruscan sarcophagus of the 4th century shows mounted Amazons in color: the archeological museum in Florence sells a postcard reproduction. Ancient literature—though no major work survives that principally deals with the Amazons—makes many references to them. The information in Robert Graves' *Greek Myths,* drawn from these ancient sources, is often suggestive, and I quote (volume two, page 125): ". . . the Amazons reckon descent only through the mother, and Lysippe had laid it down that the men must perform all household tasks while the women fought and governed.

. . . These unnatural women . . . were famous warriors, being the first to employ cavalry. They carried brazen bows and short shields shaped like a half moon; their helmets, clothes, and girdles were made from the skins of wild beasts. . . . At Ephesus they set up an image of Artemis [Diana] under a beech tree, where Hippo offered sacrifices; after which her followers performed first a shield dance and then a round dance, with rattling quivers, beating the ground in unison, to the accompaniment of pipes—for Athene had not yet invented the flute. The temple of Ephesian Artemis, later built around this image and unrivalled in magnificence even by that of Delphic Apollo, is included among the seven wonders of the world. . . ."

The playwright learned a lot from Brigid Brophy's *Black Ship to Hell* and enjoyed turning over in his mind such lines from it as these: "There are few ways in which man can be more innocently employed than in making love. In one form or another, it is to this tutelary deity [Eros] that we must commit and commend ourselves—and to his mother [Venus] who, as Lucretius pointed out, because she alone can conquer Mars potent in arms, is alone able to bless mortals with tranquil peace."

Prologue

(Agamemnon, the Greek commander-in-chief, in his tent before Troy. To him, his counsellor Ulysses.)

ULYSSES: You need me, Agamemnon?

AGAMEMNON: Does not the brawn of soldiers always need the brain of counsellors, Ulysses? We wish to end a war which has dragged on nine years. Ten is enough. At long, long last Troy's towers must come down. For which I need Achilles, son of Thetis.

ULYSSES: His brawn more pertinent than all our brains. But then–

AGAMEMNON: We don't get along, he and I. I stole his girl, Briseis. And that affair he had with the boy Patroclus – my war must stop, Greek history must wait, while he has fun?

ULYSSES: It paid off. When Hector killed Patroclus, Achilles killed Hector.

AGAMEMNON: When he fights he wins. When he fights for us, we win.

ULYSSES: Where is Achilles now?

AGAMEMNON: I have sent him out with his friend Diomede to look into these so-called "Amazons" –

ULYSSES: The female warriors hovering for weeks now on the plains yonder?

AGAMEMNON: *(nodding).* Are they on the Trojan side? Or ours? And, if on ours, are they acceptable allies? Is it possible we can't tolerate their existence but will have to wipe them out?

ULYSSES: Would you go that far?

AGAMEMNON: Even the Trojans don't contest the principles which govern our culture, our –

ULYSSES: Civilization? What principle d'you have in mind?

AGAMEMNON: "Woman is the property of man."

ULYSSES: Ah, yes.

AGAMEMNON: Who owns Helen – Paris or Menelaus, Troy or Greece? That's what our war's about! And quite enough to keep two nations busy without a third one whispering to Helen that she's no one's property but her own or, worse, that she's the property of a nation wholly female.

ULYSSES: Shall I go out and bring Achilles back?

AGAMEMNON: That's what I was coming to. Do that. Tell him we can't win the war without him.

ULYSSES: And is that true, d'you think?

AGAMEMNON: It's true if we're to win heroically. To be the hero of an heroic war, that's what's in this for him.

ULYSSES: And is there an alternative?

AGAMEMNON: *(coughing, looking to right and left).* An unheroic one. A Trojan traitor, Sinon, has a madcap scheme. He opens up Troy's gates, our men slip in, inside a wooden horse as tall as a mountain.

ULYSSES: We'd rather avoid that, of course.

AGAMEMNON: Bring Achilles back, then, and at all costs! At *nearly* all costs, ha?

ULYSSES: I'll set out at once.

I

(Encampment on the plains near Troy, Sentry on a hilltop. Diomede in the doorway of a tent—he is a still young Greek officer yet marked by nine years of war. To him, Ulysses, with troops.)

DIOMEDE: Welcome, Ulysses!

ULYSSES: Diomede!

(They embrace cordially.)

DIOMEDE: What brings you to the plains? But I can guess: you want us back in camp. Especially you want Achilles back.

ULYSSES: *(nodding).* We cannot win the Trojan War without him. Why are you both still here?

DIOMEDE: For weeks, the Amazons have roamed these windy plains, a robber band, we thought, planning some raids on our Greek army before Troy. The Trojans thought so too, and their King, Priam, sent his son Deiphobus out to them to form an alliance. The Amazons attacked Deiphobus' men and drove them back. Concluding now they were on our side, Achilles and myself went out to meet them—

ULYSSES: What are they like, these women? One hears such rumors!

DIOMEDE: They are a rumor that you don't believe till one day there they are: is it a cavalry charge or a herd of cattle gone berserk coming smack at you across the plains? And then you notice: down to the waist they are women—breasts, the whole thing—but such horse-women, horse and woman to the male eye are one. What are they like? They are like centaurs.

ULYSSES: Have you seen their Queen, Penthesilea?

DIOMEDE: *(nodding).* The first time that we saw the Amazons her figure stood out in the distance: tall yet graceful, powerful yet delicate. On a white charger, her silver armor gleaming, a white plume on her helmet, in her short snakeskin tunic, she seemed the dashing, yes, male chieftain of some tribe exotic, picturesque—her skin is dark—but, no, the body has its female curves and, look what's in her hand, ah yes, the emblem of the Amazons!

ULYSSES: A bow?

DIOMEDE: A huge bow of pure gold, the strings of which, they say, will sing out like an instrument of music announcing fortune good or bad in gay or mournful sounds.

ULYSSES: How did you find her?

DIOMEDE: She found us. One day stood there, a lion in our path, looking our troops over with the cool, appraising eye of an old soldier, her face as blank as the flat of my hand until she saw the man beside me. She stared at him as if he were someone she'd once known and must now bring back into her recollection. Suddenly the cold eye caught fire, the colorless face turned red. She jumped down from her horse and made a beeline for him, crying, "Who are you?" Achilles doesn't stammer but he stammered: "Achilles." "Achilles?" she repeated, blushing, palpitating. She was now a gawky teenage girl with a crush on the winner at the Olympic games. Then she switched back. The red face blanched, the hot eye cooled. She shouted:

"Your Queens are known
For their sharp tongues alone!
Our Queen you'll know
By the sharp arrows from her bow!"

She jumped back on her horse and, tossing her head, galloped away. All of which Deiphobus' men from across the plain had followed. Seeing our discomfiture they burst out laughing. Too soon! The Amazons regrouped into two separate troops in order to—can you guess?

ULYSSES: Fight Greek and Trojan—both at once?

DIOMEDE: Correct. And *how* do they fight?

ULYSSES: Like wildcats? One woman equalling three Greek men?

DIOMEDE: Then unaccountably not fight at all.

ULYSSES: Not fight at all?

DIOMEDE: Penthesilea fought like *ten* wildcats but, when she came face to face with the great champion whom she had sought for all along, Achilles, all of a sudden, nothing doing!

ULYSSES: How *was* that?

DIOMEDE: Here they are. Both breathing hard. A trembling pause. Each horseman poised for a final blow. Deiphobus rides up behind Achilles and trips his horse. He's on the ground. In a trice the Queen can remove this hero from both history and legend. But she doesn't.

ULYSSES: Why not? This is no fancy duel in some school with rules of fairness.

DIOMEDE: What's the matter? Is she blushing again? Oh, look, she's got a grip on her sword. Prepares a mighty blow? And it descends! On whom?

ULYSSES: Deiphobus?!

DIOMEDE: *(nodding).* Nature consists of forces and their opposites: fire fights water; water, fire. All's distinct unless one day water should burn and fire be wet as water—

ULYSSES: What did Achilles do?

DIOMEDE: Assumed a fighting posture. She followed suit, but, having dodged his first blow, grinned and rode away into the sun.

ULYSSES: And when *was* this?

DIOMEDE: Just now.

ULYSSES: Today?

DIOMEDE: An hour ago. Achilles has taken off after her, swearing he'll never leave the scent until he's dragged her off her horse by the hair. This warrior has long silky tresses! I have a dozen men on Achilles' tail. Here's one returning now. Alexis?

(A messenger has entered.)

MESSENGER: We have to fear the great Achilles is lost to us forever.

ULYSSES: What?

DIOMEDE: Quickly, your story.

MESSENGER: The Amazons beat back the Myrmidons. Achilles, though, did not fall back; instead, down a long slope ran on alone. The Myrmidons cheered. Suddenly a yawning chasm opened up before him: his chariot will plunge in the abyss! The charioteer wrenches it aside. The horses panic, back up, stagger, fall. The chariot turns over. Achilles is underneath a pile of twisted iron. The charioteer starts to dig him out. And now the Amazons arrive in the ravine. He's at the top: Penthesilea hurls her horse at the sheer face of the cliff, gets twenty feet up, the horse slips, horse and rider fall through the air to the bottom. The Amazons have now found a trail. Seconds before they reach the top Achilles gets his chariot moving. He pulls away but against those horses and those riders he can't keep the lead! He's done for!

SENTRY: *(calling from the hilltop).* There he goes! Achilles!

His chariot blazing like the sun in spring! The whizzing wheels turned into solid discs!

MESSENGER: *(calling back to him).* And Penthesilea?

SENTRY: On his heels! Sweeping across the plain at the head of her horde! My, how she rides! How firm she holds her charger with her thighs! How flat she throws her head and torso on her horse's mane! The white plume on her helmet can't keep up!

MESSENGER: Is she gaining on him?

SENTRY: Slowly but surely she is closing up the gap between them! But look! See the wide arc he's taking? She cuts across to intercept him! She's so close now, her shadow's fallen across his chariot! He wheels, yanks the reins across, as if to pull the chariot to one side with an enormous heave! Ye gods! It worked! She overshoots the mark! She is thrown clear over her horse's head! Penthesilea's down! The same with the women just behind her! Over their horses' heads they go! They are *all* down! Achilles has made a getaway!

ULYSSES: As a friend, what have you made of all this, Diomede?

DIOMEDE: I want him back in camp. For his own sake.

ULYSSES: I'm glad I can count on your support. Ask him to speak with me. I'll be here in your tent.

(Diomede leaves the tent to greet Achilles who enters amid cheers and acclamations.)

DIOMEDE: Achilles, welcome back!

ACHILLES: Friend Diomede!

(They embrace.)

DIOMEDE: All in one piece? No wounds at all?

ACHILLES: A scratch or two.

DIOMEDE: Orderlies! *(Orderlies step forward and attend to cuts and bruises on Achilles' arms and legs.)* Something has come up. But you need sleep.

ACHILLES: No, no, I'm all set to go back.

DIOMEDE: Back?

ACHILLES: To see if she's all right.

DIOMEDE: She?

ACHILLES: The Queen.

DIOMEDE: I thought the aim was to kill her?

ACHILLES: Ha? A fall from a horse won't kill her. Let me take a look.

(He starts to go back whence he came.)

DIOMEDE: Stay. *(Shouting to the hilltop:)* Sentry, can you see the Queen?

SENTRY: *(calling back).* Oh yes, sir!

DIOMEDE: Still on the ground?

SENTRY: No, no! Picked herself up. Wiped the blood off. She's still standing there.

ACHILLES: Hm. What was it that "came up"?

DIOMEDE: Ulysses is here.

ACHILLES: Ulysses?

DIOMEDE: In my tent. Will you see him now?

ACHILLES: Why not?

DIOMEDE: *(Showing him into the tent but not following him in).* I'll leave you two together then. Do drink my wine.

(Ulysses rises. The two men stare at each other, half smiling.)

ACHILLES: I know what you are about to say, Ulysses.

ULYSSES: What is that, Achilles?

ACHILLES: "All is forgiven, come home."

ULYSSES: *(nodding).* With all the risks I run of arousing your celebrated anger! Oh, dear! Can we instead drink Diomede's wine together?

(The wine is on Diomede's table.)

ACHILLES: I'll enjoy Diomede's wine.

ULYSSES: So shall I. It will reduce my fear of you. Yes, you intimidate me.

ACHILLES: And you make me nervous. It has been said: one has to keep tabs on you.

ULYSSES: Good. Keep tabs on me while I brace myself to confront Achilles. *(Raising a can of wine.)* Here's to that anger! May the Trojans – not the Greeks – suffer its consequences!

ACHILLES: And here's to your – is it cunning?

ULYSSES: Sagacity, I believe.

ACHILLES: *(raising a can of wine).* To the cunning sagacity and sagacious cunning of Ulysses!

(They are seated at the table now.)

ULYSSES: "All is forgiven, come home."

ACHILLES: Tell me the worst.

ULYSSES: My little joke. There is nothing to forgive.

ACHILLES: We just aren't forgetting past peccadilloes?

ULYSSES: But we don't assume they will be repeated.

ACHILLES: Aren't they always?

ULYSSES: Is that the latest in psychology?

ACHILLES: Ancient Greek wisdom: "character is fate."

ULYSSES: We mustn't start fencing, you and I.

ACHILLES: If the fencing's with words, you'll win.

ULYSSES: Oh, I can be straightforward, Achilles: today I have no reason not to be: we are going to agree!

ACHILLES: On what?

ULYSSES: Penthesilea.

ACHILLES: *(a double take.)* Ah! Ah! You *have* hit a bull's eye.

ULYSSES: She is not trying to become our ally against Troy?

ACHILLES: No sign of that, no.

ULYSSES: Nor does she present a serious threat to us?

ACHILLES: No-o-o.

ULYSSES: Just now, for instance, that you should pursue her was not a military necessity?

ACHILLES: It was not, no.

ULYSSES: You would be more use to Greece back with the army before Troy?

ACHILLES: Oh yes.

ULYSSES: Good. Then come back!

ACHILLES: Ha?

ULYSSES: Come back.

ACHILLES: I see. Yes, yes. Well argued. Except that "Greece" right now is Agamemnon. It would do him so much good to lose.

ULYSSES: Come now. Just because he stole your girlfriend? Didn't approve of your having a boyfriend?

ACHILLES: Those are good reasons. Or let's say: I don't approve of *him.* Would love it if a Trojan arrow got him.

ULYSSES: And if it did? There is a politics to this war that will survive Agamemnon. Perhaps you are indifferent to the Greek cause?

ACHILLES: Totally.

ULYSSES: But when I appeal to your patriotism, I am not asking that you do anything for Greece that would be against *your* interests. Though Greece needs you, your motive for returning could, would, be all your own. True, we want you to win the war for our sake. But you want to win it for your sake: that you might also win an immortal crown—

ACHILLES: Glory! Everlasting fame!

ULYSSES: Ah! At last you are agreeing with me.

ACHILLES: Following you.

ULYSSES: Then let me try again. You can loathe Agamemnon, you can have your doubts about the rectitude of our cause, or the shrewdness of our making war against Troy at all, but you still wish to play the good Greek if only because you are, of all good Greeks, the best. The model Greek. You can fume and fret over losing Briseis. You can rave and agonize over losing Patroclus. Both times you returned to the fray. You will do so now—for the third time.

ACHILLES: To secure my place in history.

ULYSSES: Not to mention song and story. *(Silence.)* I have reached you.

ACHILLES: Well argued once again. Even I would expect Achilles to say "yes" to glory, to everlasting fame. He's lived for it. Till today.

ULYSSES: And now he doesn't? What does he live for now?

ACHILLES: Penthesilea.

ULYSSES: The Amazon Queen? Ye gods, you are infatuated once again!

ACHILLES: Ha?

ULYSSES: After Patroclus the girl-boy, Penthesilea the man-woman?

ACHILLES: Oh dear, you are concocting funny little theories about me!

ULYSSES: You did run around in a woman's dress that *time.* All right. Have yet another affair! Break all records in love as you have already broken all records in war! Possess the Amazon Queen if you must! But, remember, if we need you, you need us, and will have to get to us fast if we are to serve your purpose and make you the world-famous conqueror of Troy.

ACHILLES: I am not intrigued by Troy. I *am* intrigued by a woman. She seems to be quite a fighter. Which is what I am, ha? *All* I am. I want to fight *her.* My arrows, not my lips, will kiss her cheeks. My sword and not—

DIOMEDE: *(entering).* The sentry's signalling—

ACHILLES: Yes?

DIOMEDE: A message from the Queen. She wants, well—

ACHILLES: Listen closely, Ulysses. The Amazons are men, no? They will have men's lecherous minds. Listen!

DIOMEDE: She wants to fight. Challenges you to single combat.

ACHILLES: Ha! Did you hear that, Ulysses? You must be so disappointed. She only wants to fight. *I* only want to fight. Do you mind if we—only fight?

(He goes out through the door of the tent.)

ULYSSES: Can *you* take it that lightly, Diomede?

DIOMEDE: By no means. She is a stag, and he the hound that hunts her. His teeth are sunk into her throat already. Such a stag can drag a hound up hill, down dale, fording the streams, delving into the thickets, until he's lost in the dark heart of the forest.

ULYSSES: *(shaking his head).* Could be even worse. For she may prove to be the dog and sink her teeth in him, the proud Greek stag.

DIOMEDE: And so?

ULYSSES: Take your men and follow him. Do whatever's best. Save him even by violence from himself. I will await you here.

(They embrace. Diomede leaves.)

II

(The Amazon warriors enter ceremoniously and then stand in formation to cry, "Hail to the Queen!" Attended by Prothoe, Meroe, and Asteria, Queen Penthesilea follows and takes the place of honor. Silence: then a voice, crying, "And now—the Feast of Roses!")

PENTHESILEA: *(After holding up her hands to speak).* Thank you, sisters, thank you all! And yet the honor's yours, not mine, for it is you who fought like tigresses, routing so many Greeks, taking so many prisoners! Your Queen's congratulations, heartfelt thanks! The cry I heard just now: "The Feast of Roses!" It was I who first uttered it. Prematurely. I was forgetting that the Feast can only follow victory complete. The great Greek champion Achilles is not captured yet. I've challenged him to single combat. Do you approve? *(Asteria holds up her arm.)* Asteria?

ASTERIA: I approve. The number of prisoners has been exaggerated. Also their quality. Have you taken a look at them, sisters? They are the scum of the Greek army. Where is the cream? Besieging Troy. King Agamemnon, Ajax, Menelaus—call the roll and none will answer—they have not bothered to come over here. With one exception: the great Achilles. They challenge us with a single champion. Let us accept the challenge. Take him on. Defeat him. We cannot call it victory till this fellow bites the dust!

(Meroe has raised her arm.)

PENTHESILEA: Meroe, my general?

MEROE: I differ from Asteria on the prisoners. They are good fighting men: for us, a prize. And they are many: thousands. Without vanity, without self deceit, we can call this a victory.

PENTHESILEA: Now, Meroe, I wonder. We could set out with all these prisoners on the road to Amazonia, but here's a man, Achilles, who will stage such savage sorties and such lightning raids we'd never get there. Even if we did, here is a brute who would not hesitate to enter the very Temple of Diana, tear the roses off our prisoners and make prisoners of us.

MEROE: Excuse me, Queen, you are again in error. You think he's on the loose. He's not. He is cut off. At best can furtively sneak back to the Greeks. Even when back, my spies report, he's been ordered: "Return at once to camp at Troy." As for the prisoners, where are they?

PENTHESILEA: I don't know.

MEROE: Where are they, sisters? *(Cries of: "We don't know!")* Because I've hidden them. From the Greeks. From everyone except their guards. I defy Achilles himself to find them, defy him to get on their trail even when we move on to Amazonia.

PENTHESILEA: Sisters, I am out-argued by our magnificent Meroe here, a veritable virtuoso of the wars! So be it. Let me appeal to you—and yes, even to you, dear Meroe. I have a feeling—no, no, it's more—it's an inspiration—that, all evidence to the contrary notwithstanding, this is the time to strike! How is it with renown? You seize it when it offers or it's gone. Voices tell me, and who knows but they may be the voices of goddesses, of the Mothers, even of the Great Mother, now is the time to seize Achilles by his yellow locks! And it's for me to do it. The laurel crown's an inch above my head. *(Prothoe raises her arm.)* And now Prothoe, nearest to me of all you most dear sisters!

PROTHOE: To be your friend I must be blunt, advising you: ignore those voices from within and heed the voice of reason from without, the voice of your great general Meroe.

PENTHESILEA: Prothoe, *you*—

PROTHOE: *(gently).* Queen, you are tired. Lay down your arms and rest: you are entitled. You have not made a case for fighting on.

PENTHESILEA: Prothoe knows me *too* closely, sisters. Hears what I say in my sleep. Or when distracted or just featherheaded. But why should I hide from you? Let me confess: this man diminishes me. I've been so close to him I could see my reflection in his armor: was that, I had to ask, an Amazon Queen? It seemed much less. I'll be at this man's feet till he's at mine! I shall feel conquered till I conquer *him!*

PROTHOE: We understand such feelings: they re-write the history of men and women. But have you told us all we need to know?

PENTHESILEA: What do you mean, sister?

PROTHOE: So intimate with you, I am not intimate enough. There's something I don't know.

PENTHESILEA: Your eyes look through my flesh into my heart. Very well, Prothoe, sisters all, there *is* a secret I am withholding from you. I must capture Achilles but am not free to tell you why. All I can promise is: at the right time you'll know. Are you prepared to trust me?

PROTHOE: What must be must be.

PENTHESILEA: Meroe?

MEROE: If there's an over-riding reason, let's accept that.

PENTHESILEA: Sisters all, cry Aye or Nay! *(Cries of "Aye!")* Thanks, I hope to deserve your trust. Now, Meroe, gather our forces. Go out once more against the Greeks. As for Achilles, he is *my* quarry: you are all forbidden to touch a hair of his head on any provocation whatsoever. Even I shall not slay him. To bring down this bright many-colored bird out of the Trojan sky, I'll break at most a wing and then, pressing these armored arms against his armored chest, throw him down on Trojan grass as on a bed of down. Sisters, to the field! *(As the Amazons ready themselves, Penthesilea talks to Prothoe.)* What shall I be more grateful for: that you were my conscience in the beginning or that you supported me in the end?

PROTHOE: Don't be grateful at all. Just count on me.

PENTHESILEA: That is true love. Without you I can't fight. It's both of us or neither, in fortunes good or bad. *(They embrace. Penthesilea addresses the Amazons once more before they move off.)* After this last encounter, the Feast of Roses!

III-A

(The High Priestess of Diana and a crowd of little girls with baskets of roses on their heads.)

HIGH PRIESTESS: In a circle, little ones! Sit cross-legged while we rehearse our catechism.

(They all do so.)

HIGH PRIESTESS: *(starting in on the catechism).* Who am I?

GIRL 1: High Priestess of Diana!

HIGH PRIESTESS: And who's Diana?

GIRL 2: Our goddess, our very own, goddess of the Amazons!

HIGH PRIESTESS: What makes her ours?

GIRL 3: She's god of girls. Women. Can't stand men!

("Ugh, men!" say the girls, and so on.)

HIGH PRIESTESS: So what does she do about them—the men?

GIRL 4: Keeps them away!

GIRL 5: Shoos them off!

GIRL 6: *(by rote).* Writes the words KEEP OUT in imaginary letters on the doors of her Temple!

GIRL 7: And on the gates of our capital, Themiscyra!

GIRL 8: And around the boundaries of our country, Amazonia!

GIRL 9: *(a mischievous girl).* The biggest KEEP OUT sign is on her bedroom door!

GIRL 10: *(a little tot).* Then how does she have babies?

GIRL 9: Diana doesn't have babies, silly!

GIRL 10: Why not?

GIRL 9: Because she's a virgin, stupid!

GIRL 10: What's a virgin?

HIGH PRIESTESS: Tell her, someone.

GIRL 9: A woman that doesn't have babies, dumb bell.

HIGH PRIESTESS: *(to Girl 9).* Don't be rude, Megaris. Am I a virgin, Xantippe?

GIRL 10: You don't have any babies, do you?

HIGH PRIESTESS: No, a priestess *is* a virgin. If I had a baby, I'd leave the Temple and join the army.

GIRL 10: Hey, that sounds really neat! And when you get into the army, how do you have a baby?

HIGH PRIESTESS: I can tell you when it starts: at the Feast of Roses. And where: in the Temple.

GIRL 10: *(whispering to Girl 9).* When that Feast comes up, I'm going to peek through the window.

HIGH PRIESTESS: Now quiet, everyone, while I tell you something thrilling that happened just yesterday.

(Cries of: "Oh, goody, tell us a story.")

HIGH PRIESTESS: I was standing by the Temple gate. There sped by, I could almost touch him, a man! *(Cries of: "Ugh, a man!")* A big hulking Greek called Achilles in an iron chariot with long, long scythes extending the axles of the wheels and chopping branches off like chaff as they brushed the trees. Seconds later came another chariot gaining on the first. In this one stood our Queen *(cries of: "Penthesilea!")* poised to jump on Achilles and cut him down. "Where are you going?" I cried. The question was foolish but she answered it: "To the Feast of Roses!" Well, that's my little story.

GIRL 1: The queen was counting her chickens before they were hatched! Suppose Achilles had cut her down? No victory, no Feast of Roses!

GIRL 2: That's not fair! I'm *for* our Queen!

HIGH PRIESTESS: We're all *for* our Queen. That's why we are preparing for the Feast. Are everyone's baskets full of roses? *(Cries of: "Yes!" Most hold up full baskets.) (To a girl.)* Where did you find those gorgeous blooms?

GIRL 3: I was going after one little rose on a jutting rock. As I reached for it I fell into a chasm. Down, down, down! I thought I'd die but at the bottom of the chasm – these giant roses!

HIGH PRIESTESS: Why, that's an Amazon parable! Keep trying and though you fall into a pit you will be beautifully rewarded! *(To another:)* Is your basket empty?

GIRL 4: Think so? Lift the cloth!

(When the High Priestess lifts the cloth on the basket she uncovers a single rose of great beauty.)

HIGH PRIESTESS: A single rose – but of such exquisite beauty.

GIRL 4: I spent the whole day seeking out that one rare rose the Queen would want to place in Achilles' hair.

GIRL 5: *(a tiny tot).* His hair is yellow, I bet! *(She giggles.)*

HIGH PRIESTESS: *(to Girl 4).* What a nice idea! Let's practice it. I'll be Achilles. You, Charmion, be Penthesilea.

(Charmion can be any of the girls except the two who will sing. The following song accompanies a little pantomine of Penthesilea placing a rose in Achilles' hair.)

GIRL 3: *(singing).* Into the chasm I slipped and fell
Thinking it led down to hell.
What did I find in the abyss?
Red roses beautiful as this.

(All join in this refrain:) Red roses for his yellow hair.

GIRL 4: *(singing).* The Feast of Roses comes and goes
Never forgot is the red, red rose
Which the captive king must wear
In his yellow Grecian hair.

(All join in this refrain:) Red roses for his yellow hair.

As they start to repeat the song, an Amazon captain rushes on. The music breaks off.)

CAPTAIN: What are you doing here, most reverend lady? It's not for priestesses or little girls to hear the brazen voice of war!

HIGH PRIESTESS: The war is over. We're preparing the Feast of Roses at the Queen's command.

CAPTAIN: What? That's more than strange for in a moment you will hear the Queen – amid the din of horns and cymbals – shriek her bloodcurdling battle cry!

HIGH PRIESTESS: Battle – again – and now?

CAPTAIN: Of course. She has not yet brought down Achilles.

HIGH PRIESTESS: What is one man? The victory was won, the prisoners taken!

CAPTAIN: Then you have not heard the rumor.

HIGH PRIESTESS: Rumor?

CAPTAIN: That the Queen's heart has been pierced by an arrow with a poisoned arrowhead. Such as might well have made her mad.

GIRLS: *(now on the hilltop gazing out toward the horizon).*— She's going out to fight him!—How her stallion dances!—She and the horse are doing a dance together!—She must be so excited!—Her armor's golden like his hair!—Everything gleams in the sun, I'm dazzled!—But now it's smoke!—That's not smoke, it's dust—from the hooves!—You can't see anything now!

HIGH PRIESTESS: An arrow with a poisoned arrowhead? No arrow can get through *her* armor.

CAPTAIN: Not if the archer is the god of love?

HIGH PRIESTESS: Eros? The male god of male-female love? Pah! What is an Amazon if not a woman armored against *that* arrow!

CAPTAIN: Pray for victory! Pray that it's Achilles, not the Queen, that falls!

ADJUTANT: *(offstage.)* Priestess!

HIGH PRIESTESS: Who is this?

(The Adjutant enters.)

CAPTAIN: Her Adjutant. The duel over already?

ADJUTANT: Couching their lances, Penthesilea and Achilles clash like colliding thunderbolts! The lances splinter, her helmet is off and she is thrown from her horse, striking her head on the rocky ground. Is she dead? He's standing over her with drawn sword, knowing he could make sure of it with a single blow. Why doesn't he? He's pale as Death; like Death, a mystery. She's not dead. Her eyes are opening. Now surely he must send her packing to the Underworld! Instead, he's staring at her. He is speaking: "Her eyes! Her dying eyes are reaching out and . . ." He knelt and put his arms about her shoulders.

HIGH PRIESTESS: *(shocked).* The Amazons let him *touch* her?

ADJUTANT: Under her orders not to touch him, yes. They could touch *her,* though. Prothoe snatched the Queen from his grasp. Penthesilea, as waking from a sleep, gasps. Her bosom is bleeding, her hair in disarray down her back. Gently they lead her off. But what had happened to that mystery man? Can Eros melt a heart, like his, that's made of iron? For he is throwing down his sword and shield, he is tearing off his armor, and would have followed the Queen if her Amazons had not stood in his path, a solid phalanx.

III-B

(To the High Priestess, Captain, Adjutant, little girls, the Queen, Prothoe, Asteria, Meroe, and Amazon soldiers.)

PENTHESILEA: *(in an enfeebled voice).* Sic the dogs on him! Let loose my elephants! Whip them along with flaming faggots! Get out my iron chariots, run them over him! Mow him down! The slender waist, the massive shoulders, muscled thighs, plow them all under!

PROTHOE: We must move on, Queen. Achilles follows.

PENTHESILEA: *(oblivious).* Has he no brains? Could he not see that, to get close, I have to woo him on the battlefield? Have to hurt him first, if ever I am to fold him in my arms? How could he return advances thus? The soft strings of a lyre, brushed by the warm Sirocco wind, sang my name in the night. He picked that lyre up and smashed it!

HIGH PRIESTESS: *(amazed, offended.)* Then, it is true, she is—!

PROTHOE: No, no, she is in shock! She doesn't know what she's saying!

PENTHESILEA: *(half-hearing this).* I did not say it! Did not even think it! I'm going to lead you all back home to Amazonia.

PROTHOE: Oh, bless you, Queen! I'll see that everyone is ready.

PENTHESILEA: Should ever anyone—anyone—bring into jeopardy the Amazon state, my bow, the golden bow of the Amazons, will fall moaning to the ground and break. *(She see the rose wreaths left behind by the girls, and picks up one of them.)* For the Feast of Roses? Who ordered that?

HIGH PRIESTESS: Why, you did, Queen.

PENTHESILEA: Liar! You did! We are beset with blood and butchery and all you think of, enjoying victory before it's won, is orgies! O Prothoe, what a scandal that the chaste daughters of Diana should howl with lust like unleashed dogs so that war's trumpets are not heard! *(She slashes the rose wreaths with a knife.)* Could the star on which we live be slashed to pieces thus? Along with these few flowers I'd like to rend the universe asunder!

PROTHOE: You must excuse her, Priestess, she has been ravaged by the Furies!

ADJUTANT: *(from the hilltop).* Achilles is pushing the phalanx back.

PROTHOE: We *must* move on.

PENTHESILEA: *(sitting).* I am too tired.

PROTHOE: Have you lost your wits?

PENTHESILEA: I am too weak to stand.

PROTHOE: Achilles is coming!

PENTHESILEA: Let him! Let him roll me in the mud: it is the primal matter from which I sprang, my Mother Earth. Let him drag me by the feet behind his chariot, the prey of dogs and vultures in the dust: a woman who can't dominate a man is less than dust.

(And she tears off all the trinkets from her hair and neck. From afar off, the Greeks are heard urging Achilles on, "Keep going," etc.)

ADJUTANT: Queen, you must fly, or it will be too late.

PROTHOE: I will go with you. You and I must always be together. *(But Penthesilea is weeping against a tree.)* You cannot? For I know this law of mortals: "What one cannot, that one cannot do."

HIGH PRIESTESS: But she can. No inscrutable fate detains her, only her own rebel heart.

PROTHOE: And what is more inscrutable than that? What if her rebel heart's her fate? Remember, priestess, a great prize seemed within her grasp. And now she cannot bring herself to reach for less.

HIGH PRIESTESS: A Queen must show the way to others—

PROTHOE: Sh!

PENTHESILEA: Prothoe!

PROTHOE: Yes.

PENTHESILEA: Suppose I fly. What then? What could I do?

PROTHOE: Re-open the war.

PENTHESILEA: Where is Helios?

PROTHOE: What?

PENTHESILEA: The sun.

PROTHOE: Why, overhead . . . Make peace with Troy. Head for that stretch of shore off which the Greek fleet lies at anchor. Set fire to their ships, then storm their camp. They cannot fight on two fronts. Take the whole Greek army prisoner and haul them off to our Feast of Roses. With me at your side, you'll have Achilles at your feet.

PENTHESILEA: *(still staring at the sun).* Then, yes, I'll fly—to him! I feel him circling round in rings of fire! Where are my wings?

PROTHOE: What? What?

PENTHESILEA: The rings of fire are so far off.

PROTHOE: The rings of fire? *(Penthesilea manages to stand*

up.) Ha? So you can stand. That's good. Hear me. Have you ever marked the vaulted gateway, Queen, back home in Themiscyra? Every stone of it, taken singly, pulled by gravity, wishes to fall. But that vaulted arch, though made up of these stones, wishes to stand and the gateway shall stand until its time comes and it falls as a single stone. Stand! Hold together, Queen, so long as there is stone or mortar left in you!

PENTHESILEA: Which way do we go?

PROTHOE: Across this bridge. Take my hand.

(Penthesilea does so, and they walk to the bridge.)

PENTHESILEA: There's one thing I must do.

PROTHOE: Yes?

PENTHESILEA: *(on the bridge).* Yes, heap Mount Ida on Mount Ossa, then sit on top of both.

HIGH PRIESTESS: Oh, she is gone now, gone!

PROTHOE: *(gently).* And what would you do then, my Queen?

PENTHESILEA: Why, pull him down by his yellow hair!

PROTHOE: Who?

PENTHESILEA: Helios.

HIGH PRIESTESS: Drag her. Use force.

PENTHESILEA: Not overhead. *(She is looking down into the stream.)* He's down here in the water. Take me, Helios, I come! *(She tries to throw herself off the bridge but Prothoe and the High Priestess stop her. Penthesilea faints. Prothoe leads her to a spot where she can lie down.)*

ADJUTANT: *(from the hilltop).* Achilles has broken through the phalanx!

HIGH PRIESTESS: Girls, away!

III-C

(The High Priestess and the girls have left. There remain Asteria, Meroe, and other Amazon soldiers. Prothoe is tending Penthesilea.)

MEROE: We're still under orders not to touch him!

ASTERIA: Then what shall we do?

1st AMAZON SOLDIER: Trick him, harass him somehow.

2nd AMAZON SOLDIER: Scare him.

1st AMAZON SOLDIER: How?

2nd AMAZON SOLDIER: Our game—swinging swords at each other and missing by a hair's breath.

3rd AMAZON SOLDIER: Yes! I'll graze his pink cheeks for him!

4th AMAZON SOLDIER: I'll trim his golden hair for him!

5th AMAZON SOLDIER: His sensual red lips will feel the kiss of death!

ACHILLES: *(at first heard calling from offstage, then entering).* Put up your swords! I am unarmed! Peace! I bring you peace! *(But he has entered now and they play their devilish game with him: he does not understand it but thinks he has miraculously managed to fend off real blows.)* Stop! Stop, girls, at once! Hit or get hit's the law of war: don't force me to hit *you. (Stepping back from them:)* How beautiful they are! Why would *you* make war? A single look from any of you would conquer any man in Greece!

2nd AMAZON SOLDIER: He's laughing at us.

(She moves her sword horizontally just over his head. He ducks.)

ACHILLES: Now, girls, please! Must you?

2nd AMAZON SOLDIER: Yes. And we're not girls.

3rd AMAZON SOLDIER: *(to 2nd).* Let's accidentally hit him.

2nd AMAZON SOLDIER: Right. I'm gonna slice his right ear off. *(But as she lifts her sword, her sword-arm is seized by a Greek.)*

GREEK: Shall we kill her, sir? She'd have killed you!

ASTERIA: *(To Meroe).* Hear that? Threatened with instant death, we are released from our Queen's order not to touch this man!

MEROE: Wait.

1st AMAZON SOLDIER: Let's sic the dogs on him.

3rd AMAZON SOLDIER: Bring out the chariots. Run him down.

4th AMAZON SOLDIER: Get the elephants. Drop boulders on him from their backs.

MEROE: No, no, stop! I command you. *(They stop.)*

2nd AMAZON SOLDIER: *(who has been taken by her captors where she can see their rear).* More Greeks are coming, a whole troop!

ASTERIA: You still say stop?

2nd AMAZON SOLDIER: A whole troop of Greeks!

MEROE: Now: no. We'll *have* to fight.

ASTERIA: *(confronting Achilles).* And you're *my* quarry.

ACHILLES: I'm your admirer. There's nothing I admire more than a pretty face—

ASTERIA: You have a pretty face too, young man. Has it stopped you attacking Amazons? Defend yourself! *(As she raises her arm to strike, the sword is knocked out of her hand by Achilles' companions.)* You see this, Queen?

PROTHOE: She is unconscious. She sees nothing.

ASTERIA: Note—all you other sisters—the message that men bring to women!

ACHILLES: All swords—on both sides—must be sheathed!

DIOMEDE: *(entering).* And sheathed they shall be! Amazons, you are all but surrounded.

MEROE: All but? Then there's a gap in your encirclement? Where is it? *(Her scout on the hillock points it out).* Four of you bring the Queen. The rest—there is the gap—make a dash for it! *(They start to do all this, but Achilles does not let the Queen be touched, and she is left there, only Prothoe, of the Amazons, staying to share her fate.)*

ACHILLES: The Queen is mine! *(To Diomede:)* Thank you. But now: pursue them. Take them prisoner. Bring them back. *(Diomede leads his men off.)*

III-D

(Penthesilea is still unconscious. Achilles talks to Prothoe.)

ACHILLES: You are—

PROTHOE: My name's Prothoe.

ACHILLES: It was you who—?

PROTHOE: Snatched her from your arms after her fall from her horse.

ACHILLES: Yes, and why did she fall? A horsewoman, a warrior, like her?

PROTHOE: Why for that matter was she in your arms? Why did you—say what you said?

ACHILLES: What?

PROTHOE: "Her eyes! Her dying eyes!"

ACHILLES: I thought she was dying.

PROTHOE: And what else?

ACHILLES: Ha?

PROTHOE: Did you—in that moment—fall in love with her?

ACHILLES: Did I—?

PROTHOE: Looking into her dying eyes, did you fall in love?

ACHILLES: *(ignoring this).* She is still unconscious?

PROTHOE: Yes.

ACHILLES: What happened?

PROTHOE: You saw what happened: she fell off her horse.

ACHILLES: You rescued her from me. And then?

PROTHOE: She tried to throw herself off that bridge. We prevented her. She fainted. Is still close to death. If she should come to now and find herself confronted by . . . her conqueror . . . death would be all she'd want.

ACHILLES: You are her closest friend, Prothoe?

PROTHOE: *(looking at him).* I love her in my way.

ACHILLES: What way is that?

PROTHOE: Loyalty. Sisterhood.

ACHILLES: I *am* in love with her.

PROTHOE: Ah!

ACHILLES: Is she with me? *(Silence.)* Why has she been pursuing me? *(Silence.)* There was love in her eyes. But behind it—pain. Misery. What about? *(Silence.)* You decline to say. She must speak for herself? But will she—to her conqueror? *(Silence.)* Unconscious. A second time! Does she live on the edge of consciousness as by a precipice? That first time, when she fell from her horse, I saw her swoon. She was out for minutes. In those minutes, for all she knew, I might have fallen off *my* horse and lost the fight.

PROTHOE: You didn't.

ACHILLES: What if I were to tell her that I did?

PROTHOE: What? What for?

ACHILLES: To revive her. Put some spirit into her.

PROTHOE: And when, later, she finds out?

ACHILLES: Later, she could face it: when I have told her I'm in love with her. Now, Prothoe, will you help me?

PROTHOE: You really propose to—No, no, I want nothing to do with it.

ACHILLES: Very well, I'll wake her and give her the whole truth. *(He starts to do so.)*

PROTHOE: No, no!

ACHILLES: Then you *will* help?

PROTHOE: I must.

ACHILLES: I lost. Am now her prisoner.

PROTHOE: Step behind that tree. She's coming to.

III-E

(Achilles watches and listens behind an oak tree. Penthesilea comes to, and talks with Prothoe.)

PENTHESILEA: *(opening her eyes).* Where am I? Prothoe!

PROTHOE: Yes, Queen. Don't you see the bridge, the rocky slope, the windy plains of Troy?

PENTHESILEA: No.

PROTHOE: What do you see?

PENTHESILEA: Horse's hooves. Grass. Achilles towering over me. I reach for my dagger! Achilles picks me up and hauls me off to his tent with mocking laughter!

PROTHOE: That did not happen.

PENTHESILEA: What did?

PROTHOE: *We* hauled you off. You tried to throw yourself in the river. When you fainted, there was a skirmish. Asteria was wounded—

PENTHESILEA: Ah!

PROTHOE: We would have captured Achilles but a troop of Greeks came to his rescue. Almost surrounded our people. Are pursuing them even now.

PENTHESILEA: You keep looking over your shoulder, Prothoe. Is there a giant behind that oak tree? A chimaera?

(She rouses herself and goes over to where she can look behind the tree. Seeing Achilles, she screams. He steps forward, is preparing to speak when:)

PROTHOE: Sh! Queen,—

PENTHESILEA: My conqueror here! I am betrayed! And you're the traitor! You've conspired with him—

PROTHOE: One moment, Queen—

PENTHESILEA: I can see what giant, what chimaera, we have here, armed to the teeth and in an ambush from which he would have leapt to slay me!

PROTHOE: Look again! He is *not* armed!

PENTHESILEA: Armed to the teeth, I say, and—*(But in saying this she has seen how wrong she is.)* Unarmed! Unarmed! What Grecian trick is this?

PROTHOE: What if it were—no trick?

PENTHESILEA: Ha? Then what is it?

PROTHOE: What if—Achilles does not come in hate?

PENTHESILEA: In what then—scorn?

PROTHOE: Not hate. Not scorn.

PENTHESILEA: I'm trapped? He'll have me chained up like a dog?

PROTHOE: Maybe he's here to let you chain *him* up.

PENTHESILEA: What? What? What happened in the fight? *(To Achilles:)* Don't tell me—you're my prisoner?

ACHILLES: Don't you recall?

PENTHESILEA: Falling, yes. I—

ACHILLES: *Before* you fell?

PENTHESILEA: No, I—

ACHILLES: I had already fallen! You were already victor!

PENTHESILEA: *That* is what happened? *(To Prothoe:)* Is that what happened?

PROTHOE: *(trembling).* Would Achilles lie?

PENTHESILEA: *(aside to Prothoe).* The blood is rushing to my head. Is this happiness? I, happy? *(To Achilles:)* You, my prisoner?

ACHILLES: *(nodding).* Wishing to serve a lifetime's sentence in the prison of your eyes.

PENTHESILEA: *(aside to Prothoe).* For years, I've felt this blood accumulating in my bosom, piling up, piling, till my breasts seemed at the bursting point. Now, suddenly, the blood flows free through vein and artery! *(To Achilles:)* My prisoner?

ACHILLES: Just so.

PENTHESILEA: Then welcome, dear young . . . *(To Prothoe)* I can't say "man."

ACHILLES: I am a goddess' son.

PENTHESILEA: Thetis, yes. Then welcome, god!

PROTHOE: Be moderate, Queen!

PENTHESILEA: It's time for our immoderate Feast of Roses! Their arms, their faces caked with blood, the Amazons return. Each leads a man whom she has captured by the hand. With wreaths of roses, little girls run out to meet them. In the Temple, a short-horned ox is led to the altar. The axe falls. Blood spurts. The ox falls. Handmaidens mop up the blood and spray the ground with Persian perfumes. Bugles blare and trumpets and old horns. The tables are piled high, and golden goblets overflow with wine. A rite to fill Bacchus and the gods of men with envy! In Great Diana's name we raise to ecstasies almost too much to bear the holy orgy of the Amazons!

ACHILLES: I do not understand.

PENTHESILEA: Ha?

ACHILLES: Like one of Great Jove's thunderbolts, you crashed down on our war, taking on one side, then the other, and then both. Why? Why do you fight at all when you could win with a single blow—by feminine arts—making us adore your heavenly sweetness, more than heavenly beauty?

PENTHESILEA: The daughters of your country practice such arts, pick out a lover at the Olympic games, coquetting with a nosegay held like this, and eyes demurely fixed upon the ground, or, in the nightingale-enchanted woods, sinking upon some massive thorax, whispering: "You're my man." An Amazon must seek her man out in the slaughterhouse, and take him with the instruments of slaughter!

ACHILLES: Unwomanly! Unnatural! Where could such customs come from?

PENTHESILEA: Shall I tell him, Prothoe?

PROTHOE: All? Tell him all?

PENTHESILEA: *(nodding).* In the beginning was the Great Goddess. The Mother ruled. There was no father. No god, no king, no master. That was the primal and the golden age. How it ended is not known. Darkness descends until a time when man hunted, woman stayed at home. Woman obeyed. Man gave the orders.

ACHILLES: Then—whence the Amazons?

PENTHESILEA: North, in the Caucasus, there was a tribe, the Scythians: one day, from Ethiopia in the South, an army came, black men under their black king, Vexoris, and wiped them out.

ACHILLES: All of them?

PENTHESILEA: All males. Sought them out in treetops, caves, wherever, and slaughtered them. Took over their huts, their crops, their women, while these last embraced the corpse of husband, lover, son, seized them in lust, in hate, and raped them.

ACHILLES: Poor women!

PENTHESILEA: Poor women with their baubles, ring and bangle, brooch and bodkin, themselves the chiefest bauble! But there's a day the weeping stops.

ACHILLES: What day is that?

PENTHESILEA: Daggers can be forged from rings and bangles on a woman's hearth. Tanais had a needle.

ACHILLES: Tanais?

PENTHESILEA: Whom Vexoris picked as bride. To get a needle between a man's ribs and into his heart—Tanais did that. It was the signal. A thousand needles leaped from a thousand bosoms and pricked the Ethiopians to their death! Before, they'd left no Scythian men alive. We left no Ethiopian men alive. The mountains of the Caucasus, our world, belonged to woman. We had created a nation wholly female with its own laws and sacred customs, guarded and guaranteed by its own weapons!

ACHILLES: Prodigious! More amazing than the exploits of Theseus or Hercules!

PENTHESILEA: This way we found ourselves. Our self-respect. Women became beings fully human.

ACHILLES: Such women as I never saw before! With such a Queen—!

PENTHESILEA: Lie at my feet. *(He does so.)* Let no one tell me suffering ennobles. Misfortune does not cleanse the soul. It makes you bitter—till you can't look upon a happy face without resentment. A happy child, playing on mother's lap, seems a conspiracy against your pain. Suffering can be heroic, yes, Achilles, but it is happiness that is divine. I'm happy. And plunge now in the pearly pool of pleasure to cleanse my body and my soul. How does our song go? *(She recites the lines:)*

Becalmed is the sea
The stormclouds clear
The Furies flee
The Blessed Ones draw near!

Come closer, son of Thetis. Don't be scared because I worsted you.

ACHILLES: *(rising to his knees).* Do flowers hate the sun?

PENTHESILEA: Bathe in my sunlight, little flower. But, look, you're wounded!

ACHILLES: A sword grazed my cheek.

PENTHESILEA: What fun it was to strike at you, Achilles! I never meant to hurt you. I envied the grass you fell on.

ACHILLES: The wound is nothing.

PENTHESILEA: *(half-closing her eyes).* You are a lion that the Queen of Love has trapped. She must chain you up.

ACHILLES: *(entering the dream).* What lion would not be quiet as a mouse if he had such a Queen to stroke his mane?

PENTHESILEA: Queen Venus?

ACHILLES: Queen Penthesilea. *(She has taken up wreaths and garlands and is bedecking him.)*

PENTHESILEA: You're a turtle dove. Caressing your soft feathers a little girl could tie a string to your leg and make you dance. Her feelings would be hands to stroke you with.

ACHILLES: To think I do not even know you!

PENTHESILEA: You shall. For now it's roses, roses all the way. From head to foot, from back to front, on shoulder, elbow, hand! *(She continues to deck him with roses.)* What manner of man are you?

ACHILLES: A gardener, a flower-fancier, longing to pluck the roses from *your* tree.

PENTHESILEA: When they're in bloom, pluck them, Achilles. *(She places a wreath on his head. It is the final touch.)* Roses become him, do they not, Prothoe? They glow like stars in his blond hair, they flow in streams down his strong arms! How delicate he is! Day himself when the Hours hale him from the hills at morning, the dewdrops twinkling at his feet like pearls, is not more delicate than this, dare I say it? Man. But look! His eyes are wet with tears. This "man" can cry! He's not *that* man.

PROTHOE: What man?

PENTHESILEA: The savage who slew Hector, pierced his ankles, tied him to the car, dragged him head downwards round the walls of Troy!

PROTHOE: His armour—made by Vulcan, the gods' blacksmith—shows he *is* that man.

PENTHESILEA: He is? The most ungovernable—of all men in the world—is governed now—by me?

PROTHOE: He is.

PENTHESILEA: Then—*(She kisses him.)* If anyone asks awkward questions, sir, just give my name.

ACHILLES: Pray, tell it to me again: I like to hear it.

PENTHESILEA: This ring will be your passport, take it. You might lose it, yes, but are . . . names better? Names get forgotten. Do I? Close your eyes. Can you see me—in your mind's eye?

ACHILLES: Cut with a diamond's point, your image is engraved upon my heart. Tell me your name.

PENTHESILEA: Our first Queen was Tanais. My mother, Queen Otrera, was descended from her. My name's Penthesilea.

ACHILLES: My swan shall go on singing, even in death: Penthesilea.

PROTHOE: *(sings).*

Becalmed is the sea
The storm clouds clear
The Furies flee
The Blessed Ones draw near!*

(A silence, then:)

ACHILLES: Your race—the Amazon race—how does it continue? How does it . . . perpetuate itself?

PENTHESILEA: Why, as I told you—by the Feast of Roses!

ACHILLES: Those ecstasies you spoke of? Holy orgies?

PENTHESILEA: *(nodding).* The Amazon takes her enemy prisoner, enchains him in roses and—*(She breaks off, looking at Achilles, enchained, as he is, with roses. He returns her gaze.)*

ACHILLES: Which brings the narrative up to the moment.

PENTHESILEA: *(confused).* We may not pick and choose: Amazon law ordains that we must take the first man battle throws our way.

ACHILLES: And after?

*If the performance is in two parts, the intermission falls here, and Part Two should open with another rendering of the little song by Prothoe.

PENTHESILEA: Throw him back. Send him away. Like his male offspring nine months later.

ACHILLES: I leave tomorrow then.

PENTHESILEA: Our laws shock you.

ACHILLES: Your laws? No! You! You broke those laws, did pick and choose, pursued me ever since the day we met by the Scamander. Even then it seemed you somehow knew me, loved me –

PENTHESILEA: So?

ACHILLES: Then what's *your* story?

PENTHESILEA: Did you hear that, Prothoe? Even you have not heard *my* story.

PROTHOE: Your secret? The great secret?

PENTHESILEA: *(nodding).* And it's here. *(She takes a locket from her neck. To Achilles:)* Open it.

ACHILLES: *(doing so).* My portrait?

PROTHOE: You've had his portrait – all this time?

ACHILLES: Who gave it to you?

PENTHESILEA: A Sibyl.

III-F

(Flashback. A cave. Penthesilea talks with a Sibyl.)

PENTHESILEA: *(doing so).* You sent for me, Sibyl. Why?

SIBYL: To save your life.

PENTHESILEA: I am the strongest woman in the world.

SIBYL: Woe to a world in which the strongest woman is not strong enough.

PENTHESILEA: For what?

SIBYL: To live.

PENTHESILEA: I do live.

SIBYL: To live on. I see the misery in your face. It is the sorrow of the Amazons. How long can you endure it? *(Silence.)* And the cause so clear, so crass.

PENTHESILEA: The cause?

SIBYL: You need, you want, a man.

PENTHESILEA: *(rising with a cry of outrage).* Ah! *(Getting hold of herself.)* How d'you know? What d'you know?

SIBYL: I was myself an Amazon once.

PENTHESILEA: Ah, you were—

SIBYL: An Amazon can have anything. The whole green earth could be hers. But not a man.

PENTHESILEA: And you know why.

SIBYL: So clear, so crass: because men held dominion over us.

PENTHESILEA: Still dominate—all other women.

SIBYL: All?

PENTHESILEA: All.

SIBYL: Go to the mouth of the cave. Look left. What do you see?

PENTHESILEA: *(having carried out these orders).* Someone gathering firewood. Some . . . *man.* Great Heavens, you are—his?

SIBYL: No.

PENTHESILEA: He's just a neighbor?

SIBYL: He's mine.

PENTHESILEA: What?

SIBYL: I'm not *his* chattel. He is mine.

PENTHESILEA: *(with an intake of breath).* And this is—your life? You've made a life utterly unlike—?

SIBYL: The far famed cities of men? Yes. But also: unlike the cities of the Amazons: Ephesus, Themiscyra.

PENTHESILEA: Indeed. *(Pause.)* And this way you—

SIBYL: Ended the Amazon agony. Escaped the unendurable female cage.

PENTHESILEA: Just you, though: one woman in the world.

SIBYL: And not the strongest!

PENTHESILEA: Not the—?

SIBYL: For the strongest, there would be a challenge.

PENTHESILEA: To do what?

SIBYL: To lead the whole Amazon tribe out of that cage.

PENTHESILEA: How?

SIBYL: Break, re-make, Amazon law. Show that you *can* love a man.

PENTHESILEA: What could justify that?

SIBYL: That you have conquered him in the beginning. That you remain his master to the end.

PENTHESILEA: I'll not love the first man I defeat. The strongest woman in the world deserves the strongest man. Produce him for me. I challenge *you!*

SIBYL: Done. Done! Here!

(She produces a locket and gives it to Penthesilea.)

III-G

(Continuous with III-E: Penthesilea, Prothoe, Achilles.)

PENTHESILEA: I searched the world for you. Loved you already. Loved the face in the locket from the moment I first saw it. But then to learn its owner was Achilles. To see the real him! When at last I found you there by the Scamander, the other Grecian heroes paled before you—as stars of night before the star of day. Like forked lightning when it falls upon traveller's path, or like the radiant Heavens when they burst open to amaze a priestess at her prayers, you blinded me! *(She breaks off).* What is the matter?

ACHILLES: I have practiced . . . an innocent deceit. To prepare you for the knowledge that I love you. Your Sibyl said: love him when you've conquered him. You—

PENTHESILEA: Loved you before? Yes. But till now did not confess that love . . .

ACHILLES: In our encounter, Penthesilea, you did not win. You took a fall. Are now—my prisoner.

PENTHESILEA: What? What?

ACHILLES: Unfair advantage won't be taken! In Greece you'll sit beside me on my father's throne and be the envy of the nations!

PENTHESILEA: You lied—?

ACHILLES: Marry me! Bear me a son! To keep, not send away. Ours will be such a son, Prometheus will get off his rock and hail him as a man after his own heart!

PENTHESILEA: I am—your prisoner?

ACHILLES: And here's my messenger to say your many sisters are my prisoners too. Diomede has been rounding them up.

PENTHESILEA: *(to Prothoe).* Is this what has been going on?

ACHILLES: *(and indeed the Messenger is entering.)* Are the Amazons routed?

MESSENGER: No! They drove us back and now are hurtling to the rescue of their Queen!

ACHILLES: *(ripping the roses off his body).* My chariot!

PENTHESILEA: *(watching in growing horror).* This . . . horror . . . is the same man who . . .

ACHILLES: They are still miles off?

MESSENGER: No, sir. There, on the horizon, the golden crescent of their banner!

ACHILLES: *(pointing to Penthesilea).* Take her away.

MESSENGER: Where to, sir?

ACHILLES: To our Camp. I'll join you there.

MESSENGER: *(to Penthesilea).* Get up.

PENTHESILEA: Diana! Goddess! Help!

PROTHOE: O my queen!

(Enter Diomede with troops.)

DIOMEDE: Achilles! There's but one escape route left, and that will be closed up in minutes by these frenetic females!

ACHILLES: *(to the Messenger).* Why is the Queen still here?

MESSENGER: She won't budge.

ACHILLES: Use force. Where's my lance?

PENTHESILEA: I will not go to Greece.

ACHILLES: You're snubbing me?

PENTHESILEA: *(pleading).* Achilles, you must follow me to Amazonia—

ACHILLES: *(preoccupied with his armor).* What?

PENTHESILEA: Where Diana's temple towers above the oak trees!

ACHILLES: Any temple you have built in Amazonia I can duplicate in Greece! Better to come willingly as my bride than to be dragged there as my slave! Those *are* the alternatives, ha? Well, though I didn't help rape the Sabine women—

(He lifts her off her feet. Enter Meroe, Asteria, and the Amazon army.)

MEROE: Free the Queen!

(The Amazons release her, but she moves back toward him.)

PENTHESILEA: *(tenderly).* Achilles, come with me to Amazonia.

ACHILLES: *(hesitates).* You are an amazing woman. Why don't I match your audacity and—whatever it may mean—reverse myself and—now—

DIOMEDE: Achilles! Must I save you from yourself?

(At a sign from Diomede, the Greeks pull Achilles away, as they all flee the Amazons.)

III-H

(Meroe, Asteria and the Amazon soldiers hail their Queen. The High Priestess returns, accompanied by Priestesses, and possibly by the little girls.)

MEROE: *(silencing the cheers).* Sisters, the goal is reached: the Queen is free! *(Cries of: Long live the Queen!)* Their tactic, Queen, was to defeat us while their leader held you. The aim: you and all of us in Greek captivity. When we learned that, we turned tail and in a united effort set you free.

PENTHESILEA: How can I ever thank you, Amazons? Why, Meroe, only just now I cried out to Diana for help! You all were here in seconds! It is a miracle!

(Cries of: All hail, Diana, goddess of the Amazons!)

HIGH PRIESTESS: A blessing on the goddess, on us all, and not least on our Queen!

MEROE: But we must put a healthy distance between us and these Greeks.

PENTHESILEA: Go? Go away from here?

MEROE: Without delay.

PENTHESILEA: Let me collect my thoughts. For I have thoughts that run the other way.

MEROE: What?

PROTHOE: The Queen's not well, She –

PENTHESILEA: I asked Diana's aid, and got it. Did I want it?

HIGH PRIESTESS: Is she out of her mind?

PENTHESILEA: O sisters, beware of wanting your own way, you just might get it.

MEROE: She's incoherent.

PENTHESILEA: I did not really want to be rescued!

PROTHOE: She is disturbed, she –

HIGH PRIESTESS: Disturbed? Deranged! Sisters, we must break up this gathering before worse happens!

PENTHESILEA: No. There are laws of war. Having lost to Achilles in fair fight, by one such law of war I am his prize. I *can't* be rescued: it would be illegal.

HIGH PRIESTESS: This *is* insanity.

PROTHOE: Sh!

MEROE: You don't know what you're saying! Stop, Queen, Reflect, Take it all back. We will proceed, and nothing further said.

PENTHESILEA: Return me to Achilles! Let him take me to Greece! *(Silence.)*

MEROE: Then I must tell you, Priestess, and you, Queen, the price we paid for this unwanted rescue.

HIGH PRIESTESS: You didn't—give back any prisoners?

MEROE: *(nodding).* The only way we could cut back at speed to rescue her was by surrendering *all* the prisoners.

PENTHESILEA: I am accursed!

HIGH PRIESTESS: The worst curse is the one you bring upon yourself. Meroe, Asteria, sisters all, as your Priestess and upholder of our laws, I now must say what I'd hoped I could hold back. "Play by the rules," our Queen tells us: would that *she* had! Rule One: don't pick your own antagonist. She picked Achilles, and since that hour neglected all her duties as our leader. Rule Two: when the time comes, an Amazon fights harder than men fight, fights without limit in ferocity or in endurance.When the time came to fight Achilles, she who never loses went limp and lost before she had begun. Rule Three: take no man as your lover till he's your captive and your slave. By that time the roses you bedeck him with will add to his humiliation. He will know that, though in passing you may need his swollen penis, not for an instant do you need his all-invading, all-annexing spirit. And here's the thing which in the interests of our State I would have kept quiet about forever: today while you, my sisters, were fighting for your lives and hers, this woman took the man who felled her and decking him with roses, fawned upon him.

(A murmuring among the Amazons.)

ASTERIA: Is this true, Queen?

PENTHESILEA: But I did not know—*(Her voice falters).*

PROTHOE: The Queen did not know—*(Her voice falters).*

HIGH PRIESTESS: *(interrupting).* And we don't want *your* explanations. We've had hers! Has she not repudiated her own rescue, preferring to be this man's chattel?

ASTERIA: Alas, Prothoe, she has forfeited her right to leadership.

HIGH PRIESTESS: To citizenship.

MEROE: I have to agree.

PROTHOE: Sisters, we are not men: we can't give way to mere revenge!

HIGH PRIESTESS: No. For Penthesilea I propose deposition, exclusion from the Amazon sisterhood, banishment from Amazonia and from our ranks wherever we may be.

(An approving murmur is heard.)

PROTHOE: Let me, in the name of womanly compassion, propose postponement. The Queen has gone through much. Give her one last chance: let her collect her wits and show us, if she can, she should still be our Queen!

(Short silence. Then a voice or two say: "Aye! Let's postpone! Give her a little time!" etc.)

HIGH PRIESTESS: Who is against postponement? *(Silence.)* Meroe?

MEROE: We love her, priestess, wish her something better than male justice.

HIGH PRIESTESS: Postpone till the Greeks have time to send for reinforcements?

ASTERIA: Till tomorrow.

HIGH PRIESTESS: Is that your will, sisters? *(Voices: "Aye, till tomorrow!").* Prothoe?

PROTHOE: I could have wished for more. But I agree. Come, Queen, when things cannot get worse they must get better.

(The Queen, who has not looked up during all this, now lets herself be led quietly off by Prothoe.)

IV

(Ulysses in Diomede's tent as before. Again Diomede brings Achilles to the tent but again stays outside.)

ACHILLES: *(in the door of the tent).* Again! Ulysses waiting for me in the tent. A stool. A little table. Wine. Do we play the whole scene again, Ulysses?

ULYSSES: I hope not. Remembering how it ended.

ACHILLES: I defied you. Went out once more on the trail of the Amazon Queen.

ULYSSES: Welcome back. *(Embraces him.)* No need to talk. Diomede has told me what occurred. Would you care to rest? *(He indicates a mat on the floor.)*

ACHILLES: *(shaking his head).* I *want* to talk . . .

ULYSSES: Pray do, Achilles. Talk.

ACHILLES: You were right. I fell for her. Offered her marriage, a throne! She turned me down. Offered *me* marriage, in Amazonia— Amazonia!— where *I* would be the little lady. . . . Well, while my brain is whirling with all this, along comes Diomede who, on your orders, "saves me from myself." *Your* phrase, I assume?

ULYSSES: Was it uncalled for?

ACHILLES: No. I had to be insane to get into . . . all that. I should thank you.

ULYSSES: Important is—

ACHILLES: To do the sane thing now. Pack up. Get back to camp.

ULYSSES: Well! Now you agree with me, *I* feel the shock! You . . . get to your conclusions the hard way.

ACHILLES: I'm slow-witted?

ULYSSES: You are the tortoise that out-runs the hare.

ACHILLES: *(holding up his wine).* A tortoise drinks your health!

ULYSSES: An old windbag drinks the health of the conqueror of Troy! May his name and fame live forever!

ACHILLES: Ah, yes: my name and fame.

(He is on the stool now. His head drops on to his chest.)

ULYSSES: Your eyes won't stay open. Let me help you over to the mat.

ACHILLES: *(without opening his eyes).* Not sleeping. Closing my eyes to see better. Landscape. Waterscape. Crater with dirty water in it. What's that over there? A spire, half-submerged. Fishermen have tied a boat to it. Is that a throne sticking up above the water? Oh, you know what this scene is? Troy! As it will be! That is the throne of Priam. And look! There's Helen's bed. A pair of otters are breeding in it while a dozen water rats look on, so many peeping Toms. . . . *(Opening his eyes:)* So much for the towers of Ilium. So much for all the glories of this world . . . Am I boring you? *(Ulysses shrugs).* Troy was boring me. And that has little to do with Agamemnon or his worthless cause. I'm not happy, that's all. What is happiness, Ulysses? Happiness. Felicity. And what's the big word? Beatitude. My victories were supposed to deliver it, but war is a show this actor has played too often. Victory comes too easy to him. Patroclus was something else. You riled me when you spoke of sex, Ulysses. In Patroclus' eyes—his eyes, not his cock—lay the promise of happiness. It was war, not he, that broke the promise. *(Silence.)* Are you giving me my head?

ULYSSES: Ha?

ACHILLES: Letting me talk my head off?

ULYSSES: Why not?

ACHILLES: Life has a curse on it. Even successful life has a curse on it. That's all I've learned from success. What, if anything, could lift the curse? *(Silence.)* You make me answer my own pompous questions? Very well: What could end the curse is love. Love. The love of Patroclus. The love of . . . What is love, Ulysses? *(Silence.)* Are you still there?

ULYSSES: More or less.

ACHILLES: When we ask a woman to love us, we let her know what we mean by the word.

ULYSSES: Ah? What?

ACHILLES: A quiet willingness to be subjugated. A voluntary enslavement in the cause of a higher liberation.

ULYSSES: Hm. Woman's love, yes. No male can afford to love *that* way. No male would dare!

ACHILLES: No male would dare . . .? Fascinating! Such love would require a degree of daring quite unprecedented?

ULYSSES: Men are men. Women are women. Two worlds: a higher and a lower. Who disputes that?

ACHILLES: The Amazons.

ULYSSES: Ah? Ah! *She* is still on your mind? *(He grunts).* An Amazon claims male power, and well she may if she can get away with it. But when would any male claim female powerlessness?

ACHILLES: When he truly loved and could summon . . . an unprecedented degree of daring.

ULYSSES: No good could come of it. He would destroy himself. He would damage the cause of his brothers everywhere.

ACHILLES: Well! And we were agreeing so . . . agreeably.

ULYSSES: Are we now disagreeing?

ACHILLES: Yes. Oh, Ulysses, we *are* playing that scene a second time. We have sat together. Talked philosophy. Drunk wine. After which I shall defy you and go out once again on the trail of the Amazon Queen.

ULYSSES: That's insane. Your word. You're teasing me!

ACHILLES: I was teasing myself. With the possibility of getting back into the old groove because it is . . . sane. I'll take *in*sanity. Only a failure of nerve can keep me from Penthesilea. Can Achilles lack nerve? While we were talking, I made my decision.

ULYSSES: Decision?

ACHILLES: I decided to challenge her to a second fight.

ULYSSES: You—! She will once more lose; once more not love you for it. It *is* love you want.

ACHILLES: And have taken care of.

ULYSSES: Ha?

ACHILLES: I'm going to let her win.

ULYSSES: Let her win? She's told you what *she'll* then do: take you prisoner, chain you with roses, drag you to Amazonia—

ACHILLES: Where I will be her manservant, yes, maidservant: in perfect self-surrender to find perfect love.

ULYSSES: You *are* insane. It's no use arguing with you.

ACHILLES: We *have* argued. This is what I've been argued into.

ULYSSES: Great Jupiter! Last time we saved you from yourself.

ACHILLES: On the assumption I would then fight Troy. This time—?

ULYSSES: I am at a loss.

ACHILLES: Fine.

ULYSSES: Have you thought this through?

ACHILLES: No.

ULYSSES: You are impossible.

ACHILLES: Yes. *(Going to the door of the tent and calling:)* Diomede?

DIOMEDE: *(outside somewhere).* Yes?

ACHILLES: I have a mission for you.

(He leaves the tent, going to Diomede.)

ULYSSES: I must think of something.

V

(The Queen in her tent. To her, Prothoe.)

PENTHESILEA: What is it?

PROTHOE: Diomede is here. Achilles wants to fight you again.

PENTHESILEA: He wants—? Pah! He knows that, in the state I am in, he'll win the more easily. Send Diomede away.

PROTHOE: First hear the private message that he brought: Achilles comes open-armed and empty-handed.

PENTHESILEA: Again? Open-armed, empty-handed, backed by deadly swordsmen?

PROTHOE: This time he comes alone, no guards, no archers, no one. "Coming to lose." Here are his words, "coming to make you a gift of victory because I love you. . . ."

PENTHESILEA: "Because I love you."

PROTHOE: "Giving up everything, the world's idea of Achilles, Achilles' idea of Achilles, I will go with you to Amazonia." *(Silence).*

PENTHESILEA: "Giving up. . . ." If I could believe this? Last time you joined him in deception—!

PROTHOE: I shall not do so now!

PENTHESILEA: Achilles, though—

PROTHOE: What sense could his proposal make except the sense he gives it?

PENTHESILEA: I *must* believe him?

PROTHOE: Yes. For through this action, you regain your throne. Achilles saves you in the nick of time.

PENTHESILEA: Hm. Why is bad news so easy to believe? Good news almost impossible? This news is *so* good it makes me tremble. Music is playing but I cannot hear it. Yes, yes, there it is, do you hear? The music of the spheres! *(Celestial music, albeit playing only in her soul, is here heard by us all.)* The Amazon state is saved by this good man! He's saved my throne and me. And, most incredible of all, he's made me happy, me! Picked up his bow and shot an arrow into the heart of happiness!

PROTHOE: He'll follow you to Amazonia and be your property.

PENTHESILEA: There was a moment when I was ready to follow him to Greece and be *his* property!

PROTHOE: Yes: the moment when Meroe and her warriors rescued you.

PENTHESILEA: You noticed?

PROTHOE: At the same time—

PENTHESILEA: *He* began to wonder if he might do what now he's done: surrender. Tell me, Prothoe, when a man loves a woman, must one of them always surrender—unconditionally? What if—unpermitted thoughts are crowding into my mind—what if both man and woman did so surrender—at the same moment? It almost happened!

PROTHOE: That would be equality, my Queen.

PENTHESILEA: Equality!

(A trumpet sounds.)

PROTHOE: Diomede—this is his trumpet—is about to announce the public portion of the message. Let us go outside.

(They leave their tent and are at once in the midst of the whole throng of Amazons, the High Priestess in a commanding position among them. With more trumpeting, Diomede enters.)

DIOMEDE: To Penthesilea and her Amazons, greeting! Since he lusts to carry off your Queen to Greece, while she lusts equally to carry him away to Amazonia, Achilles challenges her again to mortal combat. Fate has an iron tongue: the sword. Let the sword speak!

HIGH PRIESTESS: She is sick, worn out, wounded. Cannot take up the challenge. The Amazons won't ask her to. It's: no.

PENTHESILEA: *(flushing).* You dare speak for me?

HIGH PRIESTESS: We would not heap more troubles on your head.

PENTHESILEA: *(to Diomede).* Tell Achilles I take up his challenge.

HIGH PRIESTESS: *(to the Amazons).* She is our Queen again! Acclaim her! *(They do so).* But at least insist on some delay.

DIOMEDE: The challenger assigns to you the choice of day and hour.

HIGH PRIESTESS: Later this week.

PENTHESILEA: Tomorrow. One hour after dawn. *(The Amazons cheer).* And, Amazons, if last time I prematurely announced the

Feast of Roses, this time I confidently say: "Hold every rose you've plucked and every wreath you've woven against the outcome of this second fight!" *(Cries of: "We shall!" and more cheers.)*

HIGH PRIESTESS: Wait two days.

PENTHESILEA: Tomorrow. Diomede, be gone. *(He leaves.)* The single favor I request of everyone: a night of rest here in my tent. Sentries, Prothoe, let no one through of lesser rank or with a message less than the most urgent. Good night, all!

VI

(Penthesilea asleep in the tent. The voice of Ulysses is heard outside saying: "I come from Achilles." The sentries let him through.)

PENTHESILEA: *(waking).* From Achilles?

ULYSSES: *(in the doorway).* A trick to get me through your guards. I come from Agamemnon.

PENTHESILEA: Who are you?

ULYSSES: Ulysses.

PENTHESILEA: In this fashion? At this time?

ULYSSES: Just *in* time to prevent catastrophe for us – and you.

PENTHESILEA: What's this?

ULYSSES: I've failed to turn Achilles from this crazy scheme tomorrow. I shall turn you instead.

PENTHESILEA: Do you know Amazons?

ULYSSES: I am learning. Women ruled once. Back in remotest corridors of time. No gods. Earth mothers. Or was it One Great Goddess? But it's a man's world now, and likely to remain so for a while. Hm? Fact is fact.

PENTHESILEA: We Amazons are a fact.

ULYSSES: A small one. Agamemnon lifts his little finger and his army removes all Amazonia from the map in – how long? Thirty days? *(He sighs).* Is it sufficient to bring these generalities to your attention, or will you force me to cite unsavory particulars?

PENTHESILEA: Go away.

ULYSSES: You *will* force me. Well then, about your plan to take a man to Amazonia, there to make use of him as servant, wife, whatever: hardly one man in a million would do such things. Is Achilles that one man? A man who rose by the male virtues: aggression and ambition, to be the world's most successful pugilist, gladiator, conqueror and, if you will, predator? The dream of every school boy, the incarnation of the male ideal: Is this the man for whom you plan an apron and carpet slippers in your kitchen?

PENTHESILEA: Go. Go away. Go. Go.

ULYSSES: What must *he* be thinking at the moment? This: "When I pretend to lose, what will it mean? I've never lost. And I have shown that I can beat this female. What is she then but a child whom I allow to win? At any time in the future I could win again. She will know that. If she ever forgets I will remind her. She cannot fail to know who's up, who's down, who's master and who's slave! What more do I want? By pretending to lose I win."

PENTHESILEA: *(through her teeth).* No. No.

ULYSSES: The fight tomorrow is a fraud. Winning by such deceit – by a man's condescension – don't you despise yourself? Don't answer that. I'm threatening you now. Privy to your secret, all I need do is wake the Amazons and tell them, here and now, the fight is fixed, you're a phony winner.

PENTHESILEA: I'm going to kill you where you stand!

ULYSSES: It won't help. Diomede is in on your secret. Should any of our leaders fall in this action, Agamemnon will wipe the Amazons out. Remember that. *(Silence).* Thanks for that silence. You will now call the fight off, I feel sure.

(He leaves. Another silence: during which dawn begins to break.)

PENTHESILEA: Prothoe! Meroe! Whip my dogs till they are rabid! Light torches to burn my elephants to fury! Dawn breaks. An Amazon goes out against a man.

VII

(Achilles' tent. Achilles asleep. Diomede and Ulysses waiting up.)

DIOMEDE: The sun is up. We must wake him.

ULYSSES: First there is something I would have you know.

DIOMEDE: Yes. What were you up to in the dead of night?

ULYSSES: Let me state the conclusion: Penthesilea will call off this fight.

DIOMEDE: She – ? What did you – ?

ULYSSES: You can wake him now.

DIOMEDE: No, no, first you must tell me –

ULYSSES: Ha? Wake him.

DIOMEDE: *(again hesitates but then, sensing that he has received a military order, gently shakes Achilles.)*

ACHILLES: *(not agreeing to wake up).* No, no, don't wake me now!

DIOMEDE: *(quietly).* Are you dreaming?

ACHILLES: *(waking now).* A dream of bliss! With her! What waking bliss can match the happiness in dreams?

DIOMEDE: I must help you arm. Remember?

ACHILLES: Or was it *dis*arm? Do *you* remember?

DIOMEDE: You must at least *seem* armed!

ACHILLES: Give me a light lance. No sword. No bow. A breastplate. But no helmet. *(Diomede carries out these orders.)* And so farewell to arms: Welcome, true love!

ULYSSES: *(without looking).* A messenger.

DIOMEDE: Ours or theirs?

ULYSSES: *(without checking this out).* Theirs *(But he now looks the man over).* Hey, wait a minute. *(Astonished:)* Ours! Yes, yes?

MESSENGER: *(entering).* Penthesilea is coming!

ULYSSES: Nonsense!

MESSENGER: But she is! Running like one possessed! With maddened dogs and elephants at her heels!

ACHILLES: What? Is this true? Go look, Diomede! *(Diomede does so.)* Bringing wild animals! Why, Ulysses, this is a cave woman after my own savage heart!

MESSENGER: Prothoe tried to hold her back. She set the dogs on *her!*

ULYSSES: There's something wrong!

DIOMEDE: *(re-enters.)* It's true. She's visible from the hilltop. Dancing with dancing hounds.

MESSENGER: I heard her call the dogs her sisters, and, as she urged them on, she herself panted—panted—for blood! Her lips are flecked with foam.

ULYSSES: Tell our men to stand ready. To await my orders. *(The Messenger leaves).*

ACHILLES: Scared, Ulysses? Don't you enjoy a circus?

ULYSSES: This one won't be enjoyable.

ACHILLES: *I* enjoy it. Only regret I didn't dress up my Myrmidons as lions – which could grapple with her dogs. I could have recruited African giants to tackle her stampeding elephants.

ULYSSES: Why didn't you?

ACHILLES: I want to be different! To be the defeated swordsman, bowman, who goes out – no sword, no bow – vulnerable, defenseless, naked – against this Amazon's menagerie!

DIOMEDE: Ulysses –

ULYSSES: What was I up to in the dead of night? *(To Achilles:)* Oh, just trying – yet again – to save you from yourself.

ACHILLES: What? You –

ULYSSES: Went to Penthesilea. Yes.

ACHILLES: You bastard.

ULYSSES: Yes: I was stupid: trusting a woman . . . even an inch. Woman is an enigma, can't be figured out.

ACHILLES: The greater is the challenge. Why not pay her greater tribute?

ULYSSES: Ha?

ACHILLES: Trust her more than an inch. Trust her totally.

ULYSSES: That is suicide. Genocide: the liquidation of the entire male sex.

ACHILLES: I'm sick of words. Goodbye, Ulysses. *(He starts to leave.)*

ULYSSES: No! I can't allow this!

ACHILLES: Ha? How could you prevent it?

ULYSSES: I speak for Agamemnon! And for Greece!

ACHILLES: And?

ULYSSES: *(desperately).* All right. You don't respect him. Or your country. But you admire yourself. In Achilles' name, then, in the name of whatever he holds sacred – *(But Achilles has walked out.)*

DIOMEDE: Now what? I grab him as I did last time?

ULYSSES: Last time he let you.

DIOMEDE: We'll just have to back him up. With the few men we have –

ULYSSES: Against dogs, elephants, and that virago?

DIOMEDE: We must save him somehow!

ULYSSES: We must, must we?

DIOMEDE: You said yourself we couldn't win the Trojan War without him.

ULYSSES: *(after a short pause).* I was lying, Diomede.

DIOMEDE: You figure we *can* win the – ?

ULYSSES: Agamemnon has an alternate plan. We fall back on it at my discretion. We fall back on it now.

DIOMEDE: *(turning pale).* Yes?

ULYSSES: Achilles is great. Greece is greater. Unlike Greece Achilles is expendable.

DIOMEDE: You'd leave him at the mercy of – ?

ULYSSES: *(relentlessly).* Greece now abandons him to a tragic but, alas, unserviceable fate.

DIOMEDE: Some of us love Achilles more than Greece.

ULYSSES: You are under arrest. *(Diomede looks nervously to left and right.)* No. Under orders. On pain of death. You will make sure our men don't see him die. We two alone share Agamemnon's secret. We'll keep it. And I alone shall see – what I shall see. *(Diomede seems to turn to stone).*

VIII

(The open plain. Amazons, both warriors and priestesses. An Amazon sentry on the hilltop. Asteria is absent; the High Priestess stands with Prothoe.)

HIGH PRIESTESS: What is that cry?

AMAZON 1: "Achilles falls! Achilles falls!"

HIGH PRIESTESS: What is the shout?

AMAZON 2: Our women crying: "Victory!"

HIGH PRIESTESS: Victory? It sounds more like Defeat!

AMAZON 3: Here's Asteria. She will have seen all.

(Asteria, having entered, stands there a few moments before gathering strength to speak.)

HIGH PRIESTESS: Speak, woman, speak!

ASTERIA: Achilles came unaccompanied. No cheating this time. Something must have been agreed between them. He must have planned to surrender. *(She swallows, manages to continue:)* Armed playfully with a light lance he advances dreaming of amorous pleasures soon to come until it seems some unexpected sound distracts him. He turns his slender neck. Sometimes a young roe will hear a roar and turn and see, O horror, a lion hunting him! No time for panic. Achilles starts to run, calling: "Diomede! Ulysses!" They do not answer, and he can't get back. He is encircled by wild beasts. He looks around, like a child at hide-and-seek, for a bush, high grass, anything to hide in that the ogre might vanish and the nightmare end! On hands and knees, he crawls into the underbrush. *(Again Asteria is momentarily unable to continue.)* Some say War is a man who drips with blood and sets fire to the land of the living with the torch of death! But now War was a woman ringed with hounds that howled like hungry wolves, followed by elephants goaded on by fire. Penthesilea with her hunter's eye sights a slight movement in the underbrush. "A stag!" she cries, "a stag that can't conceal his antlers!" The golden bow of the Amazons is in her hands. She draws it, aims, shoots. In a flash her arrow's deep in Achilles' throat. Somehow he clambers to his feet, falls with a thud, slowly picks himself up, stands there teetering like some great building about to collapse, an easy target for her dogs. "Tigris," she shouts, "Leone, Dirke, Sphinx!" And with them flings herself upon his body. The golden bow falls from her hands and breaks: with a voice like some small animal in pain the bowstring sings the fall of the Amazons. Writhing now in a deep red pool—it's his own blood—Achilles touches her delicate cheek with a finger. He even gets some words out: "Is this the Feast of Roses?" A starving lioness desperately prowling empty Arctic snowfields in search of food would have heard him. She did not hear him. A bitch now in a pack of bitches, she sank her teeth in the white skin of his chest on the left side. The others chewed up his right side. When I got there, arterial blood was tumbling from her mouth. His blood.

AMAZON 1: *(to the High Priestess).* They are bringing the body. The Queen follows. She is fainting, seems not to know where she is or what transpired.

HIGH PRIESTESS: How could this be, Prothoe?

PROTHOE: Ulysses must have lied to her: told her Achilles would still be the master, told her—

HIGH PRIESTESS: *Was* that a lie? Achilles may have thought he loved her but he was a man and he despised her. She knew Ulysses was not lying.

AMAZON 2: The Queen!

(Funeral march. No one has left the stage. And now the body of Achilles, or what is left of it, is borne by Amazons on a bier. Following it, Penthesilea.)

PENTHESILEA: *(addressing the High Priestess, tonelessly).* Achilles dead. His body a bone that bitches have gnawed at. *(Pause.)* Who did it?

PROTHOE: *(coming to her).* My Queen! You must go far, far away from here. I will come with you.

PENTHESILEA: Ah yes, to the Elysium of women. It is so tranquil there. The very oak trees hold their breath. Nymphs endowed with everlasting youth wait by crystal waters on the Great Goddess. She will mend my bow. *(Silence.)* Who did it? *(Silence.)* I did it? Is that true? *(Silence.)* Your silence says it's true. *(She gives a slight cry of pain.)* How sharp the blade: cutting, cutting. Is it killing me, the *thought* that I killed him? Loved, bit him?

PROTHOE: Did Ulysses lie to you? Say Achilles mocked you?

PENTHESILEA: Have I missed something? Has everyone missed everything? Has there been an eclipse of the sun of understanding? *(Suddenly:)* Give me a knife.

PROTHOE: No one here will do that!

PENTHESILEA: *(shaking her head).* I am cut already. *(Again the slight cry of pain.)*

PROTHOE: She is delirious.

PENTHESILEA: *(running her hands down her torso).* This is the mineshaft where I found the ore and tempered it to steel in fires of Pain, steeped it in the poison of Remorse and carried it to the anvil known as Hope for sharpening. Kissing without biting. Loving, not killing. Elysium? No? Hades? Did Hope know all this when sharpening the knife? *(An intake of breath at a sharp stab of pain.)* The knife is still cutting. Through skin, flesh, and now the heart.

(With a moan, she falls to the ground.)

MEROE: She's fainted.

PROTHOE: *(after holding her a moment).* Thus all the stones of the great vaulted gateway when their time has come fall as a single stone. She is dead.

HIGH PRIESTESS: Without a knife? Set aside recriminations now and honor her in death, bury her grandly as the chief of state—

PROTHOE: The Amazon state is finished. Hers was the last attempt to save it.

HIGH PRIESTESS: What?!

PROTHOE: The pain which we have muted all these years is screaming from the body of our Queen.

(She has pointed at the Queen's body.)

HIGH PRIESTESS: Do you know what you're saying?

PROTHOE: That you can put women in a cage, but all they'll do is rage and rage and rage till they get out. Here is the secret that the Queen kept from you, sisters. A Sibyl helped her out of the female cage. Let her love a man. *Try* to love a man. But placed an impassable barrier in her way.

MEROE: What barrier?

PROTHOE: Domination. What males had done to us we'd do to them. The war of the sexes would continue but this time we'd win. She won. *(She points at Achilles' body.)*

HIGH PRIESTESS: But *had* she won? Had she really got the upper hand of Achilles? Would he not still have been master even as her captive?

PROTHOE: No doubt Ulysses made her fear so, and what a fear that is! Small wonder it turned so fast to hate, from which it sprang. What shall deliver us, sisters, ever, from this unending cycle of hate and fear?

HIGH PRIESTESS: To put such a question is subversive of—

PROTHOE: What can bring domination to an end?

HIGH PRIESTESS: Such speeches are more than your life is worth!

PROTHOE: How much is that? Haven't you asked yourself how the Greeks will take the death of their hero?

HIGH PRIESTESS: We shall fight them!

PROTHOE: And be wiped out. I'd give us fifteen days.

HIGH PRIESTESS: *(with a threatening gesture).* Prothoe—!

MEROE: Peace, sisters both, and sisters all, whether the peace of the ages or the peace of fifteen days!

ASTERIA: Even if we survive, one better than us has died. The withered oak, near-dead, survives the storm. The live oak, whose lavish leaves the gale can get a grip on, falls crashing to the ground.

PROTHOE: To our Queen, a last salute!

Epilogue

(Same setting as the Prologue. Ulysses reports to Agamemnon.)

ULYSSES: Highest priority, my dear Agamemnon, went to keeping secret it was a woman killed Achilles. Just to confuse things tidily I told several poets Achilles had killed *her.* In the epic one of them's preparing she'll be offset by the right kind of woman – sexless, dumb, and rather good at sewing – and waiting all these years in Ithaca for me.

AGAMEMNON: Who are we going to say did kill Achilles?

ULYSSES: Troy's greatest warrior now that Hector's gone: Paris.

AGAMEMNON: We've seen the last of the Amazons?

ULYSSES: Their total annihilation, which scoffers said would take us several weeks, took us ten days.

AGAMEMNON: Let's bury Troy so deep it won't be dug up for three thousand years. Where is the Trojan turncoat? Where are my carpenters? We are going to build that horse.

Wannsee
A Tragi-Comedy

Based on *Cathy of Heilbronn*

Preface: On Hoping Against Hope, or the Official Optimism and the Unofficial Pessimism

The year I wrote *Wannsee* I also addressed the graduating class of Trinity School in New York City, a class which included Eric Bentley—my son. *Wannsee* is a play for young people. For young people to act. For young people to see. Addressing the young people of Trinity School I was trying to think young, which is the opposite of bringing down an ancient's wisdom *to* the young and, as it were, from Mount Sinai. The axis of my thinking in this talk is hope/despair, optimism/pessimism. Since that is also the axis of my thinking, and my non-thinking, my para-thinking, my *imagining*, in *Wannsee*, the talk is printed here as the preface to the play.

The official optimism is that of the people who own and control our society—men of power, men of money. For instance, our politicians. They have to be optimistic to get elected. When their optimistic promises are broken, they will retire, but they would retire anyway. Meanwhile they have passed the optimistic torch to the next generation of politicians. When we have a presidential campaign, the two candidates vie with each other as to whose hopefulness can be the greater, and we, the electorate, caught with the excitement of it, lost in a euphoric cloud, vote for the man who fills us momentarily with the greater hopefulness, even though experience could have taught us that such hopes are illusory.

And politicians are not as much worse than the rest of the population as they may seem. They are of a piece with a system, and their opposite numbers in other fields have to be equally optimistic. Take soldiers. What general is ever going to say: "This is a war we shall lose"? In some situations, military defeatism has been punishable with death, which means that optimism has been made absolutely compulsory. Now optimism would not have to be compulsory if it were either plausible or natural. It is only when you are pretty sure you are going to lose a war that you have to be forced to say you are sure you are going to win it. A lot of optimism is like that. Take advertising. I often do "take" it as I ride the New York subways. I look at the people on the seats opposite. They are so glum. Facial expression ranges only from resignation to rage, from moroseness to aggression. But look on the bright side. Or rather, look up. Above the seats are the ads. They picture the same people—ourselves—our fellow Americans but in an exactly opposite mood. Gone is their manic depression. Come is their fixed elation. Their beautiful teeth proclaim their unmixed happiness. They laugh, they smile, or they show a gravity that is all poise and self-assurance: they are men and women of distinction. In short, the ads are populated by optimists, while the seats are occupied by pessimists. Such, you might say, if you are philosophers, is the relation, always, of appearance and reality. Such is the contrast, I will be content to say, between the Official Optimism and the Unofficial Pessimism.

Take religion next. As I say this, I realize it is the Christian religion I am going to "take," and this hardly seems fair when I am the guest of a school called Trinity and am standing in a church also called Trinity. Bear with me. Allow me, even in a place committed to a dogma, my rights under the First Amendment of the U.S. Constitution. For I want to say that the optimistic claims of Christianity put too much strain on credulity. One of the Church Fathers, I'm sure you have heard, said he believed in Christianity just *because* it was absurd. This would mean: the more strain is put on our credulity, the more we can and should be credulous. Perhaps this is what is implied by the colloquial expression: You better believe it.

From the New Testament—which I have just been reading in a translation called the Good News Bible, and my objection to the New Testament is that, in its ambience, the news is always good—I learn that, if I watch my p's and q's, I can achieve uninterrupted joy for all eternity. Another view, famously offered by Paul, is that I shall achieve uninterrupted joy for all eternity *without* having watched my p's and q's—amazing grace—for my taste, a little *too* amazing. It is true that the joy won't set in till after I am buried, but who wouldn't trade in half a century of misery for billions of centuries of the other thing? The New Testament may be said to be making us an offer we cannot refuse: certainly it offers an optimism beside which the other optimisms shrivel to insignificance.

Now, what of education? What of optimism in the schools and colleges? Although there is a specific optimism of education, I think the schools are more importantly a conduit for the other optimisms, including those just mentioned—the optimisms of religion, public relations, and politics. And it is on Commencement Days that one is most forcibly reminded of this, for that is when the speeches soar highest into the optimistic stratosphere. You will see now what suggested my topic to me. I am on the spot this morning—the spot where what possibly is required of me is the heady optimism of the pep talk and the inspirational sermon.

It is when one may feel propelled towards expressing the Official Optimism of the culture that one remembers its Unofficial Pessimism, and one's deeper objection is not to the Optimism per se but to the function it so often performs, namely, to mask a real pessimism, a real Unbelief, a real Cynicism. Again politics provides the most blatant examples. What greater purveyor of the official optimism was there than Richard Nixon? But when we got behind the facade to his private conversation, and his actual dealings with people, we encountered pure cynicism. Why pick on Mr. Nixon? Politics *in general* leads this double life: flowery, optimistic rhetoric in public, but in the smoke-filled rooms where business is done, a ruthlessness that reflects only cynicism. My complaint against schools is that they tend to teach the pretty rhetoric about democracy—as if self-government were something we had already achieved—and overlook the crass facts, such as that only half the electorate in our country bothers even to vote, so pessimistic are they in the face of the optimistic rhetoric of the candidates. For the unofficial philosophy of modern society, *possibly of all society so far,* is pessimism. There is a positive side to this negativism: that it shows people are resistant to propaganda. But I would add: they are so resistant to it, they believe nothing. I was taught in school, for example, that the medieval period was an age of faith. It is a conclusion derived from the propaganda of faith. I think we are entitled to question whether the faiths of the past were really believed in any more than the faiths of the present. We are entitled to wonder if they were not just, to the contrary, masks of unbelief, covers for cynicism.

What I am suggesting is that cynicism may well be the real "perennial philosophy" of homo sapiens. Perhaps "philosophy" is saying too much. It is a stance, an attitude. Einstein was saying as much when he defined man as a passive animal. So was Thoreau when he remarked that most of mankind lead lives of quiet desperation. It is this resignation—the defeatism of the mass of mankind throughout history—that I am calling the Unofficial Pessimism. If I am right, the talk about belief and affirmation is a rickety superstructure on a firm foundation of unbelief and negation.

It is hard to believe *anything* is really worth the trouble. Usually, we don't even intend to make the attempt. If we were to attempt a revolution, we would be sure from the start that it would end in disaster. Was it really just in the Nineteen Sixties and Seventies that the Russian Revolution was *discovered* to be a fiasco by Mr. Solzhenitsyn, or is it not rather the case that there is never enough faith in the first place to make such an enterprise succeed? Since everyone knows in advance that revolutions haven't a chance, they really *haven't* a chance.

The inertia of slaves and peasants is the archetype of this human passivity and hopelessness, which also is why the religions of slaves and peasants are religions of extreme, if otherworldly, optimism: "pie in the sky when you die."

Both the pessimisms and the optimisms exist also in more subtle and sophisticated forms. As graduates of an elite school you are unlikely to become peasants and will not, at least in any obvious way, be slaves, but the opportunity will be offered you to rationalize passivity into more subtle and plausible formulae or, as an alternative, to re-write some of the optimisms into exaggerations less gross and extravagant . . .

Is that any escape from the Either-Or I have been setting forth? Beside a realism so negative it eliminates hope, and a romanticism so positive it can only function as a flight from reality, is there any third possibility?

One whole school of modern literature takes the pessimism as an unquestioned premise. Indeed modern literature as a whole might be described as pessimistic, though some of the profoundest pessimists, such as T. S. Eliot, will occasionally reach out to the extreme optimisms—in this case, Christianity—as a lifebelt. Communism has functioned for some as Christianity did for Eliot.

The newer optimisms have tended toward vulgarity, ludicrous oversimplification, mindlessness. Such are the psychotherapies that offer too much too fast, like Werner Erhard's EST and Esalen group therapy, not to speak of Scientology. Such also are the simplifications of Indian mysticism brought to us in big black Cadillacs by Swamis on the make.

Against this background, pessimism is often a certificate of spiritual integrity and intellectual seriousness—as in the work of Franz Kafka, Samuel Beckett, Peter Handke, Harold Pinter, Edward Bond, and so many others. Theirs is indeed a respectable—respect-worthy—version of the Unofficial Pessimism: here the universal passivity is given a rationale and set within a vision entirely realistic. Man as a species will come and go: has come and will go. He is a speck in infinite space. His history is but a moment in endless time. Even without taking in all that, we can say, with Ernest Hemingway: "All our stories have the same ending." We die, and if there are no grounds for cosmic hope, there would seem to be only very flimsy grounds for social hope. The planet is over-populated and ecologically headed for total disaster. Objectively speaking, it is highly unlikely that mankind is going to master these problems.

Life, yea or nay? Objectively, the nays have it. It is only that, by that answer, one cannot get from today to tomorrow—not even from breakfast to lunch. Is this a fatal admission, driving one straight into the arms of a Swami or other super-Therapist? Extra Sensory Perception? The Jesus Freaks? There is no easy answer. Is there *any* answer?

Well, if one cannot get from breakfast to lunch on the word No, and one *can* get from breakfast to lunch on the word Yes, then the Ayes have it. Perforce: by the pragmatic necessity of continuing to function, continuing to be. If this is a leap into faith, it can't be helped. That much faith *is* necessary. Is there a risk to such leaps into the irrational? Certainly. What, in this life, is there no risk to? Is there also an obligation to hold the irrationality down to a minimum? That too. We must bear down mercilessly on all that might be wrong with our affirmations—their internal contradictions, their failure to accord with external facts. If we find ourselves forced into opting for romanticism over realism, let it be a realistic—a rationally tested—romanticism.

I am advocating a qualified optimism then? That does sound dull. My conclusion is, I think, both worse and better than that—worse in that it is an optimism in defiance of facts, based ultimately on need alone—better in that it should not, at that, be limited by the spirit of timidity. There need be no commitment to mediocrity or even to moderation. If the minimum commitment is to continuation, persistence, survival, the maximum commitment is to changing the world. Clearly, if we don't believe the world can be changed, that is going to be a self-fulfilling prophecy, and the world will not be changed. *It is worth seeing if it can be changed by acting on the assumption that it can.*

"Nothing to be done," say the clowns in Samuel Beckett's *Waiting for Godot,* the classic statement of the modern version of the perennial pessimism. Can Beckett live by that conviction? It is easier to believe that he lives off the Irish humor that pervades *Waiting for Godot.* He also lives off the poetic talent that illuminates all his work.

To be fair to pessimists like Beckett, it is not they who have discouraged us most. The greatest discouragement comes from entertaining false hopes *and then discovering their falsity.* Those who extend false hopes—gurus and swamis, statesmen and generals, bishops and psychiatrists, professors and schoolteachers—should think sometimes of the terrible responsibility they bear, *and the terrible guilt they have so often incurred.* Of course they are far too busy formulating their excuses and evasions. But our writers—the good ones—do think of such responsibility. One wonders if some of them ever think of anything else. Disenchantment is the main note struck throughout modern literature, and the literature of disenchantment has a moral, namely: hopelessness may be bad but it is better than false hope.

Let me comment on that moral. Hopelessness is better than false hope morally, in that honesty is better than self-deception, but it is not always better in its practical effects. To go from false hopes to no hopes may well be to jump from the frying pan into the fire. More important, it is unnecessary, if not perverse, to ask that we be despondent just in order to show that we are not fakers, when there is in us a *need* for hope—genuine hope—that will not be denied, because, as the poet said, it "springs eternal."

Ten years ago American students were in eruption. There were complaints about that from any and every quarter. What should really have been complained of was not that the students wanted to change the world and actually tried to change a few corners of it but that they allowed themselves grossly false hopes as to how and where and when. That way they brought on, quite inevitably, their own disillusionment. It would seem to be a law of our limited, "fallen" nature that if we permit unreal hopes to be raised in our hearts beyond a certain modest point, we fall headlong, at the moment of failure, into a despair that is not at all unreal. Thus, the tragedy of the student revolts is one, not of the Sixties, when they happened, but of the Seventies when they reaped their harvest of inevitable disenchantment, and when a large part of the world of school and college reverted to the old slave-mentality, the old passivity, the old defeatism, the Unofficial Pessimism—or went after the new false gods of mysticism and psychiatry . . .

A naive but necessary question: how can you know—at the time—that a hope *is* false? A naive—and perhaps dismaying—answer: often you can't.

I am so glad my audience is you: graduates of Trinity School who will soon, most of you, be freshmen in a college and all too soon after that, as the years rush by, graduates of Yale, the University of California, and where not? You have each been given an instrument to measure the falsity—or authenticity—of hopes. It is called *your intelligence,* and it has been the job of your teachers to help you develop it. Promise me that if your university has not developed it further by this time next year, you will transfer to another!

It's another naive thing to say, but we have been given urgent reason in recent years to say it: as students—not to say as teachers—we are committed to intelligence, first, last, and all the time. The kernel of education as we know it, as we respect it, can be found in a single sentence of Socrates: "the unexamined life is not worth living."

If a few minutes ago, I advocated a leap, at a certain point, into the irrational, I hurried on to declare nothing off limits for the critical, analytic intelligence, and I would add now that we of the schools and universities should not hesitate to see hostility to intellect—anti-intellectualism of any kind—as hostility *to us and to our most fundamental commitments.*

If I leave it there, someone is going to ask me afterwards if I, as an old radical, would apply this test as severely to my own people as I apply it to the anti-intellectuals of the Right. My answer is: even more severely. One must hold one's own family most strictly of all to the universal standard. Besides, how does radicalism differ from more conventional "isms" except in its willingness to apply a limitless critique to a society which others passively accept?

Be that as it may, to be hopeful and to fail to subject our hopes to all the tests the intelligence is capable of applying is to court failure and *hope-less-ness.* It is true that intelligence itself may sometimes raise false hopes. But only more intelligence can correct the errors. Thus there is hope in intelligence itself. There is no hope without it.

Hopeful people uncommitted to intelligence, unwilling or untrained to use their intelligence, cannot help us; nor can intelligent people who have abandoned themselves to despair and are sinking in the swamp of the Unofficial Pessimism. Not only are both hope and intelligence necessary, nothing can be achieved unless they work hand in hand. I rather think you must know this, or you would already have committed suicide. Don't overlook it, or you still will commit suicide. Work at it! Work with others who work at it! Refuse to work with others who won't work at it.

Remember what I told you about college. If my son Eric finds college does not meet the test here proposed, he can save me a lot of money by dropping out. Better still, a transfer can be arranged to a superior college. But quit that one! Leave a note for the Dean telling him he can look for you, the year after, at the crossroads where hope and the critical intelligence meet.

For there is also an *un*official optimism.

I lived near Wannsee for a year or so in the sixties. The emanations from the lake seemed to me real but wholly benign. One could believe angels were hovering, but not devils. Yet when I visited Auschwitz, now a museum, I was shown, under glass, the document in which an S.S. officer set the Final Solution in motion. The letterhead was Wannsee, Berlin.

I wrote this play on the shores of another lake, Erie, another angelic spot when the weather is fair. But when the black clouds rise ominously above the water, and the gale winds rise, why then the witches ride and the devils howl and the horns and cloven hoof of Satan can, at least dimly, be discerned in the sky.

Wannsee is dedicated to my friend Saul Elkin who brought me to Lake Erie and for whom I wrote the play. Under the auspices of the State University of New York, he produced it in the Pfeifer Theatre, Buffalo.

> In the course of an investigation of certain heroic figures—lone resisters to the Nazi regime—I found that prophetic dreams and even hallucinatory experiences during waking hours could occur in individuals who are clearly not psychotic. I concluded that the ability to create, in extreme situations, the fantasy of being supported by a godlike omnipotent figure should be evaluated as belonging to the assets of a healthy psychological organization.
>
> —Heinz Kohut in *The Restoration of the Self*

Cast (in order of appearance)

Kleist
A Cherub
Count Otto
Theobald, Cathy's father
Count Frederick
Cathy
Flammberg, Frederick's aide-de-camp
The Burgrave
Georg, the Burgrave's aide-de-camp
Kunigunde
Rosalie, Kunigunde's maid
Bridget, an old servant
Countess Helena, Frederick's mother
The Rhinegrave
The Emperor
Sybilla, an old crone
Nightwatchman
Several messengers
Judges, attendants, armies, crowds.

The above "cast of thousands" can be reduced to 19 players by the following device: four other angels will accompany the Cherub and help him put on the show. They will play Georg, The Nightwatchman and all the Messengers and Attendants. Judges, armies, crowds will be omitted except insofar as the same four angels can do duty for them.

Wannsee is pronounced Vahn-zay.

Prologue

(As the house lights dim, a voice is heard over the speaker system: "Our play presents the thoughts that passed—that may have passed—through the mind of the poet Heinrich von Kleist in the last hours of his life."

The lights come up on a well-dressed German, aged 34, on the afternoon of November 21st, 1811. He is polishing a revolver. The "voice over" continues:

"He has concluded a suicide pact with a young woman who has a terminal disease. This evening he will shoot her, and then himself, here beside Wannsee, a lake just outside Berlin."

A knock at the door of the lakeside cottage in which Kleist is sitting. He had been holding the revolver at arm's length and looking down the barrel. He now hastily puts it in a drawer and goes to the door without opening it.)

KLEIST: Yes?

VOICE: *(from outside the door).* Heinrich von Kleist?

KLEIST: Yes. Who are *you?*

VOICE: Hope.

KLEIST: Your name is Hope?

VOICE: The name of the firm is Hope.

KLEIST: The firm?

VOICE: Heaven.

KLEIST: Heaven!

VOICE: I don't have a name. I'm a Cherub.

KLEIST: A what?

VOICE: Remember Cherubim and Seraphim, plural?

KLEIST: Angels? The ones I've heard of do have names: Michael, Gabriel—

VOICE: Archangels. General-of-the-army Michael! Ambassador Gabriel with his secret missions to highly favored ladies!

KLEIST: *(opens the door to the Cherub, a tall young gentleman, blond, blue-eyed, handsome).* No wings, Nameless One?

CHERUB: We wear them in Heaven only, Herr von Kleist. Or in human visions of Heaven. Formal occasions.

KLEIST: And this occasion? But do sit down. Or do you prefer to flit about?

CHERUB: No cynical remarks! God is not impressed by atheism. I shall neither sit nor flit. I am quite happy standing here where I can see your very pretty lake.

KLEIST: Pretty? Many people find it murky.

CHERUB: What's it called? Yes: Wannsee.

KLEIST: Wannsee: yes.

CHERUB: What are *you* looking at?

KLEIST: You. If God is not impressed with atheism, atheism is not impressed with God and his angels. Can one be sure the Unseen is there?

CHERUB: When it's seen. You see me, don't you? And I'm a Cherub.

KLEIST: Prove it.

CHERUB: Must I?

KLEIST: It would pass the time.

CHERUB: *(shrugging).* It's my profession.

(He performs a miracle, removing in an instant the walls of the room and house, throwing off his cloak, and appearing in silver in the sky, with his wings on, calling:

Hope! Hope! Hope!

Then he undoes the miracle, removing his wings, and donning the cloak again.) Do you accept the proof?

KLEIST: You could have spared yourself the demonstration.

CHERUB: What?

KLEIST: When a drunk tells me he sees green snakes, should I tell him he does not, there are no green snakes around? No, there are green snakes around. The question is where. I would suggest: in his imagination.

CHERUB: Are you suggesting that I exist only in your imagination?

KLEIST: Definitely.

CHERUB: It's not such a bad place to be. You have a remarkable imagination, Herr von Kleist. As for the play you are about to see—

KLEIST: I am about to see a play?

CHERUB: Nor does it matter if you consider it a product of your own imagination. By Kleist or by God, it's the same play.

KLEIST: What does matter?

CHERUB: Whether it talks you out of suicide.

KLEIST: You have brought me a play that will talk me out of suicide?

CHERUB: A worthy objective, surely.

KLEIST: But you admit that you yourselves may be a product of my imagination. If you are, then *I* wrote *your* play. *Your* play expresses *my* beliefs.

CHERUB: That's what we hope.

KLEIST: You haven't followed me.

CHERUB: I have. The play expresses your *true* resolve, which is to go on living. For all the reasons you—we—know. Life is good. There's a divinity that shapes our ends . . . God's eye is on the sparrow . . . For even Faith and Charity are not enough without Hope.

KLEIST: You really haven't followed me. Even if I don't go on living, what your—my—play says might still be what I believe.

CHERUB: Then why would you be killing yourself?

KLEIST: Having lost hope, I have lost my beliefs too. Disbelieve what I believe. Believe nothing.

CHERUB: Luckily, it's not an argument I've brought you, it's a play.

KLEIST: Here and now?

CHERUB: When was the suicide to be? By sundown you will both—you *would* both—be dead.

KLEIST: What's it about then—your—my—play?

CHERUB: The setting's medieval.

KLEIST: God's favorite period.

CHERUB: Your native Germany over five hundred years ago: primeval forests, mysterious caverns, charming grottos, majestic castles . . . can we start?

KLEIST: I have nothing to lose.

CHERUB: And the world to win.

(Transformation of the scene. The Cherub repeats his miracle with a difference. The house again disappears, but this time what appears is the setting of the first episode in our story. Only one anomaly: for the moment the Cherub and Kleist are still there.)

CHERUB: In an underground cavern, somewhere in Swabia, a secret court is in session.

I

(On the wall, Insignia of the "Femgericht" or Vehmic Court—a secret, "vigilante" set-up. Lamplight. A chief judge and several co-judges are in place, seated. There are armed Attendants, standing. The Cherub and Kleist disappear as the chief judge starts to speak.)

JUDGE: Let us stand for the invocation.

(All the judges stand.)

Impotent is the arm of earthly justice, for crime is a monster that hides in the caves of the heart. One day armies of angels will smoke it out: meanwhile as God's secret agents we do what men can do in courts far underground and yet, we pray, only a *little* lower than the angels. And now, since justice is impersonal and blind, blot out your faces!

(The other judges don masks. They are already muffled in robes that conceal whatever they may be wearing underneath.)

I, Otto, Count von der Fluehe, hereby, with you, lose name and face!

(He, too, dons a mask.)

Bring in the accuser and the accused!

(Two men, blindfolded, are brought in, and their blindfolds removed. They look warily around. The judges sit.)

Which is Theobald, armorer of Heilbronn, and the accuser?

ONE OF THE TWO MEN: I am, my lord.

OTTO: *(to the other).* And you are Frederick Wetter vom Strahl, Count of the Empire, the accused?

FREDERICK: The same, my lord.

OTTO: Well, Theobald, your fame has gone before you! Everyone wants his armor fixed by you! Accuse Count Frederick but remember he also has a reputation and must defend it. Speak!

THEOBALD: In the name of God I demand that you, my lord, turn this man over to the devils who brandish their redhot spears at the gates of Hell!

OTTO: You do, do you, old man? That's a demand that might follow some dire charge. What is the charge?

THEOBALD: That the man's in league with Satan and has used all the black arts of Hell to win, no, to bewitch my daughter Catherine! That he used witchcraft and seduced her!

OTTO: And you were a witness to all this? You actually saw Satan's horns and cloven hoof—exactly, I presume, as they are carved in cedar wood above the altar at Heilbronn?

THEOBALD: *(to all the judges:)* I saw enough to bring you all to your feet shouting: "We are twelve but there's a thirteenth who's the Devil!"

OTTO: Accuse then, wild accuser.

THEOBALD: She was born at Easter fifteen years ago. Try in your mind's eye to see a child as innocent as Eve and Adam were before *their* fall. Heilbronn, made pregnant by the Swabian sky, gave birth to her or one might say she rose like smoke of myrrh and juniper from the evening of my days and grew in favor both with God and man. Try now to see the grown girl walking down the street, her straw hat all ashine with yellow lacquer, fine silver chains above the velvet of her black bodice. Do you hear the whisper pass from window to window: "Look! There goes Cathy! Cathy of Heilbronn"? She was a person of some substance even as a child. Her mother died, and so her grandfather's estate had come to her. A man of property, young Gottfried, is—or rather was—her fiancé: the wedding was to be next Easter. Had she been nobly born—as idle tongues have not been slow to rumor that she is—kings of the Orient would have come with pearls and rubies, carried by black slaves, to ask her hand in marriage! Such was my child, my lords, before this man stole her.

OTTO: He stole her, did he? By what arts? And when? Did he meet her by the spring when she drew water? Or by the pillar when she came from mass? Or did he steal up to her window in the night and hang a diamond necklace round her neck?

THEOBALD: *(shaking his head).* She'd have seen through tricks like that as fast as Our Lord saw through the Judas kiss! No, no, she knew her own back better than she knew him—or even the birthmark on the back of her neck that she got from her late mother! She'd never seen him before!

OTTO: Yet a seduction must have a time and place. She'd never seen him *before what?*

THEOBALD: The Eve of Pentecost. In my armory. He'd come there—for just five minutes—to have his armor fixed.

OTTO: Five minutes? In broad daylight?

THEOBALD: He was on his way to battle against the Pfalzgrave. I planned to serve him wine and fresh smoked ham while I was working. The door opened. There she was, a large tray on her head with food and drink upon it. But when she saw Count Frederick she dropped the tray and fell at his feet as if struck down by lightning, her forehead on the floor, her face pale as a corpse, her two hands joined in prayer. When I raised her up, she stared at him – her face now red as fire – as if he was a ghost but a ghost she'd seen before. He took her hand asked, "Whose child is she?" I finished work, and he prepared to leave. He stooped to kiss her brow – she only came up to his chest – and said: "May the Lord keep you and give you His peace, Amen." We went downstairs but just as Frederick, now on his horse, started to ride away, a slight sound just behind us made him ask: "I wonder what that was?" He rode away. From the upper room the girl had thrown herself thirty feet to the pavement, hands uplifted. Both her thighs were broken just above the ivory arch of the knee. Six endless weeks she burned with fever, helpless and close to death, and spoke no word. Even delirium, picklock of human hearts, did not unlock the secret that now obsessed her. As soon as she could walk a very little she tied her bundle and at crack of dawn set out. "Where to?" asked the servant girl. "To Count Frederick," answered she and vanished.

OTTO: Leaving everything behind? Her estate, her home, her betrothed? Did not even ask a father's blessing?

THEOBALD: She kissed my eyes as I slept. I only wish she'd closed my eyes in death.

OTTO: And since that day?

THEOBALD: The gleam in *his* eyes wound itself round her soul like a five-ply cable! She the camp-follower, he the camp! Barefoot, her short skirt fluttering in the wind, only the straw hat to hold off searing sun and drenching storm! In mist of chasms he journeys onward through deserts scorched by the noonday sun, through the wild night of tangled forests, with my girl at his heels like a bitch that has tasted her master's sweat. She who always reclined on the silkiest cushion, she who always would feel the tiniest knot in sheet or blanket, now sleeps in the straw with his horses.

OTTO: On that – on all you've said – the Court must question the accused. Is it true, Count Frederick?

FREDERICK: I turn round and see two things: my shadow and her. That much is true, my lord.

OTTO: She has a home, and should *be* there. Instead, she sleeps under your roof. Can you justify that?

FREDERICK: *(sighing).* Some twelve weeks past I was taking a nap in the midday heat some fifty miles from Heilbronn. I awoke and there she was—a rose that had fallen from the sky—fast asleep at my feet. When *she* awoke, she said: "I'm going to Strassburg on an errand." I arranged to put her back on the path and rode away. But that same night at an inn on the Strassburg road the girl was below, asking could she sleep in my stables? She was in the stables night after night as my expedition advanced, washing and mending for me, too, as if I had no one else. When we got to Strassburg and I asked her business there her blushes seemed to burn her apron up as she stammered: "Surely you know?" I sent a messenger to tell her father he could come fetch her home. When, after twenty days on horseback, he reached my castle, what did he do, my lord, but sprinkle me with holy water like a thing accurst! When he opened his arms to embrace his daughter and she called on the saints to protect her from him, flinging herself, as she did so, at my feet, he froze, seemed to turn into a pillar of salt and threw hate in my face, crying: "Satan incarnate!" Then galloped back to Heilbronn as if a thousand Satans were in hot pursuit.

OTTO: Hm. Now, Theobald, tell the court how the Count was at fault.

THEOBALD: He poisoned her! He poisoned her!

OTTO: Literally?

THEOBALD: I wasn't in the stables as a witness but wait out the nine months and you'll see what poison he fed her there!

FREDERICK: *(jumping up angrily).* Now I protest—

OTTO: One moment, Count. Old man, you change the subject and the charge. Your first charge was seduction. Then, poisoning. But now it is seduction *and* getting the girl pregnant. Yet *you* haven't waited nine months: three at most. How do you know she's pregnant?

THEOBALD: It happens every day. It's a conclusion that follows from a premise.

FREDERICK: *(more calmly).* I have a request, my lord, based on an objection.

(Theobald starts to shout, but Otto silences him.)

OTTO: Yes, Count?

FREDERICK: The objection is that the body in the case—the one that's said to be bearing my child—is not in court where the soul in the body—and this is my request—might give utterance! May I add a rhetorical question?

THEOBALD: *(shouting).* No!

OTTO: So afraid of rhetoric? Speak, Count.

FREDERICK: Can you believe I'd seduce a mere child and get her pregnant? And if you *could* think such nonsense, could you also suppose I'd be a hypocrite and stand here tying the truth in knots?

THEOBALD: Yes, yes! This is the first time you've spoken any truth!

OTTO: The court will pass the rhetoric by, but, as courts should, heed the request. Theobald brought his daughter with him: it's time to bring her in. *(He gives a sign to the attendants. Evidently Cathy has been in an ante-chamber all along, for she is brought in at once, still blindfolded.)* And now, unveil her eyes—*(Her father moves to do so but Otto goes on:)* No, let me see Count Frederick do it! *(Frederick unveils her eyes.)*

CATHY: *(going down on one knee before him).* My noble lord!

FREDERICK: *(taking a step back, and indicating Otto).* No! Your lord—your judge—is there! I'm the accused.

CATHY: You're accused?

FREDERICK: Oh yes.

CATHY: *(to Otto).* You are masked and muffled. Is it Judgment Day? If it were, he *(indicating Frederick)* would sit there and judge, and you would stand before the bar and tremble!

OTTO: Now, little girl, aren't you being rather silly? *(She fidgets.)* Stand still when I talk to you. *(She does.)* Thank you. Now tell the court: why did you do those things?

CATHY: What things?

OTTO: Drop your tray at first sight of the Count? Plunge from a high window to the street? Why did you ever since follow Count Frederick through night and fog?

(Cathy has her lips tight shut.)

FREDERICK: Cathy!

CATHY: Yes?

FREDERICK: Tell *me.* Would you tell *me?*

CATHY: Of course.

FREDERICK: May I do this, my lord?

OTTO: Do it, do it.

FREDERICK: Well now, Cathy, did I ever take your hand?

CATHY: Never.

FREDERICK: Cathy!

CATHY: Oh yes, when my father was working on your armor.

FREDERICK: Only that once?

CATHY: My hand?

FREDERICK: Or arm. Or anything.

CATHY: My chin?

FREDERICK: Did I touch your chin?

CATHY: *(nodding).* In Strassburg. I was so ashamed at . . . what you proposed.

FREDERICK: Which was?

CATHY: That I return to my father lest he die of grief! You took his side against me!

FREDERICK: Did I visit you in the stables?

CATHY: Never!

FREDERICK: You mustn't tell lies, Cathy.

CATHY: My lord!

FREDERICK: What happened in the stables five days back when it was going dark at evening?

CATHY: Oh, Jesu, I forgot. *You* came.

FREDERICK: The secret's out: I did visit you in the stables. You're done for now, Cathy!

OTTO: Oh, please! I said do it! I didn't say over-do it!

THEOBALD: Thank you, my lord.

CATHY: Father!

(Father and daughter embrace.)

THEOBALD: So you had noticed me!

CATHY: Oh, father!

OTTO: *(to Frederick).* Question the child, don't torture her!

FREDERICK: There is a saying: cruel to be kind.

OTTO: Missed the point, did I? Well, we'll try again. Count Frederick, what *was* it happened in the stables when it was going dark at evening?

FREDERICK: I kissed her, fondled her, threw my arms around her!

CATHY: *(protesting loudly).* No, no, no!

FREDERICK: *(closing the trap).* No?

CATHY: No! You spurned me with your feet!

FREDERICK: Why'd I do a thing like that?

CATHY: Father had come to take me home. I begged you to shield me from him. But you . . . just spurned me with your feet, again taking my father's side against me!

FREDERICK: Yet you stayed on in *my* castle?

CATHY: Not *in* the castle. Outside it. You chased me outside. With a whip.

FREDERICK: A whip, no less!

CATHY: Which you keep on a nail on the wall.

FREDERICK: What happened "outside"?

CATHY: By the ruined, outer wall a little finch had built a nest in an elder bush. I kept him company.

FREDERICK: Yes, you settled in right there! I had to set my hunting dogs on you to get you out!

CATHY: You never did that!

FREDERICK: No? Something yet more cruel?

CATHY: No, you just bade me leave.

FREDERICK: And you?

CATHY: Sent a message back to you.

FREDERICK: Saying?

CATHY: You let the little finch live there: if a little finch could have the franchise, why not Cathy?

FREDERICK: I've finished, milord.

OTTO: I see. And, Cathy, what was *his* message back to *you?*

CATHY: He would not rate me lower than a finch, so I could stay.

OTTO: Ah? And you stayed?

CATHY: Yes, my lord.

OTTO: I see. Frederick Wetter vom Strahl, Count of the Empire, you are acquitted. You're not guilty, sir. Theobald, armorer of Heilbronn, go home and learn some sense.

THEOBALD: *(interrupting).* He's a devil backed by devils! He is destroying her!

OTTO: Maybe I did leave one thing in the air: you never answered my questions, girl. Why did you drop your tray at first sight of the Count? Plunge from a high window to the street? Follow Count Frederick through night and fog?

(Silence. Count Otto's eyes appeal to Frederick.)

FREDERICK: D'you know why? Answer *me.*

CATHY: Yes. I – *(Slowly:)* No, I don't know why.

OTTO: *(giving her up as hopeless, shaking his head).* Count Frederick, you have some power over this girl. Use it, would you, to restore her to her father?

FREDERICK: I'll try. Now, Cathy, listen: do you love me?

CATHY: Do I live?

FREDERICK: Well, if you love me, you'll do anything to please me, won't you?

CATHY: Anything.

FREDERICK: It would please me if you went home to your father.

CATHY: *(after a pause).* I gave my word.

(But she falls down in a faint. General consternation. Count Otto strides to the prostrate body and lifts Cathy's head.)

OTTO: It isn't serious, look! She's coming to, already! You can prepare to take her home, old man.

THEOBALD: *(bitterly).* But will she stay? Bewitched is still bewitched. The girl may kill herself or – which is the same – bury herself alive in a nunnery!

OTTO: The universe has angels in it, sir, as well as devils. *(To his attendants:)* Blindfold them.

(His attendants start to blindfold Cathy, Frederick and Theobald.)

II

(Count Frederick is led blindfolded out of the cave into the surrounding forest, where the blindfold is removed. The attendants doing this return to the cave. The Count blinks in the light of the sun as it streaks through the trees.)

FREDERICK: *(raising a hand to his brow as if dizzy).* Back in the overworld! And look, there's my horse! *(Pointing through the trees.)* At any time I can ride straight back to life! But nothing is the same. What is this feeling? The feeling men have for women? *(Pause.)* Following me everywhere, she irked me, even bored me, yet just now, when I told her to go home, I didn't want her to go. While on trial for bewitching her, could it be I was bewitched by her? For this girl's soul's as sensuous as other women's bodies and I saw her soul stark naked –

dripping with unguents like the anointed bride of some Persian King mounting the marriage bed! Nothing can come of it: a Count can't marry a blacksmith's daughter, least of all a Count like me who dreams of marrying an *Emperor's* daughter!

(Horses' hoofs have been heard. Sound of dismounting. A voice says: Count Frederick.)

It's my aide-de-camp, Flammberg.

FLAMMBERG: *(entering).* Sir, you must ride home to Wetterstrahl and get your men together! War threatens!

FREDERICK: Who threatens it? Who always threatens me with war but the Loveliest Lady in the Land—so she is called: I've never seen her—the Lady Kunigunde, the great Baroness of Thurneck?

FLAMMBERG: She's behind it, yes.

FREDERICK: And in front of it, her lover, her "fiancé,"—she always says she's going to marry them—her lover bears the title of Pfalzgrave—No, she jilted him when he didn't promote her interests too successfully. Her present lover is the gallant Burgrave. Am I right?

FLAMMBERG: You'd have been right last week but now she's jilted *him* too and—

FREDERICK: Has a third lover, a third "fiancé"? One Cleopatra with three Antonies! Pfalzgrave, Burgrave and now . . . well who is Number Three?

FLAMMBERG: The Rhinegrave.

FREDERICK: *(sniffs).* The Rhinegrave! And how do Number One and Number Two feel about the new development?

FLAMMBERG: The Pfalzgrave's forgotten her already but the Burgrave declares he'll kidnap her and expose her before all the world!

FREDERICK: About her present flame, the Rhinegrave. What's she talked him into?

FLAMMBERG: She told him that some land her ancestors sold to yours long ago is hers. She showed him documents. Says he: you give this land back or it's war!

FREDERICK: Interesting. What land *is* that?

FLAMMBERG: Staufen.

FREDERICK: Staufen? Three prosperous towns and seventeen villages—who wouldn't like to own them?

FLAMMBERG: The Rhinegrave is so infatuated with her he will put all his men at her disposal.

FREDERICK: Tonight? Tomorrow morning?

FLAMMBERG: For the present they're content to feast on their infatuation! And while the happy pair run rampant in the bedroom, his troopers drink themselves under the table in the dining hall!

FREDERICK: It seems I'll have no peace from the various worthies until I take the offensive and deliver the final coup de grâce, which I will do if it means poisoning the February snow which—had you heard?—she takes her baths in!

FLAMMBERG: She takes her baths in February snow?

FREDERICK: Where is that bedroom?

FLAMMBERG: In the Rhinegrave's castle.

FREDERICK: Let's get our men together as you said, ride straight to the Rhinegrave's castle, surprise them all in their beds and under their tables and—*(He makes the gesture of throat cutting. A Messenger enters.)* Not more news—now?

MESSENGER: *(breathless).* Well, yes, sir, yes! Wouldn't you want news of Kunigunde?

FREDERICK: I *have* news of her: she's busy with the Rhinegrave in the bedroom!

MESSENGER: Not any more. She's disappeared.

FLAMMBERG: What?

MESSENGER: She took a walk in the castle grounds and disappeared.

FREDERICK: Flammberg, what was that you said about the Burgrave?

FLAMMBERG: He said he'd kidnap her.

FREDERICK: Hm. Let's hope he has. In any case without the Lovely Lady the Rhinegrave is the weaker. Let's not return to Wetterstrahl. *(Pointing to the Messenger:)* Rudolf can do that. Rudolf, go, and when you get there send all my men posthaste to fight the Rhinegrave! *(Rudolf, the Messenger, leaves. To Flammberg:)* We'll be advance scouts. Ride straight to the Rhinegrave's castle. How long will it take?

FLAMMBERG: Two days. The night between we can spend in some charcoal burner's hut in the mountains.

FREDERICK: And, on the side, keep a weather eye out for Kunigunde. *(They stride toward their horses.)*

III

(In the mountains. Night. Thunder and lightning. A charcoal burner's hut and surrounding land. In the front room of the hut, a man sleeping. Another man crosses the land to the hut and knocks on the door, loudly.)

THE MAN ON THE BED: Who is it?

VISITOR: Me, Georg, your aide de camp! Is that you, Burgrave?

(It is: the Burgrave opens the door. George looks around.)

GEORG: So this is a charcoal burner's hut? How goes it, Burgrave?

BURGRAVE: Well, *very* well. Sit down.

GEORG: You don't want to go back to sleep?

BURGRAVE: I couldn't: till I've told my story! But first—yours.

GEORG: *(sitting).* Tried to find you near the Rhinegrave's castle. Guessed you'd headed back. Guessed you'd spend the night in one of these huts. Went from one hut to another until—*(He opens his palms to indicate himself and the Burgrave together.)* What are *you* up to, Burgrave? Why here—alone?

BURGRAVE: I *was* at the castle.

GEORG: Wasn't that rather reckless?

BURGRAVE: You'd think I'd attack that bastard with all the men at my disposal?

GEORG: Of course.

BURGRAVE: But I had one servant! And so was . . . less conspicuous.

GEORG: That kind of job? When you heard the Lovely Lady had taken up with the Rhinegrave—well, the rest of us, in such a case, would have said: I'll kill her! But you said—

BURGRAVE: "I'll kidnap her and then expose her!"

(Pause.)

GEORG: *(slowly).* You've kidnapped her?

BURGRAVE: What d'you think?

GEORG: Well, she's not here.

BURGRAVE: Nor is my man. *(Pause.)* Not in this room.

GEORG: A charcoal burner's hut has a *back* room? *(He has seen a door at the back and is making for it.)*

BURGRAVE: You may peep through the keyhole.

GEORG: *(does so, takes a long look, whistles).* My God, so you did do it!

BURGRAVE: How do things look in there?

GEORG: *She* looks like an ox on the way to the butcher's block! He's gagged her – your man – tied her to the bed and now stands guard like he expected the enemy's arrival any second!

BURGRAVE: Remind me to increase his wages.

GEORG: What now?

BURGRAVE: Well, we have to ask ourselves as Christians why this empty image, this lifesize statue of a heathen goddess, should be at large diverting souls from Christ and Mother Church. What do you think?

GEORG: Pagans are fair game, I've always heard.

BURGRAVE: Let's tear the statue from its pedestal and hurl it upside down on the dungheap to demonstrate it's of the Devil. Yes?

GEORG: Hate the Devil, hate *her,* oh, yes!

BURGRAVE: I loved her, Georg, loved her but *(He sobs.)* she was unworthy of me. *(Stops sobbing.)* Georg, have you ever seen a hen hold off a rooster that's circling her all day till, in the evening, he sees she's eaten up with the scab and he wouldn't want to fuck her anyway?

GEORG: He wants to kidnap her? Kidnap and expose her was what you said, but what did you mean?

BURGRAVE: Revenge, you see, just is not Christian. Besides I want more than revenge. I'm going to take her back to the Rhinegrave's castle and expose her!

GEORG: I still don't get it.

BURGRAVE: Can't you *see* it, though? In the courtyard with the Rhinegrave and his people looking on? Me removing her . . . neckerchief?

GEORG: She wears a neckerchief?

BURGRAVE: Keeps her neck most carefully covered.

GEORG: So because you won't be so unchristian as to take revenge, with everybody watching, you remove her neckerchief?

BURGRAVE: Which is more than revenge! Am I hard to follow? Begin again. What is under her clothes?

GEORG: The most beautiful body in Swabia.

BURGRAVE: Yes? Have you ever seen this lady?

GEORG: As she walks, the very pebbles at her feet flash fire as if she'd told them: when you see me, pebbles, melt, melt! I've seen this lady surrounded by imperial knights in shining armor: and she outshone them as the sun outshines the planets!

BURGRAVE: Which is why we all love her! Have you asked yourself, Georg, why we all hate her?

GEORG: Tell me.

BURGRAVE: Well, why did she now, when lifted down from her horse, just lie there like a corpse with her lips pressed tight together?

GEORG: I don't know.

BURGRAVE: I'll tell you: so as not to lose her teeth.

GEORG: Beg pardon?

BURGRAVE: Because they're false.

GEORG: So's not to lose her false teeth?

BURGRAVE: I could hardly be her lover and not get into her mouth, ha? Well, to count the teeth in there I didn't need much arithmetic!

GEORG: Do we hate all people with false teeth?

BURGRAVE: Oh, Georg, you must study the different types of falsity! Saint Augustine mentions seventeen. Kunigunde's type eleven: the false-all-through. Teeth—*(Noise off.)* What's that?

GEORG: *(at a window).* Two men dismounting. They're coming here.

BURGRAVE: Keep them out at all costs. Make up a good story.

(The two men are Frederick and Flammberg, who also have been going from one hut to another. Flammberg knocks; Georg opens the door a crack.)

FREDERICK: May we come in, sir? *(Georg gives no answer.)* Why, on a night like this one would ask shelter from wolves in their caves!

GEORG: *(with a glance back toward the Burgrave).* Afraid not, sir. You see, my master's wife's in the back room and she's sick, she's dying, and the whole place is full of her attendants!

FREDERICK: That *is* too bad. Flammberg, we must look for another charcoal burner's hut! Good night, sir.

GEORG: Good night.

(He shuts the door. Frederick and Flammberg walk away and are momentarily lost in the darkness.)

BURGRAVE: Well, thank you, Georg, you're a very accomplished liar. Shall we sleep?

(He blows out the light as they lie down, the Burgrave on the bed, Georg on the floor. Frederick and Flammberg reappear just outside. They had evidently got separated and have just rejoined each other.)

FREDERICK: Flammberg, I lost you!

FLAMMBERG: I've been taking a look at the dying lady. She *will* die, sooner or later, in *that* condition.

FREDERICK: What condition?

FLAMMBERG: Bound, gagged, and under guard.

FREDERICK: She's bound, gagged, and under guard?

FLAMMBERG: But no death's head as yet: a blazing beauty.

FREDERICK: A beautiful woman . . . ? This man and his master must be scoundrels. My knightly oath—

FLAMMBERG: Beauties in distress! You *have* to go to their aid. However, we're two, and they're three.

FREDERICK: Does the hut have a door at the back? Wasn't that where you saw the lady?

FLAMMBERG: Yes, yes.

FREDERICK: You inspected the lock? Could easily break it? *(Flammberg nods.)* The guard you mentioned—just one man? *(Flammberg nods.)* If you surprise him, you could overpower him? *(Flammberg nods.)* Do all this while I keep the two scoundrels busy. Produce the lady in the front room when you hear the scoundrel-in-chief say "Jairus's daughter."

FLAMMBERG: Whose daughter?

FREDERICK: Jairus's.

FLAMMBERG: The girl who . . .

FREDERICK: Yes. Let's go.

(Flammberg again goes to the back of the hut. Frederick again knocks at the front door. Georg again comes to the door.)

GEORG: You—again?

FREDERICK: I have to speak with your master.

GEORG: Oh no, you haven't!

(But as he begins to try to close the door, the Burgrave intervenes.)

BURGRAVE: Let them in for one second, Georg. *(Frederick is let in.)* Hm. Where's your man?

FREDERICK: He'll be here in a moment.

BURGRAVE: What do you want, sir?

FREDERICK: Want? Oh yes, I want to know about your wife!

BURGRAVE: *(coldly).* My man Georg told you about my wife.

FREDERICK: Did he tell me the truth?

GEORG: That's an insult, Burgrave.

FREDERICK: He said your wife is dying. Is she dead yet?

BURGRAVE: *(sobbing).* Oh, sir!

FREDERICK: Want to change your story? No? Then you know what I'll do? Bring her back to life. It's been done before. In the Bible. Somebody's daughter.

BURGRAVE: *(quickly).* Jairus's.

FREDERICK: Whose?

BURGRAVE: Jairus's daughter was brought back to life!

(Flammberg enters from the back room, stands by the doorway to let someone enter.)

FLAMMBERG: The guard slithers to the floor, unconscious. The lady rises from her bed, another Jairus's daughter. Praise be the Lord!

(A gorgeous-looking young woman enters in riding dress. Neither she nor her clothes are much the worse for the treatment they have received.)

THE LADY: And if you're wondering why I don't show the signs of the rough treatment I've been receiving, why, that's just part of the miracle! How do I look?

FREDERICK: *(with open mouth).* "A blazing beauty"—Flammberg's phrase hardly does justice to beauty so potent or a blaze so dazzling!

THE LADY: Thank you. It's you I owe my life to?

FREDERICK: And God.

THE LADY: Thank both of you! I'd guess from your appearance you're under knightly oath to rescue beauty in distress?

FREDERICK: That is so.

THE LADY: Then it was not enough to give me life: you must also take me under your protection. *(Pointing to the Burgrave and Georg:)* Save me from those two ruffians! A maiden injured and reviled makes this appeal! *(She throws herself at Frederick's feet.)*

BURGRAVE: *(clapping).* Bravo! And now: Curtain! When, good sir, you were told this woman's mortally sick you were told the truth. She's . . . sick *in mind,* and thinks she's not my wife but someone else – some "maiden injured and reviled" whom I have kidnapped and whom gallant knights from the story books will rescue.

THE LADY: *(an outburst).* Liar, you –

FREDERICK: Quiet, lady. Sir, if she's not a maiden injured and reviled and if you have not kidnapped her, why did you gag and bind her?

BURGRAVE: She goes berserk and has to be tied up.

FREDERICK: In a charcoal burner's hut so far from home?

BURGRAVE: Wherever the fit comes on her.

FREDERICK: Hm. Shall we believe him, Flammberg?

FLAMMBERG: Would you give the lie to a lady?

FREDERICK: No. She's under my protection, sir. If you want her, fight for her!

BURGRAVE: Fight? Here in this hut?

FREDERICK: Or outdoors – in that thunderstorm.

BURGRAVE: Here, then.

(With the help of Flammberg and Georg, the antagonists prepare for a sword duel. They fight. Just as the Burgrave seems to have won, Frederick delivers a crushing blow on the Burgrave's head. The Burgrave falls.)

FREDERICK: So, bridegroom, go to Hell and celebrate your honeymoon down there!

GEORG: *(pale and close to tears).* He cannot speak. Blood from a scalp wound fills up his mouth.

THE LADY: *(aside).* I hope he chokes.

FREDERICK: *(to Georg).* Who is your master?

GEORG: He is the Burgrave.

FREDERICK: The gallant Burgrave!

FLAMMBERG: *(solicitous now for the Burgrave, to Georg.)* Let's carry him to this bed. *(Flammberg and Georg carry the Burgrave to a bed.)*

THE LADY: To his bed? To his grave! A grave for a Burgrave!

FREDERICK: Quiet, lady, he'll not hurt you now.

THE LADY: I'm hurt already. Water! I'm going to faint! *(As*

Frederick starts to look for water.) I'll be all right, for now I realize I'm free and you're my liberator! I've been saved and you're my savior!

FREDERICK: Who are you then if not the Burgrave's wife?

THE LADY: I'm the Lady Kunigunde, Baroness of Thurneck.

FREDERICK: No, no!

FLAMMBERG: *(from the bed).* She's Kunigunde?

FREDERICK: She's Kunigunde!

KUNIGUNDE: I though you'd be impressed but you're astonished!

FREDERICK: So will you be. I'm Frederick Wetter vom Strahl, Count of the Empire.

KUNIGUNDE: No! No!

FREDERICK: Yes! Yes!

KUNIGUNDE: Well, I'll be damned.

BURGRAVE: *(from the bed).* He is Count Frederick?

FLAMMBERG: He is Count Frederick.

BURGRAVE: Then mark my words: he'll live to rue the day he rescued Kunigunde.

KUNIGUNDE: *(aside).* If I am to escape that wolf on the bed over there I must go all the way with the alternative. *(To Frederick:)* Beloved youth, dear rescuer, receive this ring from me! More later, a far worthier reward, just now this is my all and by that token enough to demonstrate all that's mine is yours. May I call you master?

FREDERICK: *(stammering).* Are you asking, lady? that I take you back to your Rhinegrave?

KUNIGUNDE: Never! All is over between that churl and me!

FREDERICK: You don't love him any more?

KUNIGUNDE: I never loved him. I was abducted and imprisoned! I was raped!

FREDERICK: No different from the Burgrave—?

KUNIGUNDE: Or the Pfalzgrave! Why must they all do this to me? But then I blame myself, or rather I had not found myself because, I start to think, I had not found my man! *(She gazes intently at Frederick.)*

FREDERICK: I blame *my*self. I planned to slay you in your Rhinegrave's arms, to skewer you both on this one blade!

KUNIGUNDE: Instead you've saved me from two unwanted loves *(Pointing to the Burgrave.)* with one blow! Master, Savior, do what you want with me!

FREDERICK: *(to her).* I'll return with you to Wetterstrahl. Place you in my mother's quarters there.

KUNIGUNDE: Can a mere man be so magnanimous? Oh, Count—Count Frederick—you overwhelm me!

FREDERICK: Meanwhile sleep here. We'll leave at dawn. Flammberg, you go on ahead and tell my troopers the war is off.

FLAMMBERG: Leave now? In this weather? *(For the thunder and lightning have continued.)*

FREDERICK: Now.

(Flammberg leaves.)

FREDERICK: *(to Kunigunde).* Is it true, lady, you're descended from the Saxon Emperors?

KUNIGUNDE: My great grandfather was Emperor. Why?

FREDERICK: It's good to know that one so beautiful is also noble, royal, nay, imperial.

(They stare at each other. Georg continues to tend the Burgrave's wound.)

IV

(Wetterstrahl Castle. In the living quarters of Frederick's mother, the Countess Helena. Kunigunde is having her hair done by a maid in front of a dressing table with much make-up equipment on it.)

KUNIGUNDE: Rosalie! I like your name, it's redolent of roses. Rosalie!

ROSALIE: You're a tease, aren't you, milady? But it *was* lucky the Count's mother let you take your pick of her maids, because I'm the only one who, er. . . .

KUNIGUNDE: *(interrupting).* Luck or fate? Fate could be on our side, hm? *(Lightening the tone:)* A lady, after all, *must* have a maid who understands her . . . special—

ROSALIE: Points. In the face, the body . . . Talking of body, there's a lovely grotto to bathe in, here!

KUNIGUNDE: A maid must be a kind of . . . kindred spirit . . . and that's what you are.

ROSALIE: Thanks, milady, nice word, *spirit.* Same as *sprite,* isn't it?

KUNIGUNDE: *(pointedly changing the subject).* Now, Rosalie, I asked you to track down that old biddy, what's her name?

ROSALIE: Bridget.

KUNIGUNDE: The one that knows all the castle gossip. Did you find her?

ROSALIE: I have her waiting in the next room now. Would you like to see her before the Count and his mother arrive?

KUNIGUNDE: Yes, while you're doing my hair. My face is finished, isn't it?

ROSALIE: A picture of health and beauty, yes.

KUNIGUNDE: Thanks to you, dear. Bring her in.

ROSALIE: *(at the door).* Come in, Bridget. *(Bridget, an old servant, enters.)* This is milady.

BRIDGET: I saw her—we all did—when she arrived. Are you really the Lady Kunigunde, ma'am?

KUNIGUNDE: The genuine article? I hope so. Won't you sit down?

BRIDGET: Sit? In the presence of an Emperor's daughter?

KUNIGUNDE: The present Emperor is no relation.

BRIDGET: But, er, but . . .

KUNIGUNDE: My great grandfather was Emperor, yes.

BRIDGET: Hallelujah! I can go to my grave in peace!

KUNIGUNDE: How so? *(Shows her the chair to sit on.)*

BRIDGET: *(sitting).* Well, it means Count Frederick's dream has come true.

KUNIGUNDE: Dream? What dream is that?

ROSALIE: A real *weird* one. *(To Bridget:)* Tell her.

BRIDGET: December before last, the Count fell into a strange and unaccountable melancholy, which soon became a raging bodily sickness. He had such a high fever, the doctors gave him up for lost. Well, but when he was delirious, out popped all his secret thoughts. Where was the girl that could really love him? And, since life without love is death, why not be dead in earnest? He gave *himself* up for lost.

KUNIGUNDE: These are banalities.

ROSALIE: *(To Bridget who hasn't understood the interruption).* Go on.

BRIDGET: On three successive nights during which his mother never left his bedside, he told her an angel had appeared to him, crying: Hope! Hope! Hope! *(Her words here are echoed in the Cherub's voice which seems to come from the sky: Hope! Hope! Hope!)* "Well, wasn't that encouraging?" his mother asked. "No," he said, then added: "But it will prove so when I see *her* again." "And when will that be?" asked his mother. And he replied: "The angel will take me to her on New Year's Eve."

KUNIGUNDE: These are old wives' tales.

ROSALIE: But, milady, *old wives* can be—

KUNIGUNDE: Sh! Let's hear the rest.

BRIDGET: On New Year's Eve, at the stroke of twelve, he started up from his couch as if he'd seen a ghost. Then he cried: "My helmet and sword! I must go!" "Go where?" said his mother. "To her," he shouted, and fell back on the couch, dead.

KUNIGUNDE: Dead?

BRIDGET: The doctors thought he was dead. But after an interval he half rose from the couch and said: "Gone. My bride is gone. But have them say some prayers for me in church. For now I want to live again."

KUNIGUNDE: So he recovered?

ROSALIE: *(nodding).* Ah, the power of prayer!

KUNIGUNDE: About that interval. While he lay "dead." What was going on?

BRIDGET: The angel did take him—to *her.* She was in bed. In her nightshirt. Judge her astonishment when the angel and the Count appeared! "Mariana!" She called out. Mariana was a servant girl in the next room. Then she threw herself at the Count's feet, calling him: "My noble lord." She was an Emperor's daughter, the angel then told the Count and showed him a reddish birthmark on the back of her neck to prove it. Quivering with pleasure, the Count was taking her by the chin to look her right in the eye, when in came Mariana with a light, whereupon the whole vision faded.

(Pause.)

KUNIGUNDE: What a story, my word! You may have these earrings for your pains. *(She gives some ear-rings to Bridget, and waves her toward the door. Bridget prepares to leave.)* Your conclusion is that this Emperor's daughter is . . . *(She points to herself.)*

BRIDGET: Who else?

ROSALIE: Everyone agrees to that!

KUNIGUNDE: Who's everyone?

ROSALIE: Everyone in the castle. We all clapped our hands and shouted: She's the one! when you arrived here.

BRIDGET: Yes. And the bells in the steeple echoed: she, she, she!

ROSALIE: Well, *that's* just a rumor.

KUNIGUNDE: Hm. You may go now, Bridget. *(Bridget starts to speak.)* Go! *(Bridget goes.)* *You* said I was the one?

ROSALIE: Certainly!

KUNIGUNDE: Even before we'd met! That did show . . . foresight.

ROSALIE: Or . . . insight, milady.

KUNIGUNDE: What? Oh yes, insight. You are a bright girl. *(She has got up and has absentmindedly wandered over to a window and opened it. Pause.)* Have you put those things in order for the Count, deeds, letters, depositions?

ROSALIE: *(at the table).* They're in this envelope.

KUNIGUNDE: Give it to me. *(She stops, and takes a lime twig fastened outside to catch birds.)* Oh, look, isn't this from a bird's wing? Someone has put lime twigs here to catch them!

ROSALIE: That's from a finch's wing, I think.

KUNIGUNDE: The young male finch I'd been trying to lure here all morning.

ROSALIE: It was you?

KUNIGUNDE: *(not absentmindedly).* Give it to me.

ROSALIE: The envelope?

KUNIGUNDE: *And* the finch! Help me catch that finch!

(A sound is heard. Kunigunde has taken the envelope.)

ROSALIE: That'll be the Count and his mother.

KUNIGUNDE: *(indicating all the make up).* You will hide all that?

ROSALIE: That goes without saying, doesn't it, milady?

(Rosalie draws a curtain in front of the dressing table and withdraws behind it. The Count and his mother enter.)

KUNIGUNDE: *(To Countess Helena, the mother).* I kiss your hands, you care for me as for a daughter. And Count, how is your arm?

HELENA: You hurt your arm, son?

FREDERICK: A scratch from my encounter with the Burgrave. It is nothing, mother.

KUNIGUNDE: *I* recall bright drops of blood!

FREDERICK: The price I paid for you! A bargain surely?

KUNIGUNDE: Did someone say the age of chivalry was dead? But, pray, be seated, madam.

(She seats the Countess. The Count seats Kunigunde.)

HELENA: *(Before sitting).* I kiss your brow, and ask: how are you faring in our Wetterstrahl?

KUNIGUNDE: My lightest word is law! My every wish is granted!

HELENA: May we ask how you'll be living from now on?

KUNIGUNDE: In my own modest castle at Thurneck, singing the praises of your son and you!

HELENA: Mightn't that get a bit monotonous?

FREDERICK: Mother!

HELENA: And there are obstacles –

KUNIGUNDE: Discords in a harmony otherwise – what's the word – divine? These papers? *(She indicates deeds, etc.)*

HELENA: Those are the – ?

KUNIGUNDE: Deeds, etcetera, yes. I'll be the first to admit they are ambiguous! I won't defend such rights a moment longer! *(She picks up the whole batch of papers.)* Here, Count: all yours.

FREDERICK: It is my turn to speak of magnanimity! But I can't let you do this.

KUNIGUNDE: You must.

FREDERICK: I can't! Appeal your case to the Emperor: let him – decide.

KUNIGUNDE: *(shaking her head).* Countess, I appeal to you! These papers burn my fingers.

HELENA: You cannot, in a single gesture, impulsive and irrational, deed away a right that belongs to your whole family. My son's correct: the Emperor must decide.

KUNIGUNDE: You are both wrong. These are not family claims. They're mine! Mine to dispose of thus!

(She tears the papers up.)

FREDERICK: Good Heavens!

HELENA: I'd never have believed it.

KUNIGUNDE: Am I very, very bad?

HELENA: You are! This is not legal! Oh, but, my dear, such a thing does take some doing! I'll forgive you. Come here and let me kiss you once again! *(This is done.)*

FREDERICK: *(as she returns to her chair).* It's the most beautiful action I ever saw! I only pray you won't live to regret it.

KUNIGUNDE: I'll live to praise you, nay, to worship you!

HELENA: You've such a way of putting things, my dear!

KUNIGUNDE: It's high time for the wall that divides me from my savior to come tumbling down!

FREDERICK: *(fervently).* It *is* down, sister: I am now your brother.

KUNIGUNDE: Brother? No, no. Carried away? Yes: a fire has broken out inside of me that carries *all* before it! It isn't sisterly! It's—

(Silence. Both Frederick and his mother jump up.)

Alas, my simple truth has broken all the bounds of modesty. I must return immediately to Thurneck!

HELENA: *(gently).* How'll you do *that,* young lady?

KUNIGUNDE: You're right: I am dependent on those I have affronted. What shall I do? Destroy myself? *(She crosses herself.)* God is dead set against *that,* I believe! *(She draws a dagger and makes as if to stab herself. Frederick wrenches the dagger from her hand.)*

FREDERICK: Kunigunde, don't you realize I will escort you home whenever you wish?

KUNIGUNDE: You—? After what I said—?

HELENA: Of course he will, it's no more than his duty.

FREDERICK: When shall we leave?

KUNIGUNDE: At once! Tonight!

HELENA: Make it tomorrow, dear. Dine with us tonight.

KUNIGUNDE: Forgiveness, it is such a holy thing! You have forgiven me?

HELENA: There's nothing to forgive.

FREDERICK: You'll dine with us?

KUNIGUNDE: Thank you, gracious lady! Thank *you,* her more than gracious son! Give me an hour, to gain control of this unruly heart and then I'll dine with you. *(She leaves.)*

FREDERICK: Did I tell you about the girl I was falling in love with, mother?

HELENA: You were—??

FREDERICK: Well, now I needn't. She's replaced.

HELENA: *(startled, and gesturing toward the door where Kunigunde left).* Not—Surely not by—?

FREDERICK: *(sarcastically).* You want me to pick one but not this one? Not the lady Kunigunde?

HELENA: I didn't say that, son.

FREDERICK: So she will pass?

HELENA: I wouldn't say I disliked her, even.

FREDERICK: Nor would *I* say the wedding must be tonight. *(He paces the room petulantly.)* Are you aware, good mother, that Kunigunde is descended from the Saxon Emperors?

HELENA: Ah! You mean it is your dream of New Year's Eve that speaks for her?

FREDERICK: Well, it does, doesn't it?

HELENA: I wonder. Let's think further.

(Pause.)

FREDERICK: It's going to be a thrill taking her to Thurneck!

V

(Mountains. Forests. Before a hermitage. Theobald helps Cathy down the face of a cliff.)

CATHY: A hermitage! Is this . . . our journey's end?

THEOBALD: Almost. Here we shall be met by my old friend, Prior Hatto. After a night here you'll proceed to the destination you've demanded. Look! Can you make out a building in the far distance? High on the pine-clad mountain? There?

CATHY: *(peering up into the peaks).* There?

THEOBALD: No, there! D'you see it now? A white speck on a field of white?

CATHY: Ah yes! Yes!

THEOBALD: Well, that's the convent: the Convent of the Ursuline Nuns. Nothing left to do now but knock on this hermitage door and tell good Prior Hatto: "Here is old Theobald, come to bury his own child."

CATHY: *(wincing).* Don't say that, father!

THEOBALD: Why not? Is not your dearest wish to enter a convent?

CATHY: It is. Oh, it is!

THEOBALD: "Leave father and mother and follow Me." You're doing more: giving up marriage, children, grandchildren, to gaze all day upon the countenance of God!

CATHY: *(crossing herself).* He will help me.

(They sit and rest their limbs.)

THEOBALD: D'you remember, at Wetterstrahl, that ruined wall where the finch had built a nest in the elder bush near the face of the rock?

CATHY: Oh, don't, don't.

THEOBALD: Why not? Wouldn't you like to go back there?

CATHY: I couldn't.

THEOBALD: Why not?

CATHY: My lord and master has forbidden it.

THEOBALD: I could go to Count Frederick: ask him to lift that ban.

CATHY: Yes, but you wouldn't, and even if you did, Count Frederick would not consent, and even if Count Frederick consented, *I* couldn't accept the favor.

THEOBALD: *(going down on his knees to her).* I'll take you back to Wetterstrahl and tell the Count: "Let her live here! Let her follow when you ride! Let her sleep in your straw at night!"

CATHY: *(weeping).* You would do that?

THEOBALD: I would! I will!

(Cathy also kneels.)

CATHY: You've plunged a knife so deep into my breast I'm bleeding inwardly! Such love is more than I can bear!

THEOBALD: So?

CATHY: No convent. No Wetterstrahl either. Not the finch in the elderbush by the ruined wall.

THEOBALD: Where then?

CATHY: Heilbronn. Give me a husband, anyone you like. I'll forget Frederick though a grave as deep as a well be my bridal bed! *(Theobald stands up, then raises Cathy.)*

THEOBALD: You're angry with me.

CATHY: No, no!

THEOBALD: *(simply).* Shall I tell Prior Hatto you *will* enter the convent?

CATHY: *(equally simply).* Ask Prior Hatto to let us spend the night here. At daybreak, we can return to Heilbronn.

(Theobald proceeds to the door of the hermitage. There is a bell hanging outside the gate. Theobald takes the clapper: the bell clangs.)

VOICE FROM INSIDE: In the name of the Father, the Son, and the Holy Ghost, who goes there?

THEOBALD: Is that you, Hatto?

VOICE: It is I, God help me.

THEOBALD: This is Theobald, armorer of Heilbronn. *(The door opens.)*

VI

(The Rhinegrave's castle. Noise of drunken troopers from the next room. The Rhinegrave, drinking alone.)

RHINEGRAVE: Writing me a letter! I must tell my men. *(Yelling toward the next room:)* SHADDUP! *(They shut up.)* Kunigunde—remember her?—has sent me a letter. Know what I did with it? *(Rough voice: "Shoved it up your royal ass, Rhinegrave!")* Good joke and not far off: I burned her letter! *(Another rough voice: "Oh, what a deed was there, my countrymen!") (Again, just to himself):* I burned her letter, but its letters are burned into my heart: "From the Lady Kunigunde to the Rhinegrave. Compliments, Dear Rhinegrave, but in future don't put yourself out on my account. Staufen has been transferred to me by peaceful negotiation." Could that be true? If it is, I should disband my troops and forget it. If it is not . . . ? Where is my messenger? He's late. There is a rumor—he's looking into it for me—that what "peaceful negotiation" means is that she's marrying Count Frederick. *(He gives out a loud cry:)* AAAAAH! *(Then quietly:)* Sometimes a spider will roll up in its own meshes till it looks like a speck of dust: let the flies beware of that spider! Let the lady Kunigunde beware of the Rhinegrave! I'll entangle her in my web, then pounce, driving the sting of my revenge deep, deep in her unfaithful bosom: *(Again screaming:)* kill, kill, kill! *(Quiet again:)* I'll preserve her skeleton in my castle here, a relic under the rubric: Whore of Babylon! But where's my messenger? He will confirm if she's marrying Frederick. If she is, oho, she'll pay me damages! I'll turn her upside down and shake the money from her pockets!

MESSENGER: *(who has entered).* He took her back to Thurneck and next morning she found upon the coverlet when she woke a deed of gift wrapped in a letter from the enamored Count assuring her it was a wedding present if only *she* would give *him* her fair hand.

RHINEGRAVE: So. So. I see it all. She took it. Stood before her mirror, curtsied—she does sensational curtsies—and took it.

MESSENGER: The deed of gift, yes.

RHINEGRAVE: And the hand?

MESSENGER: Her answering letter—which also I have seen, ever your loyal spy—contained a little double talk, varied its colors a little like changeable silk, talked big a little, saying his sacrificial act cut into her heart like a diamond and she was too overcome with emotion to be coherent, but still, if glances talk, looks write, and holding hands can seal, the marriage contract's drawn. I heard him speak these words: "Before new moon we two will have sailed into the matrimonial harbor!"

RHINEGRAVE: No! They will not! Lightning will split their masts before they reach port!

MESSENGER: You've other plans for them?

RHINEGRAVE: This woman's deceived many in her time but now, my friend, that she's deceived the Rhinegrave, she'll never deceive anyone again! Where's my other messenger?

MESSENGER: M2? *(Calling:)* Hey, M2!

RHINEGRAVE: M2?

MESSENGER: He calls me M1. I call him M2.

(The other messenger enters.)

RHINEGRAVE: (reaching in his coat for letters.) Well, in that style, here are two letters: L1 and L2. M1, take L1 to my confessor—that's Prior Hatto in his hermitage—it informs him I'll be needing absolution at 7 this evening: I'm undertaking a very dangerous mission. M2, take L2 to Thurneck Castle, scene of the mission. Let no one see you. Don't enter till nightfall. Then seek out the governor of the Castle, my friend within the enemy's gates. This letter lets him know we'll seize the castle at midnight. All clear? L1, M1, L2, M2. Hatto. Governor. All clear, all clear?

M1: Yes, Rhinegrave.

M2: All very clear, Rhinegrave.

(They start to leave.)

RHINEGRAVE: I didn't get them mixed up, did I? Interchange the letters?

(They look at the envelopes.)

BOTH MESSENGERS: No, Rhinegrave.

RHINEGRAVE: Oh, marvellous, everything's in order. *(So they again set out.)* Oh, but they could have got mixed up earlier. Put in the wrong envelopes!

M1: Could they? By whom, Rhinegrave?

M2: Yes, Rhinegrave. Who put them in the envelopes?

RHINEGRAVE: I did. Ha, ha! Thanks for reminding me! *I* put them in the envelopes! So all is well! Ha, ha, ha!

(They leave, as he continues to roar with laughter.)

VII-A

(Kunigunde's castle at Thurneck. While Flammberg polishes weapons, Frederick is composing a song.)

FLAMMBERG: *(as Frederick picks out the tune on a lute)*. Have you got the words together?

FREDERICK: Let's see. *(He sings.)*

Who is the lady of my dreams?
The lady who is what she seems
The quiet splendor of whose dress
Mirrors her spirit's loveliness:
Kunigunde.

Whose varied virtues do not fight
In whom the opposites unite
Majesty and simplicity
Magnificence and delicacy:
Kunigunde.

Of kingly lineage thou art
And yet all woman is thy heart!
Thy beauty of bone, hair, and skin

Is matched by beauty deep within:
Kunigunde.

(He sighs.)

FLAMMBERG: As bad as that, eh? Head over heels? How about the lady?

FREDERICK: She adores me.

FLAMMBERG: Has she said so?

FREDERICK: She said so in Wetterstrahl already.

FLAMMBERG: And has repeated it here in Thurneck?

FREDERICK: Oh, I can't hold my secret in any longer! Kunigunde and I are going to be married.

FLAMMBERG: What?

FREDERICK: Before new moon, we two will have sailed into the matrimonial harbor!

FLAMMBERG: I can almost hear the patter of little feet.

VOICE: *(outside).* Open the door!

FLAMMBERG: *(moving to the window).* Who could that be?

VOICE: Open the door!

FREDERICK: *(dropping the lute).* I would know that voice in Hell!

FLAMMBERG: Yes, yes, isn't it—?

FREDERICK: That girl. Cathy of Heilbronn. Don't let her in!

(But during this conversation she has somehow got in. She stands now in the doorway. Coldly:)

Well, Cathy, what can we do for you?

CATHY: *(scared by his tone).* Nothing, nothing . . .

FREDERICK: *(loudly).* Then what are you here for?

CATHY: *(holding out a letter).* Well, it's . . . about this letter . . .

FREDERICK: Writing me letters now, ha? Well, I won't even open them.

CATHY: But . . . it's not from me!

FREDERICK: I don't care who it's from!

CATHY: It's important—urgent—!

FREDERICK: Hocus pocus! *(Furiously:)* Where is my horse whip?

CATHY: *(bewildered).* Your—?

FREDERICK: See that nail over there! There it is! *(He takes down his horse whip from a nail on the wall. Roaring:)* No loose women in this castle! We're going to keep the place clean! *(Cathy is petrified.)*

FLAMMBERG: My lord! *(Holds Frederick back.)*

FREDERICK: Get her out of here. I will not accept her letter.

FLAMMBERG: *(tries to get Cathy away).* Come.

CATHY: *(offering him the letter).* You read it, Flammberg.

FLAMMBERG: What's it about?

CATHY: The Rhinegrave's preparing to attack the castle!

FLAMMBERG: This castle?

CATHY: Yes, yes!

FLAMMBERG: When?

CATHY: Tonight, tonight!

FLAMMBERG: What? Who says so?

CATHY: The Rhinegrave! In this letter!

FLAMMBERG: How would *you* come by a letter like that?

CATHY: Providence!

FLAMMBERG: Whose eye is on the sparrow, ha?

CATHY: Chance, then: by chance it got sent to Prior Hatto. Before he could send it back by the bearer, I grabbed it, read it, and ran here with it!

FLAMMBERG: From Hatto's place in the mountains?

CATHY: *(nodding).* The murderous plan goes into effect tonight! At midnight they'll burn down the castle and everyone in it!

FLAMMBERG: You're seeing ghosts.

CATHY: The Rhinegrave's troopers are all over! Send out a scout if you don't believe me!

FREDERICK: *(intervening at last).* Give me the letter. *(He reads it aloud:) "Will be at Thurneck on the stroke of twelve. See that the gates are open. As soon as there's a blaze, I enter. The targets: Kunigunde and Frederick. Show me where they are."* The signature? Just three crosses like the bandit he is. *(To Cathy:)* How many of his troopers did you see?

CATHY: Fifty! Maybe sixty!

FREDERICK: I have a hundred! What time is it, Flammberg?

FLAMMBERG: About eleven.

FREDERICK: We can do it. Let's get our men together. My helmet! My gauntlets! *(He sets about getting ahold of these and while doing so catches sight of his whip on a table.)* What's the whip doing here?

FLAMMBERG: You just took it off the hook.

FREDERICK: Did my dogs need whipping? *(Neither Flammberg nor Cathy reply. The Count angrily throws the whip clear through a pane of glass, which crashes and tinkles.)*

CATHY: *(timidly).* I'd better be returning to Heilbronn.

FREDERICK: With a battle raging all around? No, no, you must spend tonight at the inn. Tomorrow, my carriage will be at your service.

CATHY: Thank you.

FLAMMBERG: Thank *you:* how could we ever hope to repay you?

FREDERICK: And, Cathy, you'll be needing a shawl in this cold. Take one of mine.

(He reaches for a shawl and places it about her shoulders. Meanwhile, a Messenger has entered in great haste.)

MESSENGER: A fire's been started in the east wing of the castle!

FLAMMBERG: An hour early?

FREDERICK: *(to the Messenger).* Run to my Captain. Tell him: engage these marauders at once! With all our men! Flammberg, you and I will go straight to the fire. Cathy, to the inn. Come!

VII-B

(Fire alarm—which takes the form of a horn blown by a night watchman. The scene has shifted to an esplanade before Thurneck Castle, all of which has now caught fire. Between blasts on his horn, the night watchman shouts.)

NIGHT WATCHMAN: Fire! Fire! Treachery has unlocked the gate! On tiptoe Crime has slipped inside! Murder stands with bow and arrow in our midst, and Devastation's torch lights him the way! Fire! Fire! *(Frederick and Flammberg rush on and scout around; Cathy, contrary to instructions, has followed them.)*

CATHY: *(proffering the Count's sword and lance).* Here!

FREDERICK: Cathy! I told you to go to the inn!

CATHY: You forgot these.

KUNIGUNDE'S VOICE: *(from inside the castle).* Help, help, help!

FREDERICK: My Kunigunde! Where is she?

KUNIGUNDE: Help, help!

FLAMMBERG: There she is, see! *(He points to the portal.)*

CATHY: Yes, yes, the lady's escaped through the portal!

(Kunigunde comes reeling on. The Count rushes to take her in his arms. She is almost fainting.)

FREDERICK: My Kunigunde! My Kunigunde! She's fainting.

KUNIGUNDE: No, no, I must get the portrait!

FREDERICK: What portrait?

KUNIGUNDE: Yours. The one you gave me. Rolled up in that beautiful case.

FREDERICK: Where is it?

KUNIGUNDE: *(pointing to the fire).* In there! It will burn! I must get it!

FREDERICK: No, no, I can't let you go back in there.

FLAMMBERG: No one must go in there. The fire has got to the rafters. In ten minutes – five – the roof may fall in.

CATHY: *(giving shield and lance to Flammberg).* I can slip in and out in seconds. *(To Kunigunde:)* Just tell me where the portrait is. Fast.

KUNIGUNDE: *(noticing her for the first time).* That's talking. It's in my desk, deary. Here's the key. *(Gives it.)*

FREDERICK: *(nervous).* Cathy, –

KUNIGUNDE: Hurry up!

FREDERICK: Well, Cathy, –

KUNIGUNDE: *(viciously).* And don't you hold her back!

FREDERICK: I could give you ten such portraits!

KUNIGUNDE: I need this one!

FREDERICK: *(lamely, to Cathy).* Nobody's forcing you – it seems you *like* meddling in other folks' business!

KUNIGUNDE: *(to Cathy).* Look for a *scroll* in a *case.* Know what I'll give you if you find it? A diamond!

CATHY: The room on the right?

KUNIGUNDE: The room on the left. See the balcony? *(She points.)* There!

CATHY: That's the middle.

KUNIGUNDE: The middle, then. Now run!

CATHY: God will help me! *(She runs.)*

FLAMMBERG: *(to Frederick).* Let me yank her back! It's too dangerous!

KUNIGUNDE: That castle is stone all the way! Secure as the rock of Gibraltar!

FREDERICK: *(looking desperately around for helpers).* Veit, Hans, Karl, where are you? Bring me a ladder!

KUNIGUNDE: Who is this kid? Someone you know?

FREDERICK: Well, she . . . came a long way . . . just to warn us of this attack . . .

KUNIGUNDE: Am I supposed to feel guilty we've sent her in there? *You* didn't offer to go!

FLAMMBERG: The roof—

KUNIGUNDE: You're wrong about the roof! I'd have sent her in there were she the Emperor's daughter! *(Cathy is seen at a burning window.)*

CATHY: Help, help! The smoke is choking me!

KUNIGUNDE: *(shouting).* Hold your breath and stick that key in the lock!

CATHY: It isn't the right key!

FREDERICK: *(turning on Kunigunde).* You gave her the wrong key?

KUNIGUNDE: *(to Cathy).* It's the wrong key?

FREDERICK: *(shouting).* You can't do it without the key. Cathy! Come down.

KUNIGUNDE: Oh, now I remember. *(Shouting:)* Listen! The mirror above the dressing table! There's a pin holds it to the wall! The key's on that pin!

CATHY: *(panting).* Mirror. Wall, Pin.

(Three servants—Veit, Karl, Hans—have brought a ladder.)

FREDERICK: I wish that painter hadn't lived to paint me! *(Shouting:)* Key—on pin—behind mirror!

CATHY: Where's the dressing table? I can't see for smoke!

KUNIGUNDE: Keep trying.

FLAMMBERG: The roof *is* falling in now. The whole castle is about to collapse!

FREDERICK: *(pointing).* Set the ladder there! I'll get the portrait myself.

FLAMMBERG: Don't you do it! Don't you do it!

(But Frederick is going ahead. The servants have affixed a ladder against the wall as the Count has directed. The Count is about to climb the ladder.)

FLAMMBERG: *(loudly).* Stop! Stop! The castle's falling, the castle's falling!

*(The Count and the servants retreat from the wall at speed. There is a tremendous crash. The castle has collapsed. Everyone turns away in fear. Unseen by any, the Cherub appears at the portal which has remained standing. He is flooded with silver light, wings on his shoulders, a palm branch in his hand. Cathy, carrying a scroll, comes floating through the portal. She then bows down before the Cherub, who, as in the prologue, calls: Hope! Hope! Hope!)**

VII-C

(This scene is continuous with the previous one. The tableau is exactly repeated: Cathy on her knees beneath the portal, the Cherub smiling down on her.)

CATHY: Shield me now, heavenly hosts! And help me face what is to come!

The Cherub touches her head with the tip of his palm branch and disappears.)

KUNIGUNDE: Hey, look there! Hey! Look!

(No one looks.)

Turned to pillars of salt?

FREDERICK: Our little benefactress—she is dead!

FLAMMBERG: Let's do some digging! At least we'll find the body! *(The servants follow him to the ruins.)*

KUNIGUNDE: Hey! Do you fellows ever notice what goes on? A girl for instance believed burned to death but really large as life and giggling into her apron over there?

FREDERICK: *(seeing Cathy).* God and his legions watch over you! How did you get *here?*

CATHY: I've no idea, milord.

*If the performance is in two parts, the intermission falls here.

FREDERICK: There was a castle here and you were in it! Ha? Isn't that true?

FLAMMBERG: *(returning).* Where were you when the roof fell in?

CATHY: I can't recall what happened.

FREDERICK: You have the portrait there?

(He takes the scroll from her hand).

KUNIGUNDE: Where? *(She grabs it).* Hey, where's the case? This scroll was in a case! I told you: bring the case! Where is the case?

FREDERICK: *(incredulously).* You want . . . the case?

KUNIGUNDE: *(trying to control her rage and be sweet).* Because, my love, as I told her, you'd autographed that case! Your noble signature, priceless in my eyes, is on that case! *(To Cathy:)* So why, in the name of God did you take the scroll from its case?

FREDERICK: *(weakly).* You did do that?

CATHY: No! It wasn't in a case, and I didn't know about the autograph!

KUNIGUNDE: *(screaming).* Liar! Monkey face!

CATHY: I should have stayed in the fire and put the portrait in the case.

FREDERICK: *(embarrassed).* No, no! How could *you* know what the case was worth?

KUNIGUNDE: God's not on her side! Satan steered her hand! *(She sinks down on a convenient bench to sob and swoon away).*

CATHY: The lady is so angry. I'll go back in the fire. You won't whip me for it, will you sir?

FREDERICK: *(affronted).* Cathy, you're out of your mind! Run along to the inn!

CATHY: *(aside).* I'm going back for that case.

(As Cathy moves towards the burning castle, Frederick's Messenger returns from the opposite direction).

MESSENGER: Victory! The Rhinegrave's troopers have been driven back!

FREDERICK: Great news! Where are they now?

MESSENGER: In full retreat towards the river.

FREDERICK: *(to Flammberg).* Let's outflank them, get to the river first and cut them off!

FLAMMBERG: Cut their balls off!

FREDERICK: *(grinning).* There is a lady present, Flammberg! *(To Kunigunde:)* Lady, before espousing you I gleefully espouse your cause! *(To Flammberg and Messenger:)* Let's go!

(Frederick, Flammberg and the Messenger rush away. Kunigunde has remained on the bench with her head in her hands.)

VIII

(At the river. A bridge, now smashed to bits. Shouting. Only Flammberg is visible.)

FREDERICK: *(his voice coming from the other side of the river).* Is—that—ev—'ry—bo—dy?

FLAMMBERG: *(shouting back).* Ev—'ry—bo—dy!

FREDERICK: *(same).* Then—fol—low!

(During this exchange, Cathy has entered.)

CATHY: Flammberg!

FLAMMBERG: Cathy—here too?

CATHY: Where's the Count?

FLAMMBERG: The Rhinegrave got here first. Destroyed the bridge and thought thereby he'd won. But then our whole band swam across! Yes, in full armor! An army of giants! On the other side the Rhinegrave hasn't a chance! Now I must follow. *(He prepares to swim.)*

CATHY: I'll come with you!

FLAMMBERG: Can you swim?

CATHY: No.

FLAMMBERG: What's that in your hand, Cathy?

CATHY: The case—for the portrait.

FLAMMBERG: From the burning castle?

CATHY: I searched in the ruins. God's hand guided me.

FLAMMBERG: *(taking it from her).* Intact, by Heaven! As if made of stone! What's in it?

CATHY: I haven't looked.

FLAMMBERG: May I?

CATHY: Of course.

(He opens the case and takes out a sheet of paper.)

FLAMMBERG: *(after reading).* Hm. You're right, Cathy. You must bring this to the Count. I'll swim you across.

CATHY: Bend down.

FLAMMBERG: I've all this gear to carry. Would you take off your shoes? And that dress—?

CATHY: Oh, I couldn't!

FLAMMBERG: I'll have my back to you, Cathy, don't be shy.

CATHY: No, no, no!

(She runs away leaving him with the scroll.)

FLAMMBERG: *(calling after her).* All right, keep everything on, I'll manage somehow! There isn't a bridge within a mile! *(Pause.)* Will she get lost? Will she reach the source of the river up in the mountains? Or—being the homing pigeon that she is—find her way back to Wetterstrahl?

FREDERICK: *(calling from the other bank).* Flamm—berg!

FLAMMBERG: Co—ming!

(He plunges into the river.)

IX-A

(Wetterstrahl. A spot near the outer, ruined wall of the fortress. Trees. An elderbush forms a kind of natural arbor. On the elder branches, a little shirt, stockings, etc., are hanging to dry. Nearby, Cathy lies asleep, her hands folded as if in prayer. A bird is singing: it is the finch.)

FREDERICK: *(entering but not seeing her).* The Rhinegrave's wings are clipped. So few of his men survived, he needs must be a law-abiding citizen for a while. Kunigunde, now *her* castle has burned down, can settle in mine. *(He has the case for the scroll in his hand.)* As for this case that Flammberg brought me, the case she made such a fuss about, what was inside it? Her title to Staufen. Flammberg is shocked. Thinks property is all that interests her . . . Hm. It's Cathy that baffles *me.* A good girl, yes, who should bring happiness to some burgher's heart. At the same time, a bad girl who breaks the crockery and throws herself through the window. A mad girl with a bee in her bonnet and the Devil's hand on her bosom. What shall I do with her? At my heels like a poodle, through water, through fire, she never lets up. Flammberg had tears in his eyes when he begged me to let her sleep in my stables. "I can't," I said, "she must stay at the inn, and only there till her father arrives." Cathy! Though what am I but a naked animal hiding behind a shield with a flashy coat of arms on it? Is the Devil's hand on my groin? *(He catches sight of Cathy, looks intently at her, then touches the corners of his eyes with his finger tips.)* Now there are tears in *my* eyes. The ruddy cheeks, the folded hands! Doubtless she fell asleep praying for the wretch who took a whip to her! *(Gently:)* Cathy, wake up, I have to talk to you! *(She does not respond.)* She sleeps like a top. And Flammberg says she always dreams as dogs do, and that she talks in her sleep and you know what she's dreaming of. *(Feebly:)* Cathy, wake up! *(Pause.)* Could I experiment on her? Find out what she's dreaming of? That would be a sin. *(He crosses himself.)* I shall now commit it.

(He goes down on his knees, and gently places his arms around her body. She moves as if trying to awake but then is motionless again.)

FREDERICK: Are you asleep, Cathy?

CATHY: No, honored sir.

(Pause.)

FREDERICK: Your eyelids are shut.

CATHY: Go on with you!

FREDERICK: No? Your eyes are open?

CATHY: Wide open. I see you—clear as day—upon your horse!

FREDERICK: Upon my chestnut horse?

CATHY: The chestnut? No: the gray one.

(Pause.)

FREDERICK: Where are you, dearest?

CATHY: In a lovely green meadow. Flowers everywhere.

FREDERICK: Ah yes, forget-me-nots, camelias!

CATHY: Look at these violets, a whole clump!

FREDERICK: I'll get down off my horse, and sit by you on the grass for a while.

CATHY: Please do, noble sir.

(Pause.)

FREDERICK: *(taking her hand).* Now, Cathy, you are . . . well disposed toward me, are you not?

CATHY: From the heart.

FREDERICK: Yet—what d'you think?—I'm not so well disposed toward you?

CATHY: You rascal!

FREDERICK: Rascal?!

CATHY: Because you're in love with me! I call you my lovelorn beetle!

FREDERICK: *(to himself).* How strong she is! A tower built on a rock! *(To her.)* What will come of it all, Cathy?

CATHY: Before my sixteenth birthday—before next Easter—you will marry me.

FREDERICK: *(holding back laughter).* Marry you? Who put that idea in your head?

CATHY: Mariana—She used to sweep for us.

FREDERICK: Where did *she* get it from?

CATHY: She was pouring molten lead on New Year's Eve—a secret rite of ours. She saw it in the molten lead.

FREDERICK: A prophetess?

CATHY: Prophesying: A tall, handsome knight would marry me!

FREDERICK: Who would have to be me?

CATHY: Yes.

FREDERICK: *(touched).* I think it's Flammberg.

CATHY: No.

FREDERICK: Someone else?

CATHY: No.

FREDERICK: Why not?

CATHY: In bed, that New Year's Eve, I asked God to show me the knight in a dream. At midnight you appeared—in living form as now—lovingly greeting me as your bride.

FREDERIC: Last New Year's Eve?

CATHY: The year before last.

FREDERICK: At Wetterstrahl?

CATHY: At Heilbronn.

FREDERICK: I was at Wetterstrahl.

(Pause. She sighs, tosses, mutters something.)

FREDERICK: What did you say?

CATHY: Nothing.

FREDERICK: *(to himself).* Because . . . *that* New Year's Eve—*(In a trance now.)* Did I come alone?

CATHY: No, noble sir.

FREDERICK: Who was with me?

CATHY: You're teasing!

FREDERICK: Far from it.

CATHY: A Cherub led you by the hand!

FREDERICK: A Cherub!?

CATHY: Gleaming! Sparkling! With wings as white as snow!

(Silence.)

FREDERICK: As I hope to be saved, I think you're right! Were you on a white sheet, under a red blanket?

CATHY: I was.

FREDERICK: In a thin nightshirt?

CATHY: *(uncertainly).* No . . .

FREDERICK: No?

CATHY: A thin nightshirt?

FREDERICK: Did you call Mariana?

CATHY: Yes.

FREDERICK: Yes, trembling in every limb, you slowly rose from the bed, fell at my feet—

CATHY: And whispered—

FREDERICK: *(interrupting).* "My noble lord!"

CATHY: *(smiling).* And then the angel showed you—

FREDERICK: That birthmark. Shield me, Heavenly powers! You have that birthmark?

CATHY: I certainly do.

FREDERICK: *(pulling her kerchief off).* Where? On the neck?

(Cathy gives a little cry. Frederick sees the birthmark.)

Yes! Yes! And then, as I raised your chin, to look you in the face?

CATHY: Came that confounded Mariana with a light! It was all over. I lay on the floor in my shirt—

FREDERICK: You *were* in a shirt then?

CATHY: —with Mariana poking fun at me!

(Cathy continues to sleep as Frederick thinks aloud.)

FREDERICK: I was in Wetterstrahl and Heilbronn at the same time? To think thus would to be insane. Not to think thus would be to fly in the face of the truth. And truth is sacred. I didn't dream those things: they happened. A Cherub took my fevered spirit by the hand and I—one of me—was with Cathy in Heilbronn. There are two of me! I'm double! *(Cathy murmurs in her sleep: she is beginning to wake.)* What happened later now becomes clear: when, in her father's armory, Cathy dropped the tray she had recognized me whether she knew it or not, and when she threw herself out the window she was overcome by this confrontation with the man out of her—*(Cathy is fully awake now and is beginning to look around.)*

CATHY: Count Frederick!

(She gets up, replaces the kerchief, puts her hat on, and falls to her knees.)

If you find me here by your castle wall, my gracious lord, it was just for an hour of rest. Say the word and I leave.

FREDERICK: A miracle has taken place. I am still dazzled by its blinding light. Or *am* I insane? Is the mind of man an instrument that can receive an angel's messages and get them right? IS SHE MY EMPEROR'S DAUGHTER? A silvery echo rings still in my ears: I must look into it, find the records of her birth, find if the emperor some sixteen years ago was in Heilbronn . . . *(To Cathy:)* You want to sleep in my stables? Is that what you were saying?

CATHY: Your will is mine, my lord.

FREDERICK: *(in a softer tone).* My will is that you stay in the castle. *(Cathy bows low before him.)*

CATHY: I will accept that kindness till my father can be found to take me home.

FREDERICK: Precede me to the castle. *(He guides her over the stones of the ruined wall. As she walks toward the castle, aside:)* I'll find your father, Cathy—even if he should be my emperor!

IX-B

(In the castle garden three weeks later. Grotto, Gothic style. Enter Kunigunde, draped from head to foot in a flame-colored wrap, with Rosalie.)

KUNIGUNDE: How long has Frederick been away?

ROSALIE: Three weeks.

KUNIGUNDE: Where is he?

ROSALIE: No one knows.

KUNIGUNDE: Hm. Unlock the grotto. I am ready for my bath.

ROSALIE: It wasn't locked.

KUNIGUNDE: Is Flammberg interested in you? But that can wait.

(She goes for her bath in the grotto. Countess Helena enters, also dressed for the bath.)

ROSALIE: Here so early, milady?

HELENA: I promised to show Cathy the grotto—the Count's charming little guest?

ROSALIE: Well, excuse me, but Lady Kunigunde is bathing there right now.

(She stands as if she would bar the path.)

HELENA: You had the key?

ROSALIE: The grotto was not locked.

HELENA: Because Cathy unlocked it. I gave her the key.

ROSALIE: No, no, before I let my lady in—anywhere—I inspect the premises.

HELENA: You inspected the side chambers of the grotto? You know about the concealed caves?

ROSALIE: *(stammering).* It has concealed caves?

HELENA: Look! Look!

(Cathy has come out of the grotto.)

Like a white swan rising with breast thrown forward from the blue flood of the crystal lake, how the girl gleams and sparkles! Cathy! Have you refreshed your youthful limbs?

(But Cathy is pale, and trembling from top to toe.)

CATHY: Milady! Milady!

HELENA: Good Heavens, girl, what is it?

ROSALIE: *(white as a sheet).* Where did *you* spring from? Don't say you were hiding in *there? (Pointing to the grotto.)*

KUNIGUNDE: *(calling from the grotto).* Rosalie!

ROSALIE: *(calling back).* Coming! *(To Cathy, between her teeth:)* Did you see her, yes or no?

KUNIGUNDE: Rosalie!

ROSALIE: *(to Cathy).* Better to tear your eyes out of their sockets than trust your tongue with what they've seen! *(She goes into the grotto.)*

HELENA: You're scared out of your wits! Who's in there—Death himself with scythe and hour glass?

CATHY: Promise to tell no one.

HELENA: I promise.

CATHY: The great dome in the middle of the grotto was too grand, too brightly lit for me: I slipped into a chamber at the side, and took my bath. Refreshed, revived, I went back under the dome in playful mood—What met my eyes, stepping from rim to pool, was—*(She cannot continue.)*

HELENA: Well, what? Who?

CATHY: Go to the Count and tell him the whole story!

HELENA: If only I knew it! Besides, the Count's away.

CATHY: Never reveal you got it from me! Better not to tell him at all!

HELENA: Tell him what?

CATHY: This . . . horror.

HELENA: Which?

CATHY: *(shuddering).* It mustn't be through me he's undeceived. In God's good time he'll see it all for himself.

(Noise off.)

They're coming!

HELENA: Rosalie and Kunigunde?

CATHY: Yes, yes, we must go!

HELENA: Go? What on earth for?

CATHY: Come on, you . . . you lunatic!

HELENA: Am *I* the lunatic? What *do* you mean?

CATHY: *(weeping).* Dear, sweet lady! I'm lost if she should find me! Get me away!

HELENA: Dear me, I'd better put you in Flammberg's room. He'll keep an eye on you.

CATHY: Take me there.

(Shaking her head, the Countess does so. Kunigunde and Rosalie come out of the grotto.)

KUNIGUNDE: *(atremble with fury, giving Rosalie a key).* Take this key. The powder's in the drawer below the mirror in the black box on the right. Pour it in water, milk, or wine, and as you do so say: "Come, Cathy, come!" That's one way, another is to force the issue:

grab her! Get a grip on her between your knees . . . Poison! Death! Revenge! I don't care how you do it, only do it! Get that stuff down her gullet!

ROSALIE: Well now, milady . . .

KUNIGUNDE: Poison! Ashes! Night! Don't talk: make *her* stop talking forever! When she's been poisoned, is dead and in her coffin, buried, putrescent, dispersed like a myrtle stem whispering in the wind of what she saw just now, *then* come and talk of mildness and forgiveness!

ROSALIE: *(in a low voice).* It won't help: she's already talked.

KUNIGUNDE: Poison! Confusion! Chaos! That powder's powerful enough to eat up everyone in the castle plus all the cats and dogs!

ROSALIE: You want them *all* poisoned?

KUNIGUNDE: Don't think I failed to note she made herself my rival for his heart! May I drop dead if little monkey face didn't get somewhere, didn't get *in* there, didn't get through to him. Dissolve her therefore into vapor—light mist or peasoup fog, what matter, so long as you now finally kill her!

ROSALIE: *(slowly).* I know a cook would poison her for money.

KUNIGUNDE: *(swiftly).* I'll cover him with gold. This world does not have room for her and me.

X-A

(Before the imperial castle at Worms. The Emperor on his throne. Frederick and Theobald, armed, stand ready for single combat. The Rhinegrave. The Burgrave. A trumpeter. Attendants, soldiers, onlookers. The trumpet sounds.)

EMPEROR: Frederick Wetter vom Strahl, Count of our Empire, several months ago, passing through our Heilbronn, you happened to make an impression on a foolish female. This loose woman—not even a woman: a mere slip of a girl—then *cut* loose from her father, whereupon instead of packing her straight off home you gave her shelter in or near your castle. And now you would condone that misdemeanor by spreading a blasphemous rumor: that the girl had sprung from our imperial loins. Well, my dear fellow, this is worse than ridiculous, it's contemptible, but so long as she inherits none of Swabia and keeps her distance from our court at Worms you can crown her Empress for all I care. There is someone who does care, though, *(He points toward Theobald)* since you have doubled his misfortune and not content with the daughter would make a harlot also of the mother—a lady he found faithful all her life, well knowing that the father was himself. Upon the armorer's grave complaint, therefore, we've summoned you to Worms, Count Frederick, to test your version of this sorry story in single combat. What do you have to say?

FREDERICK: *(baring his right arm).* Look at this right arm: all muscle to the bone, all bone to the rough, tough marrow! *(Pointing to Theobald:)* Now look at that white head. Sometimes, on a Swiss farmer's table you see a cheese soft, squooshy, crushed, decayed: Theobald's head will look like such a cheese if he takes *me* on. We would rather avoid that, wouldn't we, your Majesty? Now, about the way people have been putting two and two together or, rather, out of two stories making one, let's say what's supposed to have happened is but a figment of the imagination, a fabrication of my fever. Let's say, when I maintained that this man's daughter is really an Emperor's child I was ranting, raving, drivelling, dreaming. One can dream anything.

EMPEROR: So you withdraw the preposterous allegation? And, Theobald, you accept the Count's abject apology? The incident is closed!

THEOBALD: Not yet, my liege. *(He turns to Frederick.)* You bloody hypocrite! You believe she's the Emperor's bastard as the saints believe in God! Have you not in the past three weeks rummaged through parish records just to fix the date of Cathy's birth? Haven't you traced the Emperor's movements back near sixteen years hoping to find him in Heilbronn? Arrogant scoundrel! You're the incarnate spirit of parricide *and* matricide aiming to bring down the granite pillars of Mother Nature's primal temple! Who are *your* parents? Is your mother a Fury? Your father some pagan god? Your father is the Devil—which now I'll prove or hurtle headlong into endless night!

FREDERICK: How loud you bark, you dog! The dust flies and the gateposts shake! Son of the Devil, am I? Rather, girt with cold steel, the Devil's fit antagonist! I deserve well of you, old man, yet you come lurching toward me, drooling with rage and yowling bloody murder! So be it. A CHERUB ARMED IN GLORY APPEARED TO ME BY NIGHT AS I LAY SICK AND KNOWLEDGE GUSHED FORTH FROM THE SPRINGS OF HEAVEN. CATHERINE OF HEILBRONN WHOM YOU CALL *YOUR* CHILD IS *HIS*—THE EMPEROR'S.

(Stony silence. The Emperor drums on the arm of his throne with his fingers.)

Now prove me wrong! I challenge you!

EMPEROR: *(furiously).* Theobald! Be the avenging angel to this blasphemer! Trumpeter! Blow the slanderer to his death! *(The Trumpet sounds.)*

THEOBALD: *(drawing his sword).* Were my sword but a reed, were the hilt but wax, I'd cleave you now from head to foot, you poisonous mushroom! *(The trumpet sounds again. Suddenly Frederick hands his sword and sword-belt to a bystander.)*

FREDERICK: Were my helmet of glass, thin as a knife blade, fragile as an egg shell, your sword would rebound from it, as from adamant, to tell the world I speak the truth! Strike!

(Planting himself within Theobald's reach, he takes his helmet off.)

Now strike!

THEOBALD: *(shrinking back).* Put it back on.

FREDERICK: Strike!

THEOBALD: Put your helmet on!

FREDERICK: Your sword rebounds from my bare head! My eyelashes flash lightning that brings you down! *(He takes the sword from his hand, Theobald falls, Frederick stands over his body.)* And now? Shall I kick your skull *in* and let your brains *out*? *(He throws Theobald's sword at the Emperor's feet.)* Live! And may that sphinx, Old Father Time, confirm what I have said!

SHOUTS: Frederick wins! Count Frederick has won!

EMPEROR: *(rises, very pale. The crowd falls silent. The Emperor rushes out alone, leaving everyone standing. Then everyone follows him except the Burgrave. Enter Flammberg.)*

FLAMMBERG: *(hailing the Burgrave before he can follow the crowd).* Burgrave!

BURGRAVE: *(turning).* Flammberg! Count Frederick's aide de camp!

FLAMMBERG: Your head's completely healed, Burgrave!

BURGRAVE: *(pointing to the throne).* You missed this spectacle? Just arrived in Worms?

FLAMMBERG: Posthaste from Wetterstrahl. Where is the Count?

BURGRAVE: Aha! I guess it all. Your face! My former sweetheart Kunigunde is up to her old tricks?

FLAMMBERG: The question is *what* tricks. Do you know little Cathy of Heilbronn—

BURGRAVE: They say she and the Count . . .

FLAMMBERG: Something has given her a scare. But what?

BURGRAVE: Kunigunde.

FLAMMBERG: Yes. But how?

BURGRAVE: Maybe I can help you. Tell me what Cathy did.

FLAMMBERG: Nothing. Except see Kunigunde take a bath.

BURGRAVE: I beg your pardon?

FLAMMBERG: Cathy saw Kunigunde take a bath.

BURGRAVE: And that is nothing?

FLAMMBERG: It isn't much.

BURGRAVE: Depending on what Kunigunde looks like naked.

FLAMMBERG: What does Kunigunde look like naked?

BURGRAVE: What *does* Kunigunde look like naked? Are you a virgin? For you are asking secrets of the marriage bed—not marriage bed exactly—

FLAMMBERG: The lover's bed.

BURGRAVE: Kunigunde's not a woman.

FLAMMBERG: A man in disguise? There *are* men who do that, they're called—

BURGRAVE: Nor man nor woman. She's a . . . The word is hard to say. For, if one says it, one may be turned to . . .

FLAMMBERG: Salt?

BURGRAVE: Stone. Kunigunde's a mosaic—

FLAMMBERG: Stone already?

BURGRAVE: Three substances—bone, hair, and skin—three kingdoms of Mother Nature—from three kingdoms of our Europe: her teeth from a girl's mouth here in Germany, her hair from fashionable France, her rosy cheeks dug out of some Hungarian mine. Do you admire her figure?

FLAMMBERG: Curves sinuous yet firm—

BURGRAVE: She owes those curves to a shirt of steel custom made for her by a Swedish blacksmith.

FLAMMBERG: My God, if *this* is true—?

BURGRAVE: You don't believe me?

FLAMMBERG: The Count will not believe you. He adores her.

BURGRAVE: Hm. She's still in his Castle?

FLAMMBERG: *(nodding).* In his Mother's quarters.

BURGRAVE: He must have an extra key. Have him use it.

FLAMMBERG: Spy on her?

BURGRAVE: Early tomorrow morning before she has got dressed, made up and so on — and so on and so on — Her charms are great, but do you know where he will find 'em?

FLAMMBERG: All over?

BURGRAVE: *(nodding).* On a chair here, a sofa there, and especially on that damned dressing table!

FLAMMBERG: Count Frederick *will* be turned to salt!

BURGRAVE: To stone. He'll be a statue of himself, a pretty thought! A statue of Count Frederick, my old rival! Where shall we put it, Flammberg? I know: beside the charcoal burner's hut where we fought our duel. *(He starts to leave. Stopping:)* And on the marble pedestal this inscription: HE RUED THE DAY HE RESCUED KUNIGUNDE. *(Moves away again. Again turns.)* Feel free to make use of this information. *(He moves off, chuckling.)*

FLAMMBERG: So Kunigunde is a witch. Cathy's not safe even hidden in my quarters. We must . . . *(He draws a dagger.)* But no: first, the Count will want proof positive. That business with the key is good . . . I must get him back to Wetterstrahl. *(He moves swiftly on to search for the Count.)*

X-B

(Somewhere inside the imperial castle, the Emperor is alone.)

EMPEROR: She is fifteen, I hear, fifteen years three months. It is just sixteen years since I held a tournament in Heilbronn in my sister's honor, followed by hectic revels. It must have been about eleven at night . . . Jupiter rose sparkling in the East . . . Tired out from dancing, I strolled through the castle gate thinking just to relax — incognito, of course — among the people congregated in the adjoining garden. *(Pause.)* No less mighty, no less mild a star than Jupiter must have shone down on that . . . conception. In the light of fading lamps I went off with . . . who was it? . . . to a less frequented portion of the garden while the music of the dance hall in the distance wafted across in the scent of linden trees . . . What was her name? Gertrude? *(Pause.)* And now I find that Theobald's wife was called Gertrude. *(Pause.)* She burst out crying afterwards, and I took a small medallion from my breast — it had a picture of Pope Leo on it — and stuck it in her bodice to remember me by — lest I prove incognito to her too! *(Pause.)* Such a medallion has now been found in the possession of young Catherine.

(Pause.) It's a mad world, a topsy-turvy world! What should I do? If Count Frederick, intimate, as he is, with angels, can pull free of this Kunigunde I will help the angels' prophecy come true. *(He moves to the door. Calling to an Attendant outside:)* Count Otto. Count Otto von der Fluehe. *(Alone again.)* It wouldn't be good to bring the Cherub down to earth another time: he'd only let the cat out of the bag. No, no, my secret shall be locked within these walls. *(Enter Count Otto.)* We must confer, Count Otto, and then act.

XI-A

(Early next morning. Wetterstrahl. In Countess Helena's quarters. The room where we have seen Kunigunde is empty. Frederick and Flammberg enter, and the former applies a key to the lock.)

FREDERICK: *(coming into the room on tip-toe with Flammberg).* We'll hide behind this screen till she comes in.

(They hide behind a screen. Kunigunde enters from the opposite side. Coming straight from bed, she is without make-up and fine clothes: she stands revealed as an old hag, bent and hunched in body, hideous of face.)

FLAMMBERG: The Burgrave spoke the truth. You now know what she is.

FREDERICK: I wish I knew what *I* am, knew what I know, for I know nothing, can't tell black from white or north from south. There was something I was looking for in woman: call it a quiet splendor. What I embraced with rapture was loud and lurid evil. What does that make me—bird, beast, or fish? If I have a soul I wouldn't care to be alone with it in the dark. I'd like to run away, Flammberg, but where can one run from oneself?

FLAMMBERG: Someone's coming.

(It is Rosalie, entering by the same door they had. They had locked the door after them, and she unlocks it.)

KUNIGUNDE: *(springing up to meet her.)* So? Is she dead? Tell me she's dead! The poison did its work, the cook got his reward, and the whole castle is talking of the "tragedy"? Yes? Yes?

ROSALIE: Well, milady, how shall I say it? I don't want you to strangle me!

KUNIGUNDE: What? What? The cook betrayed us? Took the money and bolted?

ROSALIE: I didn't pay him in advance. I stood over him while he prepared . . . Poison Soufflé, light, exquisite, absolutely scrumptious, but . . . but . . .

KUNIGUNDE: But what? Get on with it!

ROSALIE: Everything was in place. The cook was in place. The Poison Soufflé was in place. But . . . but . . .

KUNIGUNDE: But???

ROSALIE: You won't kill me?

KUNIGUNDE: I'll kill you if you don't spit it out!

ROSALIE: *Cathy* was not in place.

KUNIGUNDE: What?

ROSALIE: I couldn't find her anywhere. The cook says the Soufflé cost a mint and you must pay for it—

KUNIGUNDE: So she's alive?

ROSALIE: Well, I don't know *that,* milady! I've lost her, that's all! We must just keep looking for her!

KUNIGUNDE: I think I *will* kill you!

(Frederick at this point rattles the key in the lock, and gives the impression he and Flammberg are just entering the room. Kunigunde sees them and screams, then runs back to her bedroom offstage.)

FREDERICK: Good Heavens, who *was* that?

ROSALIE: You burst in on us—without knocking—and with your own key?

FREDERICK: I asked: who *was* that?

ROSALIE: Who was what?

FREDERICK: Hunched, bent, leaning like the Tower of Pisa. It couldn't be—

ROSALIE: Couldn't be who?

FREDERICK: Kunigunde?

ROSALIE: Kunigunde, are you crazy? That was . . . that was . . . old Sybilla! My stepmother!

KUNIGUNDE: *(from the other room in her grande dame voice).* Rosalie!

ROSALIE: *There's* my lady now. She isn't even up yet. I must go to her. *(She leaves the bedroom, taking the dressing-table with her.)*

FREDERICK: Putting Cathy in your rooms has saved her life. Go tell her she's under my protection now as well as yours.

FLAMMBERG: You'll handle Kunigunde?

FREDERICK: By all means.

(Flammberg leaves. Frederick calls out.)

Now, Rosalie!

ROSALIE: *(re-entering).* Yes, sir.

FREDERICK: Introduce me to your stepmother Sybilla.

ROSALIE: Me—? Oh, yes. Yes, why not? I will, I will. And milady's up now. She'll be with you too. Sybilla! *(An old hag on crutches appears in the bedroom doorway.)* This is Count Frederick, Sybilla.

SYBILLA: The time of day to you, most noble sir!

(And she hobbles across the room and out. Before she is out, Kunigunde is in the bedroom doorway, and Frederick sees them both at one time.)

KUNIGUNDE: *(grande dame again).* My dear Count Frederick! Back at Wetterstrahl? And up so early?

FREDERICK: So *the witch* is double too!

KUNIGUNDE: The which is which? The *what* is double?

FREDERICK: I am double.

KUNIGUNDE: I thought you said—?

FREDERICK: You were? No, no, no!

KUNIGUNDE: I thought the *word* you said was—

FREDERICK: No, no. Some words I never say. *(With a swift change of tone.)* My dearest Kunigunde! How are you?

KUNIGUNDE: In the pink. How are you?

FREDERICK: Also in the—what color was it?

KUNIGUNDE: Pink. Is all in readiness for our wedding?

FREDERICK: No. Yes. Of course, all is in readiness for our wedding.

KUNIGUNDE: And when's the happy day?

FREDERICK: Ha? How about tomorrow? Will tomorrow do?

KUNIGUNDE: Tomorrow would be marvelous! Or wouldn't it?

FREDERICK: Oh, it would.

KUNIGUNDE: Of course it would. Marriage! Tomorrow at high noon!

(A knock at the door. Flammberg is back.)

FLAMMBERG: I must speak with the Count.

KUNIGUNDE: *(going apart with Rosalie).* By all means.

FLAMMBERG: *(alone with the Count).* Cathy isn't there.

FREDERICK: Not in your rooms either?

FLAMMBERG: And there are two troopers at the gate demanding to see you.

FREDERICK: In whose livery?

FLAMMBERG: In no livery. But with an air to them—grand, mysterious—

FREDERICK: Have *they* abducted Cathy? Let's see them. *(To Kunigunde).* Excuse us, ladies.

(Frederick and Flammberg leave.)

KUNIGUNDE: He came, he saw, he conquered. He knows all.

ROSALIE: He knows nothing. He thinks it was Sybilla, and he thinks Sybilla, whom I let him really see just now, is my dear old stepmother! Her visit was well timed: she stopped by to put fine, powdered snow from the high Alpine peaks into your bath!

KUNIGUNDE: *(not hearing).* He was looking me over. He was taking my measure.

ROSALIE: No, no. And even if some doubt did cross his mind: that you then showed yourself tall, slender, and magnificent must have struck all doubts down! Can he doubt you're the queen of women? Take heart, lady, tomorrow you will be Count Frederick's Countess.

KUNIGUNDE: I wish the earth would open up and swallow me.

XI-B

(Wetterstrahl. The main gate. Two guards. Flammberg and Frederick enter.)

FLAMMBERG: This is Count Frederick, gentlemen.

GUARD I: You are under arrest.

FREDERICK: On whose orders?

(Guard II shows a badge.)

GUARD II: You will acompany us to . . . a certain destination.

(They all prepare to leave.)

XII

(The cavern of Scene One. Frederick again on trial there, this time attended by Flammberg. Four masked judges. Attendants.)

FIRST JUDGE: *(We of course recognize the voice of Otto).* Impotent is the arm of earthly justice, for crime is a monster that hides in the caves of the heart . . . *(He breaks off.)* But let us cut short the preliminaries. Count Frederick, you are back. You were acquitted that time. This time who would acquit you? You have accused your Emperor of fathering a blacksmith's daughter! You went on – when he declared the charge ridiculous, contemptible – to give your Emperor the lie! Libel, calumny, defamation and above all lése-majesté, the highest of high treason! Hm? I hardly imagine you have anything to say this time? Hm? Hm?

FREDERICK: Perhaps not, my lord. Like you I'm overwhelmed, and yet –

OTTO: And yet what? Can there be any "yets" in such a case?

FREDERICK: The Cherub – The statement that I made came from Our Father which art in Heaven!

OTTO: And who's his deputy – your father which art on earth? Who, hm? *(Silence.)* The verdict of this court is: Guilty. Is that clear? Was any other verdict possible? No court can overrule us, either: only God could do that or the Emperor, who, in the circumstances is hardly likely . . . You take my point?

FREDERICK: Hang me. Behead me. What you will. For, no, I would not like to be a traitor.

OTTO: And could hardly appeal to the Emperor for clemency?

FREDERICK: He could never forgive me in a thousand years.

OTTO: *(He takes off mask and cloak).* But in the twinkling of an eye?

FREDERICK: Who are you?

OTTO: Otto, Count von der Fluehe. I have pronounced the verdict. The colleague on my right will now pass sentence.

(Otto rises and removes the mask and judge's robe from the colleague on his right: it is the Emperor.)

FLAMMBERG: The Emperor! No wonder you've been convicted!

FREDERICK: Sh!

OTTO: The Emperor speaks.

EMPEROR: Yes, Frederick, your Emperor has come to a conclusion. A Cherub said that Catherine was my daughter. Heaven has moved my heart to make that holy angel's word come true.

FLAMMBERG: What? What's this?

FREDERICK: Make the holy angel's word come true? How could you do that, sire?

EMPEROR: Just what *I* asked myself! And asked also: suppose that Theobald just ceded her to me?

FREDERICK: If he ceded her to you she would be yours, but then he wouldn't, ever!

FLAMMBERG: Besides, where is he? Miles away!

EMPEROR: You tell me, even if he were here, he would not do it; and he is not here. Give me more credit! Theobald, come forth. *(The "judge" on the left of Otto stands up, takes off his mask, and drops his robe. It is Theobald.)*

FLAMMBERG: Is it doomsday? Is the whole world here?

EMPEROR: Theobald, have I "lied" about you too?

THEOBALD: Never, my liege.

EMPEROR: Not even just now when I declared—what was it I declared?

THEOBALD: That I'd ceded Cathy—Catherine—to you.

EMPEROR: Thank you. *(Theobald sits.)* Cathy of Heilbronn has been reborn as my daughter, Princess of Swabia, by name, Catherina.

FREDERICK: Merciful Heavens! Then—

FLAMMBERG: May I speak, my liege?

EMPEROR: Pray do.

FLAMMBERG: That Cathy is a Princess is great news but . . . but . . . she's disappeared! She must have been abducted from my rooms . . . !

EMPEROR: Ah yes, by devils! But what is it you always say, Count Otto?

OTTO: There are also angels.

FLAMMBERG: Don't tell me . . . *she's* here too . . . ?

(Everyone stares at the only remaining masked figure.)

EMPEROR: Show yourself, Catherina! *(With the help of Otto, Cathy is unveiled.)* She has a Cherub for a friend. An Emperor can be proud to be her father.

FREDERICK: Most highly favored lady! *(He bows down before her.)* I wash your feet in my boiling tears.

EMPEROR: Aren't you forgetting something, Count?

FREDERICK: I'm dizzy.

CATHY: So am I.

EMPEROR: Sit down, my child, You, sir, come here. You were found guilty of a heinous crime. Having removed the crime, must we not relieve you of the guilt? We do so!

(He gives Frederick his ring to kiss.)

FREDERICK: I thank you from the bottom of my heart.

EMPEROR: And now, Count Otto, can we all be going? Cathy—Catherina—shall walk with me!

OTTO: Aren't *you* forgetting something now, my liege?

EMPEROR: What's that?

OTTO: An Emperor's daughter . . . must get married.

EMPEROR: At fifteen? When I've hardly met her myself?

OTTO: If she should wish to and if . . . the man wants her.

EMPEROR: Ah, but does he? Many rumors reached me that he didn't. You didn't, did you, Frederick?

FREDERICK: I do now!

EMPEROR: Haven't I done you enough favors for one day?

FREDERICK: She is yours to give, my liege, I'm humbly begging you to give her—and to me.

EMPEROR: She should be *given* away, this lovely princess? Nothing for nothing is this life's rule. You must pay. For an Emperor's daughter you must pay three times over. First, you need Theobald's approval.

FREDERICK: He'll never give it.

THEOBALD: May I speak for myself, young man? My Emperor's will is mine.

FREDERICK: Good Heavens. And thank you.

EMPEROR: Second, take Theobald into your house and care for him.

FREDERICK: Gladly. Most gladly. Let me embrace you, Theobald! *(They embrace.)*

EMPEROR: And, thirdly, you need Catherina's consent.

FREDERICK: But she *always* wanted me.

EMPEROR: Do you want him now, Princess?

CATHY: Is this a dream? I'm so confused.

EMPEROR: Frederick will unconfuse you, won't you, Frederick? For both her fathers give her now to you.

FREDERICK: Both her – ? Oh, had I ten lives to give to these two fathers I'd give them and die laughing – after the wedding night, of course! And now one kiss on these ambrosial lips. *(He kisses her.)*

EMPEROR: Now *we'll* be going, Frederick. Talk to Cathy. *(All leave except Frederick and Cathy.)*

FREDERICK: Confused? You? You've always known my heart as well as yours!

CATHY: You are in love with me.

FREDERICK: With all five senses, totally, forever. A stag, tormented by the midday heat, that tears the soil up with his antler points, does not more hungrily pant to throw himself into the forest stream whose mighty current will sweep him along than now *I* pant to – to –

CATHY: To what?

FREDERICK: Why, to throw myself into the stream of these your youthful charms!

CATHY: But, er, but –

FREDERICK: Oh, I have abused you! Manhandled you! I know! I blush for shame!

CATHY: You mustn't! It's not so! I reached in my memory and find nothing!

FREDERICK: We're going to be so happy, Catherina. May I tell you **how** happy, my Princess?

CATHY: I just wish to ask . . .

FREDERICK: Soon shall the feet that followed at my heels, so sore and weary, be shod in silk and gold! The head that once got scorched by summer sun shall be covered by a silvery canopy! Later, when trumpets call me to the wars, Arabia will send its noblest steed in gilded harness for my girl to ride, and where the finch has built its nest in the elder bush a charming summer house shall rise where I can loll with Cathy on my return!

CATHY: Oh, I adore you, Frederick, but . . . is not tomorrow . . . your wedding day?

FREDERICK: Is not tomorrow – ?

CATHY: *(in a strangled voice).* Your wedding. With another.

FREDERICK: Ah, yes, *that* wedding with . . . *that* other . . . Just at high noon, with pomp and circumstance, the wedding procession will set out toward the church. For the occasion I will devise a glittering entertainment in which you, dear, shall counterfeit a goddess.

CATHY: I am confused again.

FREDERICK: My mother's got a costume that's just right for you: opulent, regal, iridescent. Will you wear it, Cathy?

(Pause.)

CATHY: You wish me to?

EMPEROR: I do. I do.

CATHY: *(holding her apron before her eyes).* Then I will. I will.

FREDERICK: You will be wearing pearls and emeralds outshining every woman there—with no exceptions. The dress has a quiet splendor, as have you.

CATHY: I think I must have something in my eye.

FREDERICK: Show me! *(He looks.)* The something in your eye is . . . tears. *(He kisses them.)* Let's be going, Cathy. The storms are nearly over. Soon now the sky must clear.

XIII

(Before the imperial castle in Worms, as in X-A. The Emperor again on his throne in the center. With him, Count Otto, Count Frederick, the Rhinegrave, the Burgrave, Georg, Flammberg, Theobald, Attendants. Under a portal on the right, Kunigunde, Rosalie, Sybilla, and their people. On the terrace to the left, Cathy and Countess Helena and attendants including Bridget. Both Kunigunde and Cathy are dressed as brides. Church bells are ringing until Count Otto, acting as Master of Ceremonies, raises his hand for them to stop.)

OTTO: Flammberg will be the herald.

FLAMMBERG: *(reading ceremoniously from a scroll to everyone assembled in the square).* Be it known by these presents that Frederick Wetter vom Strahl, Count of the Empire, today celebrates his marriage with Catherine, Princess of Swabia, daughter of our illustrious lord, the Emperor!

KUNIGUNDE: *(aside to Rosalie).* That Flammberg of yours, has he taken leave of his senses?

ROSALIE: *(aside to her).* Or shall we soon be taking leave of ours?

OTTO: *(to everyone).* And may the marriage bed be blest with healthy children! *(Looking around:)* Now where's the bride?

ROSALIE: Here, noble sir!

OTTO: Where is that?

ROSALIE: *(indicating Kunigunde).* Here, sir!

OTTO: We do not see her. Herald, show us the bride!

(Flammberg walks across the square to where Cathy and the Countess are standing.)

FLAMMBERG: Hail to the bride: Cathy of Heilbronn, Catherine, Princess of Swabia!

(Everyone except Kunigunde and her party cries: Hail to the bride!)

OTTO: Now let the bride speak.

CATHY: *(all eyes on her).* Me, my lord? Whose bride am I?

OTTO: Let the bride's father speak.

EMPEROR: *(to Cathy).* A Cherub wooed him for you, don't you recall? Would you carc to exchange this ring with him? *(He holds up a wedding ring.)*

OTTO: *(looking at Theobald).* Let the bride's father speak again.

THEOBALD: *(gently).* Will you give your hand to Count Frederick, Cathy?

OTTO: Let the bridegroom speak.

FREDERICK: *(who has his lute with him, singing).*

Of kingly lineage thou art
And yet all woman is thy heart!
Thy beauty of bone, hair, and skin
Is matched by beauty deep within:
Catherina!

Will you have me Cathy?

CATHY: God and all his saints protect me!

(She falls half-fainting into the arms of the Countess.)

OTTO: The Emperor will give the bride away.

EMPEROR: Take her, Count Frederick! Take her to the altar!

(Otto gives a signal to the bell-ringer, and the bells start ringing. Almost at once, Kunigunde gives a counter-signal.)

KUNIGUNDE: Stop! *(The bells stop.)* An end, at last, to this charade! Sybilla, Rosalie, and I are what we are. *(The three stand revealed as witches and hideous faces and crooked bodies.)* We have a thousand weird sisters within call: already they surround your church. The wedding, with whatever bride, is off.

EMPEROR: *(stammering).* No, no, I am the Emperor and I say: the wedding's on, the procession will set out!

KUNIGUNDE: Try it. Just you try it. Your path to the church is barred. Even if your bride and groom slip through, d'you know the consequence?

EMPEROR: What?

KUNIGUNDE: Their wedding's accursed! Their marriage bed can only bring forth monsters!

CATHY: No! No! Count Otto, say it, say it!

OTTO: *(taken aback).* Say it? Say what?

CATHY: Then *I* will: THERE ARE ALSO ANGELS!

KUNIGUNDE: Where? I don't see any!

CATHY: Ask once more. I dare you.

KUNIGUNDE: Greatest of all the angels, the only one that's a prince in his own right, is the fallen angel, Satan, and what he's prince of is this world which is and shall remain a colony of Hell! What other angels are there?

CATHY: Once more please!

KUNIGUNDE: What other angels are there?

(The Cherub appears, in the victorious posture of Archangel Michael as sculpted by Jacob Epstein before Coventry Cathedral. Kunigunde and her weird sisters vanish.)

CHERUB: Satan may be prince of this world below, but angels swoop down from the World Above to foil him, exchanging one letter for another in the post, extracting your children from the fire when your house burns down, providing you all when you come to the end of your rope with a new rope!

(Two shots ring out. Kleist and the Cherub appear but not in the hut at Wannsee, as in the prologue, just in abstract space suggested by pin spotlights.)

CHERUB: Yes, it was at that point that you fired two shots and killed the lady and yourself.

KLEIST: And I was wrong?

CHERUB: Time changes one's perspective. In the generations that followed yours the world unlearned witches, emperors, Cathies of Heilbronn, and, in an age when it is rumored that God Himself has committed suicide, even a Cherub can believe you had a point.

KLEIST: In killing myself? Not in writing the play?

CHERUB: Exactly so.

KLEIST: Besides, that play was not convincing. The plot was improbable, the tone ironical, from beginning to end.

CHERUB: It's true.

KLEIST: So even you—symbol of hope, incarnation of my own hopefulness—are now cleaned out, hope-less? *(The Cherub extends his palms to express—What else is possible?)* Can you guess what my very last thought was? My final state of mind?

CHERUB: Complete despair.

KLEIST: It would be logical, would it not? Symmetrical: a real suicide, a real despair; an unreal play, an unreal hopefulness. Is it possible, though, that the suicide was the melodrama, and the hopefulness in the play the bedrock of my reality?

CHERUB: What was your very last thought?

KLEIST: This. *(Kleist and the Cherub disappear, and the lights come up again on the crowd gathered for the wedding in medieval Worms—only the three witches are missing. Wedding march. Then a tableau: at its center, Frederick placing the ring on Cathy's finger.)*

Afterword: In the Matter of Eric Bentley

(An interview with the Voice of America.)

VOA: Do you think of yourself as Eric Bentley the critic? Or Eric Bentley the playwright? Or under some third or fourth heading? Your work has been in more fields than one, but do you think of yourself as mainly one thing?

EB: Yes: a writer. The term is broad enough to embrace several kinds of writing. My non-writing activities, even teaching, I would consider, for me, subordinate. Performing—yes, I have sung in nightclubs, and have recorded Brecht songs and the like—was subordinate. So was stage directing.

VOA: Would you divide up for us—or join together, if you prefer—the different kinds of writing you have done? We see for ourselves—glancing at the list of your publications—what they are. You have been a theatre reviewer for a magazine, and a critic and historian of the drama on a fairly grand scale. You gave the Norton Lectures at Harvard and published them as *The Life of the Drama.* You've translated European playwrights—Brecht, Pirandello. . . . Then, in the Seventies, we began to see plays of your own on stage: *Are You Now Or Have You Ever Been* at Ford's Theatre, here in Washington, D.C.—and hasn't that play recently been published and produced in West Germany? . . . Is this all one person?

EB: Or do I have ghost writers on my payroll? No. On the contrary, I myself sometimes write under another name. . . . Whatever shows up in a person in later life has been there all along. The public may not have known but the person himself couldn't avoid knowing. Well, I'm what today's students would call a theatre nut. Stage struck, if you will. Yes, even after everyone has proved that the theatre is finished, that the future is with television or what not! Does the future interest me? Possibly. Does the theatre interest me? Definitely. That's the difference. Some people have to imbibe peanuts all the time. Others have to do endless crossword puzzles. I have to *make theatre.*

VOA: But such a compulsion, surely, doesn't inevitably make a person both a critic and a creator?

EB: Then let me tell how all that evolved. As an infant, one sees performers, and picks up the art of acting—in my case it was seaside Pierrots on a beach in North Wales. So I didn't begin as a writer. I began as an actor, as did so many other writers. . . . Then comes education. School gave me the chance to do somewhat more mature acting but, more importantly, shifted my interest somewhat from *acting* to—not yet *writing* but certainly to *conceiving* and *comprehending,* not to mention a certain degree of *knowing.* School and university. I went all the way through with that—to the Ph.D. And my earliest publications reflect the process directly: me informing myself—and passing the information on.

VOA: Turning again to this list of your publications, are the early, scholarly titles on the lines of graduate papers, doctoral dissertations?

EB: Oh yes. A B. Litt. thesis I wrote at Oxford never saw the light except as a couple of essays in a review. My Yale doctoral thesis, revised, became my first published book, *A Century of Hero Worship,* a study in the history of ideas.

VOA: Then came a book still in print which many of us read in college days, *The Playwright as Thinker,* 1946. Was that your first book written for others and not as part of your own education?

EB: I hope others find it properly addressed to them and their interests, but in the first instance I did the work on that ms, yes, in order to inform and educate myself. And you're getting warm now. I had at last got to what was always going to be my subject: theatre. This was my first book about it. I had discovered my ignorance. Theatre was my subject but I knew nothing about it. My job at the time was teaching at Black Mountain College. May I teach drama? I asked. I had been teaching history. And it was the kind of college where they gave a teacher his head. I got all the drama books out of the Library, took notes, talked, listened to student discussion; then wrote *The Playwright as Thinker.*

VOA: The book came out of books, then, not out of theatre, not out of performance?

EB: Unavoidably.

VOA: You would have preferred it otherwise?

EB: I didn't say *that.* I just said (in effect) that I didn't *get* it otherwise. And Nietzsche taught me to try to love my fate. Well, my fate has been to miss out on . . . so many things. But there was always a book in my hands. Several books. I like to live surrounded by books, and I do live surrounded by books.

VOA: Not surrounded by actors?

EB: Come right out with it!

VOA: As a dramatic critic, are you over-literary? Some people after all wouldn't concede that theatre is primarily literary. Or even verbal.

EB: Things of *mine* have even been quoted to that effect. But I don't believe I want, here and now, to endorse them. If I'm outlining the evolution of my own consciousness, I should, instead, concede that, as its title suggests, *The Playwright as Thinker* did propose a literary theatre.

VOA: Playwrights primarily thinkers?

EB: No. Does the title suggest *that?* The book does not go so far. Doesn't say "only thinkers" or even "primarily thinkers," only that even playwrights think, drama is not mindless.

VOA: Did someone say it was?

EB: You bet your life. At the time everyone was saying it was. Especially George Jean Nathan—himself, the best mind, the brightest intellect (Stark Young was the finest sensibility) among the drama critics of the day.

VOA: But were you *anti*-theatrical?

EB: Absolutely not. I was just saying theatre needn't be mindless.

VOA: But, for you, the script was always the heart of the matter, was it not?

EB: The play's the thing? Ye-e-es, I have generally been happiest with theatres where the play was the thing: where the inspiration radiated outwards from the playwright—a Molière, an Ibsen, a Brecht.

VOA: So that the others are judged as interpreters of the playwright and condemned if they "misinterpret" him?

EB: I was happiest in a theatre where that was the assumption, yes. But I also had occasional "happiness" from something different: the idea of a silent theatre—mime, silent film. Dance as a theatrical art in its own way. Opera which, however dramatic it may become, does not give the librettist the place of honor . . .

VOA: All of which is discussed in *The Playwright as Thinker?*

EB: Much of it is. But I hadn't finished putting my views

together at that time. My views would develop *after* that time.

VOA: The emphasis changed, didn't it? From thinkers and from literature to executors—is that the word?—and performance? Your next books—as of the early Fifties—reflect this change even in their titles: *In Search of Theatre, The Dramatic Event, What is Theatre?*

EB: And I had indeed been moved, in the meanwhile, from the library stacks to the critic's seats on the theatre aisle.

VOA: You *were* moved—you didn't just go?

EB: I was placed there by editors who asked me to review shows. I accepted—to get free seats, yes, to get paid for writing, yes—but above all to get into the next phase of my life. What I needed before was educational background: first, in history and languages; second, book knowledge of dramatic literature. Now I needed to see those dreams acted out. I needed to learn what acting was like—any acting, to begin with. Then I would need to find out how far the art of acting can go—what the best actors can manage to achieve.

VOA: You say "acting." Is that a good synonym for "theatre"? What about directing, stage design, choreography, music?

EB: Indeed! Sometimes I think music is the key to all the rest. Especially rhythm—it's everything. When I work in the theatre, I feel that my theatrical sense is underpinned chiefly by my sense of movement as I know movement from music. Wagner said his operas were endless melody, and I think that is what any of the temporal arts should be . . .

VOA: Yet when you said drama, you spoke of writers; and when you say theatre, you at once speak of actors.

EB: Yes. The musicians are not the principal people in the dramatic theatre: the actors are. My only qualifier is that an actor should be a musician too in a profound sense—not the player of a violin, necessarily, but the possessor of rhythmic sense as fine as a violinist's. Or a dancer's.

VOA: For the sake of his gestures? Body movement?

EB: For everything. When Ina Claire spoke a comic line, it had a rhythmic subtlety and precision like that of Horowitz playing Chopin.

VOA: So you made it your business to see actors. Ordinary but also *extra*ordinary actors. This was in the late Forties, early, middle Fifties?

EB: And, when I could, ever since.

VOA: You made yourself an expert on the texts early on? Then you spent at least ten years becoming expert on the *performance* of texts? From *In Search of Theatre,* I note that this search took you outside the U.S. back to your native Britain and thence to France, Germany, Italy? Is acting equally bad—or good—in all countries?

EB: Countries with a strong theatrical tradition have a marked advantage: Sweden, Germany . . . But I was not making a comparative study nation by nation. Just looking for what was outstandingly good anywhere.

VOA: You were the discoverer of the Berlin Ensemble? Also Felsenstein's Komische Oper in East Berlin?

EB: Let's say I turned up at quite an early date. With Brecht I was already associated before he founded the Berlin Ensemble in 1949: I simply followed him to Berlin, where he told me the only other company worth seeing was the Komische Opera Company. And Brecht introduced me to Felsenstein who had just founded *that* company. Through Felsenstein I learned what opera could do with theatre—what opera would be if it was not the more boring thing that it generally is. If not more boring, less dramatic.

VOA: And Brecht? Or is that the sixty-four dollar question?

EB: It's my fate anyway, to be asked that question, and, as I say, I try to love my fate.

VOA: A vision of Jesus made clear to St. Paul what religion would be for him from then on. Did meeting with Bertolt Brecht make clear to you what theatre would always be for you from then on?

EB: I did pick up more about theatre from BB than from any other person I have ever met. Yes. Yes.

VOA: His celebrated theories?

EB: No. No. His savvy, his talent, his genius, *anything* but his theories. What's more: in Brecht—in my relationship with him—I lived that whole transition from theatre as book to theatre as performance. You see, I read him first. No one was performing BB back then. But I also talked with him. Then—last phase—I saw his work on stage, beginning with his own production of *Galileo* in Hollywood in 1947. Following through with his *Mother Courage* in Berlin, 1949. And when BB directed *Courage* in Munich, 1950, I assisted him and was at all rehearsals.

VOA: There's a notation on the desk here—one of our staff must have written it—"For Bentley nothing has happened *since* Brecht. Anything later he rejects on Brechtian grounds."

EB: Well, well, is that the younger generation knocking at my door? Scary. I am supposed to have rejected everything since BB's death in 1956? No, no, I seem to remember giving *Waiting for Godot* a favorable write-up, was not always unfavorable to Ionesco, Dürrenmatt, Frisch in the Fifties and Sixties . . . And today do not reject all of Pinter, Shepard, Albee, Mamet. . . .

VOA: To use your own word *happy,* have you been as "happy" with any playwright since the Fifties as you were with Shaw and Brecht before that?

EB: A weighty question indeed! You are mentioning men who made the greatest possible impact on me as a youth. Can any later impact equal something of *that* sort?

VOA: Well, but did Brecht put you in blinkers, and prevent you seeing the things that are invisible to Brechtianism?

EB: I have to hope not. But I see *some* force in your implied argument. When I glance back over my critical work of the past several decades, I do see that some writers took a beating from me mainly because they were not Brechtian enough: I did not do full justice to the non-Brechtians, to writers of, say, a surreal or subjectivist tendency. Today, I think some of my criteria were over-austere, Puritanic.

VOA: Too didactic?

EB: Am not sure on that. What I do see is a certain prejudice against, say, Jean Cocteau, Christian Bérard, Cecil Beaton, a theatre I too easily dismissed as decadent . . .

VOA: Did you mean homosexual?

EB: Oh dear, another weighty question!

VOA: Not to be too personal, but also in our notes is that, in the Seventies, you championed Gay Liberation in speeches, essays, songs, plays . . . Not to mention your dramatization of the trials of Oscar Wilde.

EB: You are giving me too much to respond to all at once: let me take one of the easier points. In the days before Gay Liberation, a lot of . . . well, especially the designers were gay and had a style that was even called gay—it certainly signalled the authors' gayness to their audience. I called it the Bonwit Teller Window style. Beaton, Messel, Bérard, Raoul Péne du Bois, and many others. "Gay" colors, so-called, lavender, pink, yellow. Now these colors and that style were the opposite of Brecht. And was I not a Brechtian, *the* Brechtian? A contradiction here, then? Only if it is assumed that homosexuals as such are addicted to lavender, pink, and yellow. I for my part had been seduced by BB's blacks, greys, and browns. So I wasn't exactly getting in position for Gay Liberation, was I? But then what's wrong with black, grey, and brown?

VOA: You were not a regular theatre reviewer for very long, were you? On the *New Republic?*

EB: Only four years, '52 to '56.

VOA: What was the next step?

EB: Well, throughout these various periods of my life, I was teaching—mostly at Columbia University. And some of the writing I did reflected the teaching experience.

VOA: No longer just the learning experience?

EB: Perhaps I was *learning* to *teach*. Anyway, at the end of the Fifties, Harvard asked me to give the Norton Lectures. I said: on what? They said: tell our students what theatre means to you. Bull's eye! They had sent their arrow right at what had always been my own target! It was a challenge, and today my attempt to meet it survives as the book *The Life of the Drama*, my main contribution to *theory* in my field. For those who are interested in how long things take, let me mention that such a theoretical book had been my project when first I got a Guggenheim Fellowship in '48. *The Life of the Drama* didn't come out till '63. Even theory takes a long time to mature, at least with me. Ideas are not what I start out from: they emerge, and rather reluctantly, from observation, from experience.

VOA: Is it possible to encapsulate such a large book for us here?

EB: I should hope not. What I can do is cite what surprised me most about it when it was done. My friends had said it would be an elaboration of Brecht's ideas. I myself thought it might be Aristotle's *Poetics* as rephrased by a Freudian—I was being "analyzed" in those years. What surprised me was that the philosophy of theatre in the book wasn't either Brecht (my father) or Freud (my guru at the time) but Pirandello, one of a number of Europeans I had translated. He saw life as role playing.

VOA: But by 1980 isn't that idea a commonplace of psychiatry?

EB: Except that the psychiatrists earn their money by promising *a release* from role playing. You discover the real you, remember? Nothing different there from what you learned at mother's knee! The different thing in Pirandello was: *all* life is role playing. No way out. All the men and women *merely* players . . .

VOA: But is that true? Or perhaps we should only ask: did you *take* it to be true?

EB: I took it to be an explanation of theatre, or as near to such an explanation as we shall ever get. Theatre provides an image of life, *the* image of life, because *life is a theatre.*

VOA: "All the world's a stage." That's not Pirandello, it's Shakespeare.

EB: Shakespeare didn't mean it. Pirandello did. For Shakespeare, or maybe just for his Jaques who says the line, the notion is merely illustrative. At best a comparison: life reminds one of drama in one or two vivid ways. No problem is seen therein. In Pirandello it is all problem, even agony—that one cannot escape play-acting. If there is any truth in that, then theatre embodies the profoundest pain and conflict—a whole destiny.

VOA: Then you do believe Pirandellianism is true!

EB: Obviously I am convinced there is something to it. Much. But what I was most convinced of was that it brought me to the center of my particular subject, the subject of my life's intellectual-spiritual effort.

VOA: Just Pirandello? No other helpers?

EB: I have written an essay—which perhaps should have been in *The Life of the Drama* but which I hadn't yet conceived at the time—about a latter-day Pirandellian, J. L. Moreno.

VOA: The founder of Psychodrama?

EB: Exactly. Terrible writer. Which is why so few have read him. If only he had wielded a more eloquent pen, either in German or English, I think he would today be regarded as one of the leading psychologists of this century.

VOA: But if he expressed himself badly, how do you know what he thought?

EB: Not just from his books, it's true. I knew *him.* And I witnessed his group therapy sessions.

VOA: You don't mean you found some sort of Final Answer in Moreno, the way others have in . . . well, VOA must not name names, but we are thinking of some of the bigname gurus?

EB: No. Not at all. I was interested in confirmation for Pirandello, dramatist and philosopher of drama, in the work of a clinician with patients. Life is dramatic: that is a very general notion but there are many fascinating specifics to it—in the details of role playing, of drama building. Drama is important because all human beings dramatize all the time. It seems to be the only way to reach out, to try to grasp, to visualize oneself and others, to recapitulate the past, to plan the future. Scenarios. Enactments. A dramatist is just a man who makes a *work of art* out of constructs which all of us put together inartistically.

VOA: Hearing you say that, I do seem to be hearing a man reaching a conclusion he has been seeking all his life.

EB: No, no, no, just a fruitful hypothesis congenial to the modern mind. Aristotle might have found it boring. Besides, my life hadn't ended when I wrote about Pirandello and Moreno in the late Sixties.

VOA: You went on to become a playwright?

EB: Thank you. But I shan't venture to claim, either, that playwriting was the culmination of everything I had ever done. Just my attempt, at long last, to try my hand at the work I had long regarded as central in my chosen field.

VOA: Did this seem sudden when it came? I know some people thought it rather a . . . plunge.

EB: It wasn't. I had approached it timidly, gradually. As a translator, mainly. Jerome Robbins told me once he had to dream himself the author when he studied a play he was going to direct. I always dreamed myself the author when I translated. That was *why* I translated—notable addition to my dream life! A sort of Walter Mitty fantasy when the author I translated seemed immeasurably greater than myself! Sometimes it was a relief to translate the less sublime authors. Or the less sublime works of the more sublime authors. And touch them up a bit. There's creativity for you! "Additional lyrics by . . ." And that is how one injects oneself into the pages of Art. I must have been ambitious to do that for I was becoming progressively more meddlesome. Translations were becoming adaptations. Next step: my own name under the title and above the phrase "based on. . . ."! I was now a playwright.

VOA: You have written a well-known play, *Are You Now Or Have You Ever Been,* to which these remarks don't seem to apply.

EB: No? It is not quite "a play by Eric Bentley" because none of the dialogue is original. I took it all from the historical record. Just edited, arranged. Interpolated comment. Its first producer wanted to say, "Collated by Eric Bentley," but I said a collation was a luncheon or at best high tea. . . .

VOA: Which plays of yours are definitely plays—and of yours?

EB: Is *Measure for Measure* Shakespeare's?

VOA: How d'you mean?

EB: It is "based on" another play. And how about Brecht's *Threepenny Opera?*

VOA: Based on *Beggar's Opera?*

EB: But still Brecht's. His stamp unmistakably on it. Let others decide—don't ask me—which of "my" works has my stamp on it.

VOA: Does playwriting do anything for you which was not done for you by your other writing?

EB: It practically kills me. It's so much slower. So many drafts, so few pages to show after many months' work.

VOA: You're sustained by the ambition to be creative, to do the more difficult thing, to be at last at the center of theatre art as you see it?

EB: Often I am not sustained. I throw up my hands. I scream. But there are seductions. For me, the writing of dialogue is seductive. I enjoy thinking up what people say, or should say.

VOA: So dialogue is a basic?

EB: What a person does when he doodles is his basic! And I am composing dialogue all the time! Second-guessing my friends: preparing their excuses, their witticisms. A natural ghost writer. When I am wakened from a dream at night, the wakener is always interrupting a torrent of (often awful) dialogue—pretentious, sometimes nonsensical, turgid doubletalk.

VOA: You are a Shavian playwright then: drama is dialogue?

EB: Wrong: here at any rate I am Brechtian. Although my doodling is dialogue, my doodles don't turn into plays. I have to plot and plan. In fact, that's how my playwriting differs from my other writing. The other stuff flows. Stream of consciousness. Compulsive chatter. But as for drama, I always think of Racine saying that, once he'd plotted the entrances and exits, the rest was easy. Oh, those entrances and exits—plot 'em right and you're Racine!

VOA: It's the entrances and exits that impose structure?

EB: For Racine. That's not actually how things come to me. The influence on me—as to this—was Brecht's *directing.* Tell the story, he said, Brecht the playwright had begun by telling it himself.

VOA: A play of yours—on Galileo, on Wilde—is full of ideas—dialogue at a rather high level of abstraction—

EB: I have room for all that. I hope I have room for all that. Even so, what I was mainly doing in both those plays – *The Recantation* and *Lord Alfred's Lover* – was threading my way from incident to incident. Telling what happened. Inwardly, sometimes: What happened *inside* my people. But never to the neglect of story in the most obvious and external sense. Galileo recanted. What chain of events led up to that? This was the urgent and ever-present question for the playwright, not what Galileo said in class.

VOA: Is there any way of recapping your remarks on this latest phase of your work?

EB: No need to be pompous about the development I've been outlining. I would hate it if my narrative followed the banal pattern of success story: I'm not that successful a playwright. I wasn't scaling ever higher heights or even undertaking more and more complex tasks. For that matter, *is* playwriting more complex? I doubt that anything is harder than being a really good critic. And, conversely, one thing in the kind of playwriting that attracts me, is simplicity. Naiveté. In plays I find I can expose more elemental parts of myself, things that sophistication would cover up in my scholarship and criticism. . . . One of my plays ends on the word "shameless," and I think that a great source of attraction to me, in the kind of playwriting that I do, is a certain *shamelessness.*

VOA: No fig leaf?

EB: No fig leaf at all.

Eric Bentley, by Lamont O'Neal